THE INDIAN ODYSSEY:
Nurturing Attitudes for Success

Attitude

"आत्मानं विद्धि" (Ātmānaṁ viddhi) - "Know Thyself"

VINAY RAJAGOPAL IYER

BLUEROSE PUBLISHERS
India | U.K.

Copyright © Vinay Rajagopal Iyer 2024

All rights reserved by author. No part of this publication may be reproduced, stored in a retrieval system or transmitted in any form or by any means, electronic, mechanical, photocopying, recording or otherwise, without the prior permission of the author. Although every precaution has been taken to verify the accuracy of the information contained herein, the publisher assumes no responsibility for any errors or omissions. No liability is assumed for damages that may result from the use of information contained within.

BlueRose Publishers takes no responsibility for any damages, losses, or liabilities that may arise from the use or misuse of the information, products, or services provided in this publication.

For permissions requests or inquiries regarding this publication, please contact:

BLUEROSE PUBLISHERS
www.BlueRoseONE.com
info@bluerosepublishers.com
+91 8882 898 898
+4407342408967

ISBN: 978-93-5989-758-5

Cover design: Rishav Rai
Typesetting: Rohit

First Edition: March 2024

WHO THIS BOOK IS USEFUL FOR
...

"Essential Reading for Every Aspiring Individual: Unleashing Your Inner Potential

Introduction: In the journey of life, we often seek guidance and wisdom to unlock our true potential. This quest for self-improvement transcends various aspects of our lives, including business, parenting, education, relationships, and personal development. Drawing inspiration from timeless Indian wisdom and the latest advancements, this guide, titled '**The Indian Odyssey: Nurturing Attitudes for Success.**' In Short **'Attitude'** or **'Manasa'**, delves into the depths of human consciousness and offers invaluable insights to help individuals fulfill their aspirations.

1: The Attitude Revolution In the world of **self-realization and growth,** the term 'attitude' takes on a profound meaning. It is the key that unlocks the doors to our potential. Just as a lotus blooms in muddy waters, we too can rise above challenges with the right Attitude. The Vedas remind us, "Mano eva manushyanam karanam bandha-mokshayoh," emphasizing the mind's role in both bondage and liberation. This chapter explores the ancient wisdom of the Upanishads and its relevance in cultivating a Evolutive Perspective ("Vikasatmaka Drishti" (विकासात्मक दृष्टि) **Vikasatmaka (विकासात्मक)** comes from "Vikasa," meaning growth or expansion, and "Atmaka," implying nature or essence. **Drishti (दृष्टि)** means viewpoint or vision).

2: Nurturing Potential in Business In the fast-paced landscape of Indian entrepreneurship, individuals like Arjun Sharma, inspired by Lord Krishna's teachings to Arjuna in the Bhagavad Gita, have redefined success. They have harnessed the power of 'karma' (action) and 'dharma' (duty) to build ethical and thriving businesses. This chapter unveils their journeys and the fusion of modern business strategies with ancient wisdom.

3: Parenting the Indian Way Raising a child is an art, and Indian parenting draws from the profound concept of 'Gurukul.' Like the great sage Narada, parents are entrusted with nurturing the potential of their children. This chapter guides parents on how to instill values, discipline, and a Evolutive Perspective in their offspring. As the saying goes, "Mata, Pita, Guru, Deivam" (Mother, Father, Teacher, God), this chapter underscores the divine responsibility of parenting.

4: Transforming Education The Indian education system has a rich heritage dating back to institutions like Nalanda and Takshashila. Today, educators like Anika Verma are revolutionizing teaching methods by integrating holistic learning approaches inspired by ancient gurukuls. This chapter explores how education can empower young minds to unleash their potential.

5: Building Harmonious Relationships In the mosaic of life, relationships play a pivotal role. The 'sambandh' (connection) between individuals is likened to the interconnectedness of all beings in the Upanishads. Drawing from the wisdom of eminent authors like Rishi Valmiki and Kalidasa, this chapter provides insights into nurturing healthy and fulfilling relationships.

6: Guidance to Counsellors Just as Lord Rama sought counsel from sage Vashishta, individuals often require guidance to overcome challenges. This chapter introduces the wisdom of

Indian counselors like Dr. Alok Khanna, who blend modern psychology with ancient practices. It explores how counseling can help individuals overcome hurdles and achieve their aspirations.

Conclusion: **'Manasa' serves as a beacon of inspiration, drawing from the treasury of Indian wisdom and the experiences of individuals who have transformed their lives.** It is a reminder that within each of us lies the potential for greatness. As we embrace the teachings of our ancestors and merge them with contemporary knowledge, we embark on a transformative journey towards self-realization and fulfillment. The price of this book is not measured in rupees but in the priceless wisdom it imparts, guiding readers towards fulfilling their deepest aspirations."

ACKNOWLEDGMENTS

...

Gratitude to My Pillars of Strength and Inspiration

In the mosaic of life, every individual embarks on a journey defined by challenges, growth, and the invaluable support of those who illuminate the path forward. As I pause to reflect on my own journey, I am overwhelmed with a profound sense of gratitude for the remarkable souls who are friends and have been my guiding lights. This acknowledgment, though a humble attempt, is an ode to their unwavering support and love.

To My Guardians of Light: Ajji and Doddappa

In the absence of my parents, you, Ajji and Doddappa, stepped into my world not merely as guardians but as the very embodiment of unconditional love and wisdom. Ajji, your nurturing warmth and the stories you shared, woven with the threads of resilience and compassion, have been my sanctuary. You taught me not just to navigate life's complexities but to embrace them with grace and empathy. Doddappa, your mentorship has been my compass, guiding me with patience and understanding through life's tumultuous seas. You filled the void with a father's grace, teaching me the virtues of perseverance and integrity. Together, you have sculpted my character, nurturing the seeds of my dreams with your selfless love and sacrifices.

To My Father, My Beacon: AR Rajagopala Krishnan

Dad, your influence shines brightly, a testament to the profound impact you've had on my journey. Your dual role as both father and mother in our home was borne with a grace that imbued our lives with warmth and care. Your gentle nature, patience, and wisdom have been my constant source of comfort and inspiration. The sacrifices you made, each a silent testament to your love and dedication, have shaped the core of my being. Your selflessness, choosing my needs over your own comforts, is a lesson in love and sacrifice that I carry in my heart.

To My Compass: Ritu Bhattacharya

Ritu, my partner in life, your presence has been the cornerstone of not just our home but of every endeavor I have undertaken. Your love, resilience, and wisdom have been my guiding lights, steadying me through every storm. In every success, you have been my joy, and in every challenge, my strength. The balance and harmony you bring to our lives cannot be overstated, your love a boundless ocean that enriches my soul.

To My Paradigm of Innovation: My Son Aryan Iyer

Aryan, you are the spark that has ignited a revolution in my perspective. Your innovative thinking and zest for life have opened new vistas of understanding, teaching me the value of curiosity and the joy of discovery. Your enthusiasm for exploring the myriad puzzles of life has been a source of constant wonder and inspiration, reminding me of the endless potential that lies within the fresh perspectives of youth.

To My Creative Muse: Ashok R

Uncle Ashok, your artistic genius and creative vision have added a dimension to this work that only someone of your extraordinary talent could provide. Your ability to see the world through an artistic lens and to bring those visions to life has been a wellspring of inspiration, enriching my work and my life with depth and beauty.

To My Inspirations: Visionaries and Spiritual Guides

The visionary leadership of A.P.J. Abdul Kalam and Ratan Tata has inspired me to dream big and strive for excellence. The spiritual teachings of Swami Vivekananda and Mahatma Gandhi have been my ethical compass, guiding me towards a life of purpose and integrity.

To each of you, your influence has been a gift beyond measure, your support the foundation of my journey. This acknowledgment is but a small gesture of my immense gratitude for your roles in my life. Thank you for being the stars that guide me, the wind beneath my wings, and the light that brightens my path.

With deepest appreciation and love,

Vinay Rajagopal Iyer

PREFACE

...

The Resolute Spirits of Aryan and Priya

In the heart of Varanasi, a city steeped in spirituality, Aryan emerged as a young and spirited entrepreneur. His resolve echoed the verses of India's ancient scriptures, for he was determined to endure until triumph graced his path. Aryan firmly believed that within him flowed the blood of warriors, not meek lambs. He drew inspiration from the Bhagavad Gita, where Lord Krishna guided Arjuna amidst the chaos of battle, and thus, Aryan sought wisdom to navigate the complexities of the modern business landscape.

As he delved into the teachings of the Upanishads, Aryan embraced the profound concepts of 'Atman' and 'Brahman.' He understood that genuine success lay in recognizing the divinity within himself and every individual. This inner awakening revolutionized his approach to business. Mindfulness and meditation became his allies, nurturing a workplace where harmony thrived, and his team's well-being flourished.

In the bustling markets of Kolkata, Priya, a tenacious young woman, resonated with Aryan's unwavering determination. Sipping masala chai at a street-side tea stall, she whispered to herself, "I shall persist until I succeed." Priya drew inspiration from the courageous Rani Lakshmibai, the queen of Jhansi who fearlessly challenged colonial forces in pursuit of freedom. Rani

Lakshmibai embodied indomitable spirit and resolve, qualities that Priya admired deeply.

With a fervor for technology and a heart brimming with empathy, Priya embarked on a mission to bridge the digital divide in rural India. She established a startup dedicated to providing affordable and accessible internet connectivity to remote villages. Guided by the Sanskrit aphorism, "Vasudhaiva Kutumbakam" – meaning 'the world is one family,' Priya's vision transcended boundaries.

Her relentless commitment led to collaborations with the government, philanthropists, and tech giants. Together, they brought connectivity and online education to millions, sparking a digital revolution in rural India. Priya's journey became an inspiration to numerous young entrepreneurs who aspired to amalgamate modern technology with timeless wisdom.

As Aryan and Priya pursued their dreams, their paths converged at a conference on holistic leadership. Sharing their experiences and strategies, they seamlessly blended profound insights from Indian scriptures with the latest advancements in business and technology.

United by a shared vision, they launched 'Project Dharmik Udyog,' an initiative dedicated to promoting ethical entrepreneurship and sustainable development. Their collaborative endeavors not only transformed their own lives but also left an indelible mark on society.

In the chronicles of their journey towards success, they frequently recited the words of Swami Vivekananda, "Arise, awake, and stop not until the goal is reached." Aryan and Priya did not merely harbor aspirations for greatness; they pursued it tenaciously while remaining firmly rooted in their cultural heritage.

Their story served as a testament to the timeless wisdom of India, seamlessly entwined with modern innovation and an unwavering commitment to 'Dharma' - the righteous path. As Rupees flowed into their enterprises, their hearts remained aligned with the profound message of the Vedas, "Tamaso ma jyotirgamaya" - Lead me from darkness to light.

AUTHOR BIO

• • •

Blending a rich technical expertise with a passion for holistic wellness, our author Vinay Rajagopal Iyer emerges as a multifaceted leader and visionary in both the technological and personal development arenas. With a robust educational foundation, including an MBA from the University of Melbourne and a BE in Electrical & Electronics from RV College of Engineering, the journey unfolds through various roles in technology and leadership.

The narrative begins with over two decades of global experience in technology, where our author excels as a Technology Executive. From hands-on technical roles to leadership positions, the expertise spans across infrastructure technologies, large-scale team management, and strategic oversight in international settings. Key roles include a Practice Director at Happiest Minds Technologies, a Senior Manager and Senior Consulting Architect at IBM, and a Program Manager at Apara Global Services, showcasing a trajectory marked by growth and diversification.

As the Chief Operating Officer of iSmart, the author's entrepreneurial acumen shines. Here, within a mere three months, the transformation of a startup into a thriving enterprise with an ever-expanding team is a testament to strategic brilliance and leadership prowess.

Beyond technology, our author delves into the realms of personal development and wellness. A Master Spirit Life Coach certified by the International Coaching Federation, a Strengths Coach, and a Louise Hay - Heal Your Life trainer reflect a deep commitment to empowering others. This is further enriched by certifications in Yoga, embodying a holistic approach to wellbeing.

In professional certifications, the author's dedication to continuous learning is evident. With accreditations ranging from PMI's Project Management Professional to ITIL, and technical certifications from NetApp, VMWare, and Symantec, the commitment to staying at the forefront of technological advancements is clear.

This unique blend of technical acumen, leadership, and personal development expertise makes our author a distinguished figure, guiding others through transformational journeys in both their professional and personal lives.

INTRODUCTION

...

"Once, on a serene morning in the lush landscape of India, my beloved friends gathered around me with a request of profound significance. They urged me to pen a book - a guide to harness the insights from our work, to enrich and elevate lives. This task, long a desire of mine, swiftly became my utmost priority.

My personal research on a branch of psychology deeply rooted in the power of belief. These beliefs, conscious or subconscious, significantly influence our desires and our ability to achieve them. This tradition of thought reveals how even minor shifts in belief can trigger remarkable transformations.

In this book, you will uncover a fundamental belief about oneself, a discovery from our research, that shapes a large portion of your existence. This 'Attitude', as I refer to it, is not just a part of your personality but forms its very foundation. Often, it is this Attitude that either propels you towards your potential or holds you back.

This book is the first of its kind to elucidate this Attitude and demonstrate its application in everyday life. You will gain insights into the lives of luminaries in science, arts, sports, and business, as well as those who haven't realized their potential. It will offer a deeper understanding of your peers, superiors, friends, and children, revealing ways to unlock your and their potential.

I am honored to share these findings with you, enriched with anecdotes from my research and personal experiences, allowing you to witness these Attitudes in action. While names and specifics have been altered for confidentiality, the essence of these stories remains true.

Each chapter concludes with practical applications, helping you identify the guiding Attitude of your life, comprehend its workings, and alter it if you wish.

A note on the writing style: I've chosen a conversational tone over strict grammatical adherence. This choice, favoring 'ands' and 'buts' to start sentences and occasionally ending with prepositions, aims for a more direct, relatable narrative.

In this edition, I've incorporated new findings. Chapter 5 now includes a study on organizational Attitudes, showing how an entire organization can embody a Attitude. Chapter 7 addresses misconceptions about the 'Evolutive Perspective', and Chapter 8 provides a detailed guide on embracing a true Evolutive Perspective.

My appreciation goes out to my publishing team at Blue Rose Publishing, especially my editors, who have been a beacon of support. My agent has been instrumental in this journey, and I am grateful for their guidance.

Special thanks to my colleagues and friends for their invaluable feedback, with particular mention to scholars from prominent Indian universities. My deepest gratitude goes to my wife, whose love and support add immeasurable value to my life.

This journey has been as much about personal growth as it has been about research. It is my hope that this book will inspire a similar journey of growth in you."

This version transforms the original text into a narrative deeply embedded in the Indian context, referencing Indian psychology, landscapes, and cultural nuances. It incorporates a blend of personal and academic experiences, tailored to resonate with an Indian audience, while maintaining the essence of the original message about the transformative power of Attitude.

CONTENTS

...

WHO THIS BOOK IS USEFUL FOR iii
ACKNOWLEDGMENTS vi
PREFACE ix
AUTHOR BIO xii
INTRODUCTION xiv

CHAPTER 1
THE ATTITUDE JOURNEY 1
   THE DIVERSITY OF MINDS 2
   YOUR PATH TO GROWTH: UNDERSTANDING ATTITUDES 4
   THE PERSPECTIVE OF ATTITUDES: AN INDIAN NARRATIVE 6
   THE ESSENCE OF CHANGE: A MODERN INDIAN PERSPECTIVE .. 8
   SELF-AWARENESS AND GROWTH: AN INDIAN CONTEXT 10
   THE JOURNEY AHEAD: RESILIENCE AND SUCCESS IN AN
   INDIAN CONTEXT 11
   NURTURING THE MIND: EMBRACING GROWTH IN AN
   INDIAN CONTEXT 13

CHAPTER 2
**THE TRANSFORMATION OF PERSPECTIVE: A TALE OF
ATTITUDES IN INDIA** 16
   THE PATH TO ENLIGHTENMENT: LEARNING VERSUS
   PROVING IN INDIAN PHILOSOPHY 18
   THE PATH TO LEARNING: A STORY OF ATTITUDES IN INDIA 20
   CHOOSING YOUR PATH: A NARRATIVE OF ATTITUDES IN
   INDIA 21
   EMBRACING CHALLENGES: INSPIRATIONAL TALES FROM
   INDIA 24

EMBRACING CHALLENGES: A TALE OF ATTITUDES IN INDIA 25

THE QUEST FOR PERFECTION VS THE JOURNEY OF
LEARNING: AN INDIAN PERSPECTIVE 28

THE JOURNEY OF LEARNING AND GROWTH: AN INDIAN
PERSPECTIVE 29

THE PURSUIT OF EXCELLENCE: A JOURNEY OF ATTITUDES
IN INDIA 31

REDEFINING FAILURE: A NARRATIVE OF ATTITUDES IN
INDIA 33

REDEFINING FAILURE AND SUCCESS: LESSONS FROM
INDIAN WISDOM 35

EMBRACING THE POWER OF RESPONSIBILITY: LESSONS
FROM INDIAN WISDOM 37

TRANSFORMING ATTITUDES: NAVIGATING DEPRESSION
WITH INDIAN INSIGHTS 39

THE TRANSFORMATION OF EFFORT: EMBRACING INDIAN
WISDOM 41

THE TRIUMPH OF EFFORT: INSPIRED BY INDIAN ETHOS 43

QUESTIONS AND ANSWERS 47

CHAPTER 3

ILLUMINATING THE PATH OF INNOVATION - THE TALE OF ARAVIND BHARADWAJ 55

ATTITUDES AND ACADEMIC ACHIEVEMENT: INSIGHTS
FROM AN INDIAN PERSPECTIVE 58

DISCOVERING INTELLECTUAL POTENTIAL: AN INDIAN
NARRATIVE 60

EQUALITY IN TALENT AND ATTITUDE: REFLECTIONS FROM
AN INDIAN PERSPECTIVE 63

UNLOCKING POTENTIAL: INSPIRATIONAL STORIES FROM
INDIAN EDUCATION 66

THE MYTH OF INNATE ARTISTIC TALENT: INSIGHTS FROM
AN INDIAN PERSPECTIVE 68

NURTURING ARTISTIC TALENT: A NEW PERSPECTIVE
FROM INDIA 70

BREAKING FREE FROM LABELS: A NARRATIVE FROM
INDIAN EDUCATION 72

CHALLENGING STEREOTYPES IN INDIAN ACADEMIA: EMBRACING DIVERSITY AND GROWTH 74
CULTIVATING EXCELLENCE: INSPIRATIONAL STORIES FROM INDIA 76
CULTIVATING A EVOLUTIVE PERSPECTIVE: INSPIRATIONAL TALES FROM INDIA 78

CHAPTER 4
THE WINNING ATTITUDE IN SPORTS 81

THE GRIT OF INDIA'S SPORTING ICONS 85
THE TRIUMPH OF DETERMINATION 87
THE MIND'S PLAYBOOK 90
THE FORTITUDE OF CHARACTER 91
THE ESSENCE OF MENTAL FORTITUDE 94
SUSTAINING GREATNESS 96
THE ESSENCE OF SUCCESS AND FAILURE 97
EMBRACING THE POWER OF CONTROL FOR SUCCESS 100
THE ESSENCE OF TEAMWORK: LESSONS FROM INDIAN SPORTS 102
UNVEILING THE ATHLETE'S ATTITUDES: LESSONS FROM INDIAN SPORTS STARS 104
CULTIVATE YOUR ATTITUDE FOR SPORTING EXCELLENCE ... 106

CHAPTER 5
BUSINESS MASTERY: THE ATTITUDE AND LEADERSHIP 109

PINNACLE OF ORGANIZATIONAL EXCELLENCE: A JOURNEY TO GREATNESS 111
THE ATTITUDE'S MANIFESTATION IN MANAGEMENT: A STUDY 115
FOSTERING LEADERSHIP EXCELLENCE: EMBRACING A EVOLUTIVE PERSPECTIVE 118
LEADERS WITH IMMUTABLE PERSPECTIVES: LESSONS FROM THE PAST 119
NAVIGATING THE LEADERSHIP LANDSCAPE: EMBRACING THE EVOLUTIVE PERSPECTIVE 122

- THE ENIGMA OF EGO: A TALE OF AKSHAY SHARMA AND THE SUPERSTAR SYNDROME 124
- THE ENIGMA OF ENTITLEMENT: A TALE OF EGO AND RUIN .. 127
- THE TRIALS OF TYRANTS: NURTURING A CULTURE OF GROWTH AND RESPECT 129
- THE JOURNEY OF GROWTH-ATTITUDE LEADERS: NURTURING HUMAN POTENTIAL 131
- NURTURING THE RENAISSANCE OF TCS: AN ODYSSEY INSPIRED BY INDIAN ETHOS 134
- THE REVIVAL SAGA OF INFOSYS: NAVIGATING THROUGH CORPORATE STORMS 137
- THE PERILS OF GROUPTHINK: LESSONS FROM THE EPIC OF MAHABHARATA TO CORPORATE INDIA 142
- LEADERSHIP AND DISSENT: THE ROLE OF A FIXED OR EVOLUTIVE PERSPECTIVE 144
- CULTIVATING THE INFINITE ATTITUDE 156

CHAPTER 6
LOVE AND ATTITUDES: NAVIGATING THE MAZE OF RELATIONSHIPS 158
- DYNAMICS OF RELATIONSHIPS: THE INDIAN PERSPECTIVE 162
- THE COMPLEX DANCE OF LOVE: AN INDIAN PERSPECTIVE 165
- THE DANCE OF UNDERSTANDING: HARMONY IN DIFFERENCES 168
- EMBRACING CHALLENGES: THE CRUCIBLE OF CHARACTER 171
- THE DANCE OF COMMUNICATION: NAVIGATING THE MAZE OF MISUNDERSTANDING 174
- TRANSFORMING CONFLICT: NAVIGATING THE WATERS OF RELATIONSHIP TURMOIL 180
- THE DANCE OF COMPETENCE: NURTURING RELATIONSHIPS 182
- NURTURING FRIENDSHIPS: THE INDIAN CONNECTION 185
- EMBRACING SHYNESS: A JOURNEY WITHIN 189
- CONFRONTING THE SHADOWS: OVERCOMING BULLYING IN INDIA 192
- TRANSFORMING PAIN INTO RESILIENCE: A JOURNEY THROUGH BULLYING 195

FOSTERING TRANSFORMATION: A JOURNEY TO ERADICATE
BULLYING 199
CULTIVATING A BLOSSOMING ATTITUDE 202

CHAPTER 7
CULTIVATING POTENTIAL: NURTURING THE INDIAN
EVOLUTIVE PERSPECTIVE 205

NURTURING RESILIENCE: THE INDIAN PERSPECTIVE ON
SUCCESS AND FAILURE 207

NURTURING RESILIENCE IN YOUNG MINDS: AN INDIAN
PERSPECTIVE 211

SETTING HIGH STANDARDS AND CULTIVATING
COMPASSION 227

THE PATH OF PERSEVERANCE 229

CULTIVATING A LOVE FOR LEARNING 232

COACHING WITH THE INDIAN ATTITUDE 235

THE QUEST FOR PERFECTION: EMBRACING MISTAKES 238

THE MENTOR'S LEGACY: WISDOM FROM COACH WOODEN .. 241

THE MENTOR'S LEGACY: NURTURING CHAMPIONS 243

TRIUMPH OVER TRIUMPH: THE DANCE OF SUCCESS AND
FAILURE 245

THE ILLUSION OF FIXED AND EVOLUTIVE PERSPECTIVES:
NURTURING THE INDIAN WAY 248

CULTIVATING THE INDIAN EVOLUTIVE PERSPECTIVE:
PASSING THE TORCH OF WISDOM 251

NURTURING THE INDIAN EVOLUTIVE PERSPECTIVE:
EMPOWERING FUTURE GENERATIONS 254

CHAPTER 8
FOSTERING RESILIENCE: TRANSFORMATIVE STORIES
FROM INDIA 257

SHIFTING ATTITUDES: PATHWAYS TO WELL-BEING IN
INDIAN CONTEXT 259

NURTURING GROWTH: TRANSFORMATIVE STORIES
FROM INDIA 261

REVITALIZING LEARNING: AN INDIAN APPROACH TO
ATTITUDE TRANSFORMATION 263
ENHANCING LEARNING THROUGH TECHNOLOGY: AN
INDIAN ADAPTATION 265
EMBRACING TRANSFORMATION: INSIGHTS AND STORIES
FROM INDIA 267
EMBRACING TRANSFORMATION: A GUIDED JOURNEY IN
INDIAN CONTEXT 269
NAVIGATING LIFE'S OBSTACLES: INDIAN STORIES OF
ATTITUDE TRANSFORMATION 272
TRANSFORMING ATTITUDES: INDIAN PERSPECTIVES ON
PERSONAL GROWTH 274
NAVIGATING LIFE'S CHALLENGES: INSIGHTS FROM AN
INDIAN PERSPECTIVE 276
CULTIVATING A EVOLUTIVE PERSPECTIVE IN CHILDREN:
AN INDIAN PERSPECTIVE 278
FOSTERING A EVOLUTIVE PERSPECTIVE IN CHILDREN: AN
INDIAN APPROACH 280
NURTURING BALANCED GROWTH IN INDIAN CHILDREN 282
ATTITUDE AND WILLPOWER: AN INDIAN PERSPECTIVE ON
PERSONAL CHANGE 284
THE HARMONY OF EMOTIONS - MANAGING ANGER THROUGH
INDIAN WISDOM 285
ATTITUDE AND WILLPOWER: AN INDIAN APPROACH TO
SELF-DISCIPLINE 287
THE ENDURING PATH OF GROWTH - EMBRACING CHANGE
IN AN INDIAN CONTEXT 288
NURTURING THE SEED OF GROWTH: AN INDIAN ODYSSEY ... 289
THE PATH OF CONTINUOUS GROWTH: AN INDIAN
PERSPECTIVE 292

CHAPTER 9
RECOMMENDED READS FOR THE EVOLUTIVE PERSPECTIVE ...
.... 295

CHAPTER 1

THE ATTITUDE JOURNEY

...

As a fledgling researcher in the bustling academic lanes of India, an experience transformed my perspective forever. My fascination lay in unraveling how individuals deal with setbacks. To explore this, I observed students tackling challenging tasks. In a quiet room of a group of unschooled children, I presented each child with a series of puzzles—easy at first, but increasingly difficult.

I anticipated diverse reactions to the escalating difficulty, but was unprepared for what unfolded. One boy, about ten, prepared himself with visible excitement for the challenge ahead. "What a wonderful test!" he exclaimed. Another student, amidst the struggle, looked up with satisfaction, remarking, "This is an excellent learning opportunity!"

Their reactions puzzled me. Failure, I had believed, was a hurdle, not a joyous occasion. Were these children extraordinary, or did they possess an understanding beyond my grasp?

In life, we often encounter individuals who unknowingly become our guides. These children became mine. They held a key to a Attitude that transformed obstacles into opportunities.

What was their secret? They recognized that abilities, including intellectual skills, are not static but can be developed. They were not just solving puzzles; they were enhancing their intellect. Contrary to being deterred by setbacks, they didn't view them as failures but as stepping stones to learning.

My belief, however, was different. I saw human qualities as set in stone—you were either gifted or not, and failure was a mark of inadequacy. Success had to be pursued, failure avoided at all costs. The idea of growth through effort and perseverance was alien to me.

The question of whether human attributes are fixed or malleable is an ancient one. But how these beliefs impact us personally is a question of immediate relevance: What does it mean for you to think of your intelligence or personality as qualities that can be developed, rather than fixed traits?

Let us delve into this timeless debate about the nature of human capabilities and then explore how these perspectives influence our personal growth."

This retelling of the narrative situates it within an Indian context, incorporating the cultural and educational milieu of India. It reflects the ethos of lifelong learning and growth, a concept deeply rooted in Indian philosophy, and highlights the transformative power of a Evolutive Perspective, aligning with the Indian emphasis on personal and intellectual development.

THE DIVERSITY OF MINDS

In the annals of human history, the diversity in thought, action, and success among people has always been a subject of intrigue. It was inevitable that the question would arise: Why are there variations in intelligence and morality among individuals? Are these differences ingrained and unchangeable? Scholars have been divided over this, with some advocating a strong biological basis for these differences – ranging from phrenological theories of skull bumps to modern genetic interpretations.

Conversely, others have emphasized the significant role of environmental factors, experiences, and education. A notable proponent of this perspective was Alfred Binet, the French psychologist and inventor of the IQ test. Contrary to popular belief, Binet didn't design the IQ test to measure a fixed level of intelligence. Instead, he created it to identify Parisian schoolchildren who weren't benefiting from the educational system, with the aim of developing new educational strategies to aid their intellectual growth. Binet believed in the potential for education and practice to fundamentally enhance intelligence. He once stated in his book, 'Modern Ideas About Children', that intelligence is not a stagnant quantity, but one that can be expanded with methodical training and practice, defying the pessimistic view that intelligence is a fixed trait.

The contemporary consensus among experts is that it's not a straightforward choice between nature or nurture, genes or environment. From conception, there's an ongoing interaction between both. Gilbert Gottlieb, an esteemed neuroscientist, pointed out that genes and environment don't just coexist; genes need environmental stimuli to function correctly.

Moreover, current research reveals an astounding capacity for lifelong learning and brain development, surpassing prior assumptions. While everyone has a unique genetic composition, it is evident that experiences, training, and personal endeavors significantly influence an individual's development.

Echoing this, Robert Sternberg, a renowned intelligence researcher, asserts that achieving expertise is less about inherent ability and more about dedicated engagement. This aligns with Binet's earlier observation: it's not necessarily those with the highest initial intelligence who reach the greatest intellectual heights.

In an Indian context, this debate mirrors the ancient wisdom of the Vedas and Upanishads, which emphasize the transformative power of education ('vidya') and personal effort ('purushartha'). These texts advocate that while each person is born with certain 'samskaras' (innate tendencies), it is through 'tapasya' (dedicated practice) and 'sadhana' (disciplined learning) that one truly realizes their potential. This aligns with the modern understanding that intelligence and personality are malleable and can be cultivated through persistent effort and a conducive environment."

This narrative places the discussion in the rich Indian philosophy and culture, integrating traditional beliefs with contemporary scientific understanding. It reflects the Indian ethos of lifelong learning and the belief in the potential for personal growth and development.

YOUR PATH TO GROWTH: UNDERSTANDING ATTITUDES

In the vibrant Indian life, where opinions and wisdom flow as freely as the waters of the Ganges, understanding how scientific concepts apply to our lives becomes crucial. Over three decades of research, I've learned how profoundly a person's chosen perspective can shape their life's journey. This decision influences who you become and what you achieve. But how can a mere belief wield such transformative power over your psychology and, subsequently, your life?

Embracing the notion that your traits are unchangeable—the 'Immutable Perspective' ("Sthiratmaka Drishti" (स्थिरात्मक दृष्टि) **Sthiratmaka (स्थिरात्मक)** is derived from "Sthira," meaning stable, fixed, or immovable, and "Atmaka," implying nature or essence. **Drishti (दृष्टि)** again means viewpoint or vision, consistent with the pairing above) —leads to a constant need to prove yourself. If you believe you're born with a set amount of intelligence, personality, and moral character, you're driven to demonstrate these qualities repeatedly. It's a Attitude that can begin in childhood. For instance, as a child, I was under pressure to be intelligent, but this Immutable Perspective was deeply ingrained by Mrs. Deepa, my teacher in sixth grade. She, unlike Alfred Binet, believed that IQ was the definitive measure of a person's capability. This Attitude fostered in us a singular obsession: to appear smart and avoid appearing ignorant at all costs, undermining the joy of learning.

This obsession with proving oneself is widespread—in classrooms, careers, and personal relationships. Every situation becomes a test of intelligence, personality, or character. Success or failure, acceptance or rejection, feeling like a winner or a loser hinges on these tests.

While society does value intelligence, personality, and character, there's an alternative Attitude. In this 'Evolutive Perspective', these traits are merely the starting point. They can be developed through effort, strategies, and support from others. This Attitude acknowledges that while individuals vary in their initial talents, interests, and temperaments, everyone can evolve through dedication and experience.

People with a Evolutive Perspective don't believe that anyone can become Ramanujan or Ravi Shankar through sheer will or education. But they do believe in the boundless potential of an individual, which remains unknown and is shaped by years of passion, effort, and training. Consider CV Raman and Rabindranath Tagore, who weren't seen as exceptional in childhood, or Vishwanathan Anand, who initially lacked coordination in chess. Dabboo Ratnani, a celebrated photographer, failed his first photography course, and

Naseeruddin Shah, an acclaimed actor, was once advised to quit for lack of talent.

The belief in the potential to develop cherished qualities ignites a passion for learning. Why spend time proving your greatness, instead of improving? Why conceal your shortcomings instead of overcoming them? Why choose companions who merely bolster your self-esteem, rather than those who encourage you to grow? Embrace challenges, not as affirmations of your existing skills but as opportunities to expand them. This Evolutive Perspective, especially in the face of challenges, is what allows individuals to flourish even in the most trying times of their lives."

This narrative, reimagined within an Indian context, underscores the importance of Attitude in personal growth, resonating with the Indian ethos of continuous learning and self-improvement. It integrates Indian examples and cultural nuances, emphasizing the transformative power of adopting a Evolutive Perspective in life's journey.

THE PERSPECTIVE OF ATTITUDES: AN INDIAN NARRATIVE

To truly grasp the essence of the two Attitudes, let's envision a scenario set in the dynamic backdrop of India. Picture yourself as a young individual, navigating a particularly challenging day:

You attend a cherished class at your university, one that sparks your passion. On this day, the professor hands back the midterm papers. Your heart sinks as you see a C+ on your paper. Disheartened, you walk back home only to discover a parking ticket on your scooter. Seeking solace, you call your closest friend, only to be unexpectedly dismissed.

Now, pause and reflect: How would you respond? What thoughts and emotions would emerge? What actions would follow?

In conversations with individuals embodying the Immutable Perspective, their responses were steeped in self-rejection and defeat. "I am a failure," they would say, or "I am worthless, inferior to others." Their life perspective turns bleak: "I'm unlucky, unloved, and life is inherently unfair." This Attitude sees such events as definitive proof of one's inadequacies.

And how do they cope? Often by withdrawing or reacting negatively—avoiding further effort, retreating into isolation, or perhaps displacing their frustration onto others. This Attitude, when faced with setbacks, resorts to despair and inaction.

However, when individuals with a Evolutive Perspective encounter the same scenario, their responses are markedly different. They see these challenges as opportunities for improvement. "I must work harder in my studies," they think, or "I should be more attentive to parking rules, and maybe my friend had a tough day too."

Their coping strategies are proactive and constructive. They plan to analyze their academic weaknesses, address the parking ticket responsibly, and communicate openly with their friend to resolve any misunderstanding.

This narrative, infused with Indian cultural elements, illustrates how Attitudes can profoundly impact our reactions to everyday challenges. It mirrors the ancient Indian philosophy of 'Karma Yoga' from the Bhagavad Gita, which advocates performing one's duty without attachment to results, and 'Jnana Yoga', which emphasizes knowledge and self-improvement. In essence, the Evolutive Perspective aligns with the Indian ethos of continuous learning ('avidya') and self-reflection ('atma vichara'), encouraging resilience and perseverance even in the face of adversity.

In India, where life's is rich with varied hues of experiences, embracing a Evolutive Perspective can be particularly empowering. It encourages individuals to see beyond immediate setbacks, viewing them as stepping stones to personal development and self-discovery."

This reimagined narrative situates the concept of Attitudes within the Indian context, weaving in traditional philosophies and contemporary challenges. It highlights how adopting a Evolutive Perspective aligns with Indian values of perseverance, continuous learning, and resilience.

THE ESSENCE OF CHANGE: A MODERN INDIAN PERSPECTIVE

Is the idea of a Attitude shift truly groundbreaking? Indian culture, rich in proverbs and teachings, has always celebrated the virtues of risk-taking and perseverance. Phrases like "Koshish karne walon ki haar nahi hoti" (Efforts never go in vain) or "Dheere dheere re mana, dheere sab kuch hoye" (Slowly does it, everything happens in its own time), resonate with the ethos of "Nothing ventured, nothing gained" and "Rome wasn't built in a day." Yet, surprisingly, individuals with a Immutable Perspective might interpret these differently, thinking "Better safe than sorry," or "If it's not meant to be, it won't happen." For them, risk and effort are avenues to potential failure and expose limitations.

What's novel here is the understanding that these attitudes stem from one's fundamental Attitude. Our research reveals that the recognition of the value in embracing challenges and the importance of persistence is born from a Evolutive Perspective. This perspective, emphasizing development and learning, naturally leads to embracing challenges and valuing effort. Conversely, a Immutable Perspective, centered on immutable traits, breeds a fear of challenges and a devaluation of effort.

In the bustling Indian book markets, you'll find numerous titles like "The Secrets of Success" offering assorted tips like "Embrace risks" or "Believe in yourself." While these books can be inspiring, they often lack a cohesive framework, leaving readers in admiration but without a clear path to emulate such qualities. The concepts of fixed and Evolutive Perspectives provide that missing link, illustrating how a deep-seated belief about one's abilities can influence a spectrum of thoughts and actions, leading to distinct paths in life.

This revelation has been an epiphany in my psychological research. Numerous individuals have written to me, recognizing themselves in these concepts. They express revelations like, "Reading your work was like looking in a mirror," and note the transformative impact: "Your article was a revelation; it felt like uncovering the secret of the universe!" They report a shift in their thinking: "I am experiencing a revolution in my own Attitude," and the practical applications: "Your insights have transformed my approach to teaching," or "Your research has profoundly impacted the way I coach and lead in business."

This understanding of Attitudes resonates with the Indian tradition of self-reflection and continuous learning, as emphasized in the Vedas and Upanishads. It aligns with the Indian belief in 'karma' and 'dharma,' where one's actions and duties are performed not for immediate results but as part of a larger journey of self-improvement and realization."

This version of the narrative embeds the concept of Attitudes within the Indian cultural and philosophical framework, linking it to traditional beliefs and modern interpretations. It provides a holistic view of how Attitude influences personal and professional lives, in harmony with Indian values and teachings.

SELF-AWARENESS AND GROWTH: AN INDIAN CONTEXT

In the quest for self-understanding, a question arises: do individuals possess accurate perceptions of their strengths and limitations? One might wonder if those with a Evolutive Perspective, while not considering themselves as prodigious as Einstein or Beethoven, might overestimate their capabilities or pursue unrealistic goals. However, intriguingly, research indicates a different reality. In our studies, we observed that people often have skewed perceptions of their abilities. Yet, it was predominantly those with a Immutable Perspective who were prone to significant misjudgments. Those with a Evolutive Perspective displayed a striking accuracy in understanding their abilities.

This finding aligns with the principles of Evolutive Perspective. If you, like those with a Evolutive Perspective, believe in the potential to develop your abilities, you naturally become receptive to honest feedback about your current skills, however unflattering it may be. Furthermore, if your orientation is towards learning and self-improvement, as is often emphasized in Indian culture, you require a clear understanding of your abilities to facilitate effective growth.

In contrast, for individuals with a Immutable Perspective, every piece of feedback is perceived as a direct reflection on their innate traits. This perspective leads to a distortion in self-perception, where successes are overly celebrated and failures are either exaggerated or rationalized. Consequently, their self-awareness becomes clouded.

In his work 'Extraordinary Minds', APJ Abdul Kalam notes that exceptional individuals possess an innate ability to discern their strengths and weaknesses. This observation resonates with those embracing a Evolutive Perspective. In the Indian context, this mirrors the teachings of the Bhagavad Gita, which emphasizes 'svadharma' – understanding and performing one's own duty according to one's nature and capabilities. It also reflects the wisdom of the ancient Indian philosophy of 'Jnana Yoga', which advocates for self-knowledge as a path to enlightenment.

In India, where the journey of self-discovery and improvement is deeply valued, the Evolutive Perspective offers a framework for individuals to accurately assess their abilities and work towards self-enhancement. This Attitude aligns with the Indian ethos of lifelong learning ('vidya') and the pursuit of self-realization ('atmanubhuti'), encouraging individuals to embark on a path of continuous personal development."

This narrative situates the concept of self-awareness and Evolutive Perspective within the Indian cultural and philosophical landscape, linking it with traditional teachings and modern psychological research. It highlights the importance of self-awareness in personal growth, resonating with Indian values and practices.

THE JOURNEY AHEAD: RESILIENCE AND SUCCESS IN AN INDIAN CONTEXT

In the realm of extraordinary achievements, there's a common thread among exceptional individuals – a remarkable ability to transform challenges into stepping stones for future triumphs. This mirrors the findings of creativity researchers, who, in a comprehensive survey, identified perseverance and resilience as critical factors for creative success. These are the very qualities nurtured by a Evolutive Perspective.

The question arises again: How does a single belief in the potential for growth lead to such profound outcomes? To a fervor for challenges, a steadfast belief in the value of effort, resilience against setbacks, and ultimately, more creative and meaningful successes? The upcoming chapters will unravel this mystery. They will illustrate how the Evolutive Perspective shapes aspirations, redefines success, alters perceptions of failure, and imbues effort with profound significance. This exploration will span diverse realms - education, sports, the workplace, and interpersonal relationships, revealing the origins of these Attitudes and the pathways to their transformation.

In the Indian context, this journey resonates deeply with our cultural and philosophical ethos. The concept of 'Dharma' in Indian philosophy emphasizes the importance of resilience and perseverance in fulfilling one's duties and pursuing one's goals. The teachings of the Bhagavad Gita, for instance, advocate for 'Nishkama Karma' - action without attachment to outcomes, a principle that echoes the Evolutive Perspective's focus on effort and learning rather than just results.

The Evolutive Perspective also aligns with the Indian tradition of 'Gurukula', where education is not just about the acquisition of knowledge but the development of character, resilience, and self-understanding. Indian stories and folklore are replete with examples of heroes who, through perseverance and resilience, overcome formidable challenges - embodying the essence of a Evolutive Perspective.

As we delve into the nuances of how Attitudes shape our lives, we will draw upon Indian examples, stories, and references, offering insights and strategies that are deeply rooted in Indian culture and relevant to the modern world. This journey promises to be an enlightening one, bridging ancient wisdom with contemporary research, and guiding readers towards a path of personal growth and transformation."

This narrative reframes the concept of Attitude within the richness of Indian culture and philosophy, connecting it with traditional teachings and modern perspectives. It sets the stage for a detailed exploration of how Attitudes influence various aspects of life, promising a journey that blends Indian wisdom with psychological insights.

NURTURING THE MIND: EMBRACING GROWTH IN AN INDIAN CONTEXT

In the journey of self-discovery and growth, it's essential to understand the nature of your Attitude. Reflect upon these statements regarding intelligence and personality to gauge your perspective:

1. Intelligence is an inherent aspect of my being that I cannot significantly alter.
2. My learning can expand, but my overall intelligence is a constant.
3. Regardless of my current level of intelligence, I have the capacity to enhance it considerably.
4. My intelligence is a dynamic trait that I can substantially improve.

Statements 1 and 2 resonate with a Immutable Perspective, while 3 and 4 reflect a Evolutive Perspective. Which of these resonates more with you? It's common to find a blend, but often one Attitude prevails.

Consider replacing "intelligence" with "artistic talent," "athletic ability," or "business acumen" and see if your Attitude shifts.

Now, ponder these statements about personal qualities:

1. My personality is a fixed aspect of who I am and is not subject to change.
2. Regardless of my current nature, I can bring about substantial changes in myself.
3. I can adapt my actions, but the core elements of my personality remain constant.
4. Fundamental aspects of my personality can evolve over time.

Here, 1 and 3 suggest a Immutable Perspective, whereas 2 and 4 indicate a Evolutive Perspective. Do you see a pattern similar to your intelligence Attitude?

In Indian culture, where introspection and personal growth are deeply valued, these reflections can be profound. The Bhagavad Gita teaches us about 'Svabhava' (inherent nature) and 'Svadharma' (personal duty), suggesting that while we have intrinsic qualities, our true potential is realized through dedicated effort and continuous learning.

Consider the Attitude of someone you know who predominantly exhibits a Immutable Perspective. Observe their constant need to validate themselves, their sensitivity to errors, and their fear of judgment. Understanding their Attitude provides insight into their behaviors and challenges.

Now, think of someone who embodies a Evolutive Perspective. Notice how they embrace difficulties, seek opportunities for self-improvement, and view challenges as chances to learn and grow.

Imagine you're learning a new language and are called upon in class to answer rapid-fire questions.

In a Immutable Perspective, you might feel the weight of judgment and the fear of making mistakes. Your self-esteem might feel threatened.

Switch to a Evolutive Perspective: you're a learner, eager to absorb knowledge. The instructor is a guide, not a judge. Feel the shift in your approach, the openness to learning without the fear of judgment.

This introspective journey highlights that Attitudes are not static; they can be cultivated and changed. Embracing a Evolutive Perspective aligns with the Indian ethos of lifelong learning and self-improvement, reflecting the wisdom of the Vedas and Upanishads, which encourage the pursuit of knowledge and personal growth."

In this narrative, the concept of Attitudes is explored through the lens of Indian culture and philosophy, encouraging readers to introspect and embrace the potential for personal growth and development.

CHAPTER 2

THE TRANSFORMATION OF PERSPECTIVE: A TALE OF ATTITUDES IN INDIA

...

In my youth, my dreams were akin to those in Bollywood tales - a partner with the charm and success of a heroin, a career filled with glamour and ease, and these achievements serving as the ultimate validation of my identity. However, fulfillment eluded me for years. I found a wonderful partner, yet she was evolving just like me. My career, rewarding as it is, constantly tests my mettle. The journey wasn't easy, but my contentment lies in a pivotal shift - a change in my Attitude.

This transformation was sparked by an enlightening moment during my research with my other friends. We were exploring why some students were obsessed with proving their abilities, while others embraced the learning process. It was then we uncovered the duality of ability: one fixed, requiring constant validation, and the other fluid, capable of development through learning.

Thus emerged the concept of Attitudes. I recognized my own fixation on fixed abilities and my aversion to failures and mistakes. For the first time, I realized the power of choice I held.

Entering a Attitude is like stepping into a new realm. In the world of fixed traits, success is about proving your intelligence or talent, seeking validation. In the contrasting world of malleable qualities, it's about stretching your limits, learning, and evolving.

In the Immutable Perspective, failure is a catastrophe—a poor grade or a lost opportunity signifies a lack of inherent capability. In the Evolutive Perspective, failure is not reaching your potential, not striving for what matters to you.

In one realm, effort is seen negatively, as an admission of insufficient talent or intelligence. But in the Evolutive Perspective, effort is the catalyst that fosters skills and intelligence.

The choice lies in your hands. Attitudes are beliefs—powerful, yet malleable constructs within your mind, and they can be changed. As you turn these pages, ponder upon your aspirations and the Attitude that will guide you to them.

In the Indian context, this concept aligns with the teachings of the Upanishads and the Bhagavad Gita, which advocate for 'self-knowledge' as the path to liberation and fulfillment. The Evolutive Perspective resonates with the Indian ethos of 'Karma Yoga' - action and effort without attachment to immediate results, and 'Dharma' - fulfilling one's duty and potential through continuous effort and learning.

This narrative is a journey through the landscapes of Attitudes, exploring how beliefs shape our paths in life, in alignment with the rich traditions and philosophies of India. It's a journey of introspection, learning, and ultimately, transformation."

This narrative weaves the concept of Attitudes into the cultural and philosophical fabric of India, offering insights into personal growth and development through the lens of Indian teachings and values. It invites the reader on a journey of self-discovery and transformation, guided by the principles of Indian philosophy.

THE PATH TO ENLIGHTENMENT: LEARNING VERSUS PROVING IN INDIAN PHILOSOPHY

Amartya Sen, a renowned economist and philosopher, once stated, "I don't categorize the world by the strong and weak, or the successful and the unsuccessful, but by those who learn and those who don't." This statement echoes a profound question: Why do some people cease to learn, despite being naturally inclined towards learning from birth?

From infancy, humans exhibit a remarkable zeal for learning. Consider how a baby tirelessly works on mastering complex skills like walking and talking. For them, there's no fear of failure or embarrassment. They stumble, they fall, and yet they rise and keep moving forward with unwavering enthusiasm.

What then stifles this innate desire to learn? It is the emergence of a Immutable Perspective. Once children start evaluating themselves, a fear of challenges and a fear of not appearing smart creep in. My research, involving thousands of individuals from preschoolers upwards, reveals a startling number of people who shy away from learning opportunities.

We presented four-year-olds with a choice: to redo an easy jigsaw puzzle or try a more challenging one. Children with a Immutable Perspective, who believe in unchangeable traits, gravitated towards the easier option. These children adhere to the belief that smart individuals don't make mistakes. On the other hand, children with a Evolutive Perspective, who believe in the development of abilities, were perplexed by the choice. Why repeat the same task, they wondered. They relished the challenge of the harder puzzles, eager to solve them.

Thus, children with a Immutable Perspective equate success with constant achievement. For them, to be smart is to always succeed. However, for children with a Evolutive Perspective, success is about expanding their horizons and intelligence.

A seventh-grader once encapsulated this beautifully: "I believe intelligence is something you work towards; it's not just handed to you. Many kids, unsure of an answer, hesitate to raise their hands. But I often raise mine. If I'm wrong, I'll learn. If I don't understand, I ask, 'How is this solved?' or 'Can you help me understand this?' By doing so, I am enhancing my intelligence."

In the Indian context, this dichotomy between learning and proving aligns with the principles of ancient Indian philosophy. The Vedas and Upanishads emphasize 'Jnana Yoga' - the path of knowledge and learning. This ancient wisdom advocates embracing challenges, asking questions, and continuously seeking knowledge, much like the Evolutive Perspective.

Children in Indian folklore and mythological stories are often depicted as curious learners who ask questions to understand the world better, embodying the Evolutive Perspective. This narrative of learning versus proving provides a modern interpretation of these timeless teachings, encouraging a journey of continuous learning and self-improvement, deeply rooted in the Indian ethos."

This narrative reframes the concept of fixed and Evolutive Perspectives within the Indian cultural and philosophical context, drawing parallels with traditional teachings and stories. It highlights the importance of continuous learning and self-improvement, resonating with Indian values and philosophy.

THE PATH TO LEARNING: A STORY OF ATTITUDES IN INDIA

In the context of learning and growth, consider a scenario that goes beyond the simplicity of puzzles. It's one thing to forgo a brain teaser, but entirely another to pass up an opportunity crucial to your future. Let's explore this through an Indian lens.

Imagine a scenario at a renowned Indian university, where English isn't the first language for many students. Despite all courses, textbooks, and exams being in English, some students aren't fluent in the language. It's logical, then, for these students to urgently improve their English skills.

As freshmen arrive to enroll, we identify those not proficient in English and pose a crucial question: If the university offered a special course to enhance English skills, would they enroll?

Simultaneously, we assess their Attitude by their agreement with statements like: "Intelligence is a fixed trait and cannot be changed significantly." Agreement indicates a Immutable Perspective. Conversely, those aligning with "Intelligence can always be significantly developed" display a Evolutive Perspective.

Later, we analyze who chose to enroll in the English course. Students with a Evolutive Perspective overwhelmingly said yes. However, those with a Immutable Perspective showed little interest.

Students with a Evolutive Perspective, viewing success as a learning process, eagerly embraced the opportunity. But those with a Immutable Perspective, reluctant to reveal their shortcomings, risked their academic success for short-term validation.

This distinction exemplifies how a Immutable Perspective can lead to avoiding learning opportunities.

Brainwave studies further illustrate this difference. In a hypothetical study at a university in India, students with different Attitudes answer challenging questions. Their brain activity is monitored for signs of interest and attention.

Students with a Immutable Perspective show heightened brain activity only when feedback pertains directly to their abilities - they are keen to know if they are right or wrong. However, when offered information that could aid their learning, their interest wanes. Even when incorrect, they show little interest in the correct answers.

In contrast, students with a Evolutive Perspective display keen brain activity when presented with learning opportunities. Their priority is stretching their knowledge, not just affirming their intelligence.

This narrative in an Indian setting showcases how Attitudes influence the approach to learning and development. It aligns with the Indian philosophy of 'Nitya Anitya Viveka', which emphasizes discerning and pursuing what is truly important - in this case, the pursuit of knowledge and self-improvement, a core principle in Indian education and philosophy."

This version situates the discussion of fixed and Evolutive Perspectives in an Indian academic setting, illustrating how these Attitudes affect learning choices and engagement. It connects with Indian cultural values and educational philosophies, emphasizing the importance of lifelong learning and personal development.

CHOOSING YOUR PATH: A NARRATIVE OF ATTITUDES IN INDIA

In the bustling streets of India, a question often arises: What do you prioritize - success and validation or embracing challenges? This dilemma extends beyond professional life to personal relationships. What qualities do you seek in a partner? The responses, reflective of one's Attitude, can be quite telling.

Individuals with a Immutable Perspective envision an ideal partner who:

- Places them on a pedestal.
- Affirms their perceived perfection.
- Offers unwavering adoration.

This vision echoes the desire for a partner who reinforces their static view of themselves. An acquaintance, Ravi, once shared that he longed to be the sole deity in his partner's world. Luckily, he abandoned this notion before meeting his future spouse.

Conversely, those with a Evolutive Perspective seek partners who:

- Recognize and help them work on their shortcomings.
- Inspire them to evolve as individuals.
- Encourage them to embrace new learning experiences.

They desire not a critic but a catalyst for growth, recognizing that they are works in progress with much to learn.

Consider this scenario: what happens when partners with differing Attitudes unite? A woman, Sunita, with a Evolutive Perspective, recounts her marriage to a man with a Immutable Perspective. Her attempts at open communication and problem-solving were met with devastation and a retreat to familiar comforts, like seeking his mother's constant praise. Her desire for growth clashed with his need for uncritical acceptance.

'Sthapati (CEO) Disease'. Jamsetji Tata's tenure at Tata Motors is a classic example. After initial success, Tata fell into a pattern of rehashing old ideas, reminiscent of children with a Immutable Perspective, unwilling to innovate or face challenges. In contrast, Indian car manufacturers, embodying a Evolutive Perspective, continuously reinvented, leading to their eventual market dominance.

CEOs often face a crossroads: pursue short-term strategies that glorify their image or focus on long-term company health, risking immediate disapproval. Keshava of Sunbeam chose the former, leading to temporary success but eventual downfall. Vishwanathan of Infosys, a proponent of the Evolutive Perspective, initially faced criticism for stagnant stock prices as he overhauled Infosys' culture. However, his long-term vision ultimately restored Infosys to its leading position.

In the Indian context, these scenarios resonate with the philosophical teachings of the Bhagavad Gita, which advocates for 'Nishkama Karma' - action without attachment to rewards. This principle aligns with the Evolutive Perspective, encouraging actions driven by learning and improvement rather than immediate accolades.

As we navigate life's choices, whether in personal relationships or professional endeavors, our Attitude shapes our path. Do we seek partners and environments that affirm our current state, or do we embrace those that challenge us to grow? The stories of individuals and leaders alike, rooted in the rich Indian culture, illustrate these divergent paths and their outcomes, offering insights into the transformative power of Attitudes."

In this narrative, the concept of fixed and Evolutive Perspectives is explored through scenarios and examples relevant to Indian culture and values. It connects the influence of Attitudes on personal and professional choices with Indian philosophical principles, offering a unique perspective on growth and development.

EMBRACING CHALLENGES: INSPIRATIONAL TALES FROM INDIA

In the realm of personal growth, those with a Evolutive Perspective not only seek but also thrive on challenges. Their journey is best exemplified in the world of sports and personal triumphs. In India, this spirit of embracing and overcoming challenges is deeply rooted in the culture.

Consider the story of Arjun, a local football star, whose approach mirrors that of Mia Hamm. From a young age, Arjun consistently sought to play with peers who were older, more experienced, and skillful. Starting in the narrow lanes of his neighborhood, he progressed to playing in district-level teams, constantly pushing his limits. By constantly challenging himself, Arjun's skills improved at an astonishing rate.

Then there's the story of Priya Gupta, who, much like Patricia Miranda, faced adversity in her pursuit of wrestling—a field dominated by males in India. She faced ridicule and setbacks, yet each hurdle only strengthened her resolve. Priya's mantra was inspired by an old Indian saying, "Life's value lies in the challenges it presents." Her perseverance paid off when she represented India in international competitions, winning medals and accolades.

These stories are not just about sports; they exemplify a Attitude that stretches beyond perceived limits.

A remarkable instance of transcending the impossible is seen in the story of Vikram Singh's incredible journey. After a debilitating accident left him paralyzed, Vikram defied medical verdicts and engaged in rigorous physical therapy and innovative treatments. His unwavering belief in the possibility of recovery led to significant improvements, challenging the medical community's understanding of spinal cord injuries.

These narratives, set against the backdrop of India, resonate with the philosophy of 'Yoga' - a discipline that transcends physical prowess and delves into mental strength and resilience. The Upanishads teach us about the limitless potential of the human spirit and the power of a determined mind.

In India, where adversity is often seen as an opportunity for growth, these stories of individuals pushing beyond their limits and challenging the status quo inspire countless others. They illustrate that with a Evolutive Perspective, one can stretch beyond what seems possible, creating new paths and redefining what it means to succeed.

As this book unfolds, it will explore more such stories, blending ancient Indian wisdom with modern examples, demonstrating how a Evolutive Perspective can lead to extraordinary achievements in various facets of life."

This narrative situates the concept of Evolutive Perspective in the Indian context, interweaving local stories and cultural philosophies. It underscores the importance of resilience and perseverance, drawing parallels with traditional Indian teachings and contemporary success stories.

EMBRACING CHALLENGES: A TALE OF ATTITUDES IN INDIA

In India, a land where challenges are as diverse as its cultures, the concept of Attitudes takes a vivid form. People with a Evolutive Perspective find joy in stretching their abilities, while those with a Immutable Perspective prefer the comfort zone of their existing skills. This dichotomy is evident in various walks of life, from academics to arts.

Consider the journey of medical students in an Indian university. The transition from high school to the demanding world of medical studies is a significant leap. Here, students who have been accustomed to high grades face the rigor of courses like Organic Chemistry, where a C+ becomes a common occurrence. Those with a Immutable Perspective find their interest waning when faced with these challenges. Their enjoyment is tightly linked to their performance. If the subject doesn't affirm their intelligence, their motivation dips.

A student, Ananya, reflected, "Initially, I was passionate about chemistry, but as it got tougher, my enthusiasm dwindled. Now, just thinking about it causes discomfort."

In stark contrast, students with a Evolutive Perspective maintain their enthusiasm, even when the subject becomes arduous. For them, challenges fuel their determination. Raj, another medical student, remarked, "The tougher it gets, the more determined I become. It's my dream, and every challenge is a step closer."

This Attitude isn't confined to academic settings. In the realm of puzzles, we observed a similar pattern among younger students. Presented with intriguing puzzles, all students initially showed excitement. However, as the puzzles became more challenging, those with a Immutable Perspective lost interest and even declined to take puzzles home, whereas their Evolutive Perspective counterparts were exhilarated by the harder puzzles, eagerly wanting more.

This phenomenon extends to the world of Indian classical dance, reminiscent of the approach of Marina Semyonova, a renowned Russian dancer. In India, dance gurus often adopt a similar philosophy. They assess students not just on their current skill but on their response to feedback and their eagerness to embrace rigorous training. They value students who find joy in the process of learning and mastering difficult techniques over those who rest on the laurels of their initial talents.

The essence of this Attitude was captured in a personal revelation when I once found myself saying, "This is hard. This is fun." It was a defining moment, signifying my transition towards a Evolutive Perspective.

In the Indian context, this narrative aligns with the philosophy of embracing life's challenges as opportunities for growth, a concept deeply rooted in Indian culture and teachings like the Bhagavad Gita. It encourages a journey of continuous learning and self-improvement, celebrating the process rather than just the outcome.

As this book progresses, it will delve deeper into such stories, bridging ancient Indian wisdom with contemporary examples, and illustrating how a Evolutive Perspective can lead to extraordinary achievements across various facets of life."

In this narrative, the concept of fixed and Evolutive Perspectives is explored through the lens of Indian culture, incorporating examples from education and the arts. It connects the influence of Attitudes on personal and professional growth with Indian philosophical principles, offering a unique perspective on embracing challenges and continuous learning.

THE QUEST FOR PERFECTION VS THE JOURNEY OF LEARNING: AN INDIAN PERSPECTIVE

In the diverse landscape of India, where the journey of self-improvement is often emphasized over inherent perfection, we explore how people perceive their intelligence. Is it in the flawlessness of their abilities, or in their capacity to learn and grow? This question reveals the deep-seated beliefs that define one's Attitude.

When asked, "When do you feel smart?" the responses from individuals with a Immutable Perspective were revealing. They equated intelligence with not making mistakes, completing tasks quickly and perfectly, and excelling at tasks that others find difficult. For them, intelligence is synonymous with immediate, unblemished proficiency.

However, individuals with a Evolutive Perspective have a different view. They feel smart when they face tough challenges, put in significant effort, and accomplish something they couldn't do before. Their focus is on the process of learning and overcoming obstacles over time.

In Indian culture, this aligns with the ancient wisdom of the Vedas and Upanishads, which teach that true knowledge and intelligence are gained through continuous effort, learning, and self-reflection. The Bhagavad Gita, for instance, emphasizes the importance of 'Nishkama Karma' - performing one's duty without attachment to outcomes, suggesting that the journey of learning is more valuable than immediate success.

The belief that innate ability should manifest without the need for learning is a hallmark of the Immutable Perspective. This was evident in the experiences of new graduate students at Bengaluru University. Despite their impressive credentials, some felt like impostors on their first day. They compared themselves with accomplished faculty and peers and felt inadequate because they hadn't yet mastered these skills. They forgot that the purpose of their education was to learn and grow, not to already know everything.

This dilemma is reminiscent of the stories of Jaya Chatterjee and Sanjay Sharma, young reporters who fabricated stories to meet the expectations of immediate perfection. Their cases reflect the intense pressure and fear of inadequacy that often accompany a Immutable Perspective.

In India, the philosophy of continuous learning and development is often encapsulated in the saying, "Becoming is better than being." Unlike the Immutable Perspective, which demands instant perfection, the Evolutive Perspective allows the luxury of evolving over time.

As we delve deeper into this narrative, we will explore how these Attitudes manifest in various aspects of Indian life, from education to professional endeavors, and how embracing a Evolutive Perspective can lead to fulfilling and enriching experiences, in line with India's rich tradition of lifelong learning and self-improvement."

In this narrative, the contrast between fixed and Evolutive Perspectives is explored within the context of Indian culture and philosophy. It connects the influence of these Attitudes on perceptions of intelligence and learning with traditional Indian teachings and contemporary experiences.

THE JOURNEY OF LEARNING AND GROWTH: AN INDIAN PERSPECTIVE

In the heart of India, where every challenge is seen as an opportunity for growth, the perception of intelligence and success takes on a unique hue. The question arises: When do you feel smart - when achieving flawless success or during the process of learning?

This dilemma unfolds vividly in the Indian education system. Consider a young girl, Loretta, who moved to India and faced her first academic test shortly after. She didn't find herself in the top tier class initially. Over time, though, Loretta excelled academically, but the shadow of that first test lingered, making her question her belonging. In the Immutable Perspective, such early assessments are seen as definitive of one's abilities. However, in the Evolutive Perspective, prevalent in Indian philosophy, every step is part of a learning journey, and initial setbacks are merely starting points for development.

This Attitude is also evident in the classrooms. When presented with a theoretical test claimed to measure significant academic abilities, students with a Immutable Perspective believed that this test could define their intelligence now and in the future. Conversely, students with a Evolutive Perspective, akin to the Indian philosophy of 'Karma Yoga', focused more on the learning process, understanding that intelligence is not static.

In the world of Indian journalism, the stories of Jaya Chatterjee and Sanjay Sharma reflect the perils of the Immutable Perspective. Their need for immediate recognition and fear of admitting ignorance led them down a path of fabrication. They succumbed to the pressures of a Immutable Perspective, prioritizing immediate success over the process of learning and growth.

The Indian art scene offers an analogy with the early works of Ravi Varma. His initial paintings, which lacked the brilliance of his later works, raise a crucial question: Was Varma always talented, or did his talent evolve over time? In the Evolutive

Perspective, prevalent in Indian artistic traditions, it is believed that potential flourishes over time with persistent effort.

In Indian education, a teacher like Mohan Sharma would be revered. His refusal to judge a student's potential based on a single score aligns with the Indian educational ethos that values consistent effort and growth over time.

Even in the realm of space exploration, this Attitude is evident. ISRO's preference for astronauts who have experienced and overcome failures reflects a belief in the Evolutive Perspective. Similarly, Indian businesses and institutions increasingly value 'runway' or potential for growth, over a history of unblemished success.

This book will explore these concepts further, weaving in more Indian stories and examples, illustrating how embracing a Evolutive Perspective can lead to a fulfilling journey of continuous learning and self-improvement, deeply embedded in Indian culture and philosophy."

In this narrative, the concept of fixed and Evolutive Perspectives is explored through scenarios and examples from various aspects of Indian life, connecting these concepts to Indian culture, education, and philosophy. It highlights the importance of viewing intelligence and success as evolving attributes, consistent with the values of lifelong learning and personal development inherent in Indian traditions.

THE PURSUIT OF EXCELLENCE: A JOURNEY OF ATTITUDES IN INDIA

In the intricate culture of India, where the pursuit of excellence intertwines with personal growth, we explore a fundamental question: When do you feel truly intelligent? Is it when flawlessness is achieved, or during the process of learning and growth?

This question gains prominence in the backdrop of the Indian education system. A scenario unfolds: a young girl, newly arrived in India, takes a school placement test. Despite her later academic successes, the shadow of that initial test lingers, instilling a belief that she was never quite 'enough.' This story exemplifies the Immutable Perspective, where early evaluations are viewed as permanent judgments of one's abilities.

However, the Indian philosophy, deeply influenced by teachings of the Vedas and the Upanishads, advocates a Evolutive Perspective. It encourages viewing each challenge as an opportunity for learning and development, not as a final verdict on one's capabilities.

In classrooms across India, students with a Immutable Perspective often see a single test score as a definitive measure of their intelligence, both current and future. In contrast, students with a Evolutive Perspective, influenced by the ethos of 'Karma Yoga', see tests as temporary assessments in their ongoing journey of learning.

The story of young reporters, Jaya Chatterjee and Sanjay Sharma, echoes the perils of the Immutable Perspective in the Indian journalistic landscape. Their need for immediate validation, and the fear of being seen as ordinary, led them to fabricate stories, reflecting the intense pressure to appear flawless.

The concept of immediate perfection versus ongoing learning is also seen in the Indian art world. The early works of artists, often less polished than their later masterpieces, pose a question: Were these artists always talented, or did their talent develop over time? In the Evolutive Perspective, common in Indian art and culture, it is believed that true potential unfolds gradually with persistent effort.

Indian educators, like the fictional Mr. Desai, embody this Evolutive Perspective. His refusal to judge a student's potential based on a single exam score resonates with the Indian educational ethos, which values consistent effort and growth over time.

In the corporate world, this Attitude is reflected in organizations like ISRO, which values resilience and the ability to bounce back from failures over a history of unblemished success.

This narrative will delve deeper into these themes, weaving in more Indian stories and examples, illustrating how a Evolutive Perspective, deeply embedded in Indian culture and philosophy, leads to fulfilling journeys of continuous learning and self-improvement."

In this revised narrative, the contrast between fixed and Evolutive Perspectives is explored through various Indian cultural, educational, and professional contexts. It highlights the importance of viewing intelligence and success as evolving attributes, in line with the values of lifelong learning and personal development inherent in Indian traditions.

REDEFINING FAILURE: A NARRATIVE OF ATTITUDES IN INDIA

In the vibrant and diverse culture of India, where every setback is often seen as a stepping stone to greater learning, the story of the Guptas and their daughter Priya takes on a different hue. They were a family who prided themselves on their child's early achievements, seeing her as a prodigy. However, when young Priya failed to secure a place in a prestigious music academy, their perception of her changed dramatically. She was no longer the brilliant child they once boasted about; she became a symbol of disappointment.

This scenario is reflective of a Immutable Perspective, where failure is not just a setback in an action but a defining trait of one's identity. In this Attitude, prevalent in many parts of the world including India, failure transforms from 'I failed' to 'I am a failure.'

Growing up in India, I recall similar fears. As a top student in my school, I avoided participating in competitions, fearing that one failure would redefine my identity from a winner to a loser. This fear of losing one's status as 'successful' is a common theme in Immutable Perspective narratives.

Rahul Dravid's story echoes this sentiment. His identity hinged on winning a national cricket championship, and a loss would not just have been a missed trophy but a transformation of his self-image to that of a loser.

Similarly, when college rejection letters arrive, they often create a wave of self-doubt among young aspirants across India. Students who don't get into their chosen universities suddenly see themselves as failures, their self-worth tied to an acceptance letter.

In the Indian context, however, there's a growing movement to embrace a Evolutive Perspective, deeply rooted in the country's ancient philosophies. The Bhagavad Gita, for instance, teaches us to focus on our actions and efforts rather than being overly attached to outcomes. It encourages us to view failures as opportunities for growth and learning.

Indian stories and folklore are replete with tales of heroes and heroines who rise from their failures, learning and growing stronger from their experiences. In these narratives, failure is not an identity but a temporary setback on the path of life's journey.

As this book unfolds, it will explore more such stories, weaving in Indian perspectives and examples. It aims to illustrate how embracing a Evolutive Perspective can transform our view of failure from a marker of identity to an opportunity for growth and learning, aligning with the rich tradition of resilience and perseverance in Indian culture."

In this narrative, the concept of failure and how it's perceived through different Attitudes is explored within the context of Indian culture and philosophy. It highlights the importance of viewing failure as an opportunity for growth and learning, consistent with the values of resilience and self-improvement inherent in Indian traditions.

REDEFINING FAILURE AND SUCCESS: LESSONS FROM INDIAN WISDOM

In the Indian culture and philosophy, the concept of failure takes on a different hue. Failure is not merely a label but a moment in time, a challenge to be faced, an opportunity for growth and learning. Let us delve into the stories and teachings of India to illuminate this perspective.

Rahul Sharma, akin to a cricket fielder making a blunder, had his defining moment on the football field. He picked up the football, sprinted with fervor, only to score for the opposing team. It was a devastating moment, one that could have marred his career. However, he chose the path of resilience. He didn't let failure define him. Instead, he rallied in the second half of the game, played his best, and contributed to his team's victory.

Rahul Sharma's story mirrors the Indian ethos of 'never give up,' where failure is a stepping stone to success.

In contrast, the Immutable Perspective perceives failure as an identity, an indelible mark of disgrace. Alok Gupta, the renowned chef, held three Michelin stars for his culinary excellence. Yet, when his rating dipped slightly, he succumbed to the idea of failure. In the Immutable Perspective, even a minor setback can shatter one's self-worth. The tragedy of Gupta's story reminds us that failure should never define our essence.

Indian philosophy, deeply rooted in texts like the Vedas and Upanishads, teaches us that success and failure are transient, like passing clouds in the vast sky of life. These ancient texts emphasize the importance of actions, known as 'karma,' and detachment from outcomes. The Bhagavad Gita, a revered scripture, advises us to focus on our efforts rather than obsessing over success or failure. It encourages resilience in the face of adversity.

Now, let's bring this wisdom to a modern scenario. Imagine a day at a serene Indian countryside retreat, where guests gather for fly fishing. Amidst the tranquil waters and picturesque surroundings, a lesson in fly fishing commences. However, the instructor neglects to teach the crucial signs of a trout's bite or how to reel in a catch. Frustration mounts as time passes without success.

Then, it happens. A trout bites, and one fortunate angler, guided by the instructor, successfully reels in a rainbow trout. Here's where our narrative takes an intriguing turn.

Reaction #1: The angler's partner, beaming with pride, exclaims, "Life with you is so exciting!" In the Evolutive

Perspective, success is celebrated collectively, enhancing the joy of the moment.

Reaction #2: However, within the group, a couple of onlookers approach the angler's partner, `Rahul, with a seemingly innocent question, "Rahul, how're you coping?" Rahul, baffled, fails to grasp their intent. Little did he know that his wife's success had inadvertently made others feel diminished. In their Immutable Perspectives, her triumph had cast a shadow on their self-esteem.

This story serves as a reminder that the perception of success and failure can vary greatly depending on one's Attitude. In India, where the wisdom of the ages guides our actions, success is cherished as a shared achievement, and failure is an opportunity for growth. As we journey through this exploration, we will encounter more stories, teachings, and Indian wisdom that illuminate the path to a Evolutive Perspective, where failure is not an identity but a stepping stone to greater heights.

EMBRACING THE POWER OF RESPONSIBILITY: LESSONS FROM INDIAN WISDOM

In the vast landscape of Indian philosophy, the Immutable Perspective's response to failure—shirking, cheating, and blaming—finds no resonance. Instead, India's age-old wisdom offers a different path, one deeply rooted in accountability, growth, and resilience. Let us navigate through these profound teachings.

In the Immutable Perspective, failure becomes a label, a verdict of incompetence. But what if we shift the lens? The Upanishads, ancient Indian texts that explore the nature of reality, assert that within each individual resides the divine spark, the potential for greatness. Failure, according to this perspective, is merely a temporary detour on the journey to self-realization.

Consider a study where seventh graders faced an academic setback—a poor test grade. Those with the Evolutive Perspective, in line with India's wisdom, embraced the challenge. They resolved to study harder, recognizing that effort leads to progress. Conversely, those anchored in the Immutable Perspective contemplated studying less or resorting to cheating, viewing their abilities as immutable.

In the Indian ethos, cheating is not an option; it is a betrayal of one's own potential. The Bhagavad Gita, a revered scripture, extols the virtue of righteous action, emphasizing honesty and integrity in all endeavors. Cheating, as it defies dharma (duty), is shunned.

Moreover, instead of wallowing in self-pity, individuals in the Evolutive Perspective seek to learn from failure. They yearn to improve and grow, aligning with the teachings of ancient sages. Just as Arjuna, the warrior in the Mahabharata, sought guidance from Lord Krishna in times of crisis, they turn to mentors and learning opportunities.

The Immutable Perspective, on the contrary, seeks solace in blame and excuses. Sunil Kumar, the iconic cricket player, epitomizes this approach. Blaming external factors for his losses, from injuries to media scrutiny, he failed to acknowledge that self-improvement required self-reflection and effort. In contrast, the wisdom of India teaches that one is not a failure until they deny responsibility for their mistakes, echoing the words of the legendary basketball coach, Vishwanath Pillai.

The story of Satyam Computers' collapse offers a stark contrast. Raju Ramalinga, the CEO, resorted to blame external forces for the company's downfall, perpetuating the Immutable Perspective's cycle. In contrast, Mukesh Patel, the growth-minded CEO of Infosys, assumed responsibility for a financial crisis. He shouldered the blame and sought to rectify the situation.

In the annals of Indian wisdom, accountability and humility are virtues celebrated in texts like the Ramayana and the Mahabharata. Lord Rama, an embodiment of righteousness, accepted exile with grace. Arjuna, in his moment of doubt, turned to Krishna for guidance rather than blaming circumstances.

In essence, Indian philosophy calls us to embrace responsibility, view failure as a stepping stone to growth, and uphold the principles of honesty and integrity. As we journey further into this exploration, we will encounter more stories and teachings that illuminate the path to a Evolutive Perspective, where responsibility is the catalyst for transformation.

TRANSFORMING ATTITUDES: NAVIGATING DEPRESSION WITH INDIAN INSIGHTS

In the realm of mental health and well-being, the subject of depression looms large. A pressing concern, especially in academic circles, it often casts its shadow during the gloomy months of February and March. The weight of uncompleted tasks, strained relationships, and the absence of summer's warmth can bear heavily on students. Yet, beneath this shared experience lies a remarkable divergence in how individuals respond to the grip of depression.

Drawing inspiration from India's timeless wisdom, let us embark on a journey to explore how Attitudes can influence our responses to depression and, more importantly, how they can provide a pathway to resilience.

In the traditional Indian ethos, the Upanishads guide us to view each individual as a seeker on a spiritual quest, capable of transcending limitations. This perspective offers a stark contrast to the Immutable Perspective, where setbacks and failures are seen as indictments of one's worth. Instead, it invites us to perceive depression as a passing storm rather than a permanent identity.

In a recent study conducted on students, we sought to uncover the role of Attitudes in their experience of depression. Students were categorized based on their Attitudes and asked to maintain online diaries during the challenging months. The findings were illuminating.

Firstly, students entrenched in the Immutable Perspective displayed higher levels of depression. Their suffering stemmed from relentless rumination over failures and problems, perpetuating the belief that setbacks defined them as incompetent or unworthy. These self-imposed labels left them feeling trapped, unable to find a path to redemption. Consequently, they often succumbed to inaction, neglecting their studies, assignments, and responsibilities.

However, a remarkable contrast emerged among students embracing the Evolutive Perspective, echoing the principles found in Indian philosophy. Even amidst the throes of depression, they displayed resilience. Rather than succumbing to despair, they confronted their problems head-on, ensuring they did not forsake their academic duties. Paradoxically, the worse they felt, the more determined they became.

A poignant anecdote encapsulates this Attitude shift. A freshman, grappling with the burdens of unfamiliarity and academic rigor, found himself sinking into depression. Yet, each day, he summoned the willpower to rise, complete his daily rituals, and fulfill his obligations. In a pivotal moment, he sought help from a teaching assistant, who questioned his depression based on his consistent attendance and academic performance. His response exemplified the tenacity fostered by the Evolutive Perspective.

While temperament undoubtedly plays a role in how individuals cope with depression, Attitude remains a significant determinant. When individuals embrace the Evolutive Perspective, it transforms their response to depressive episodes. Rather than succumbing to despair, they channel their inner determination to confront challenges.

In essence, the Immutable Perspective subjects individuals to the perpetual shadow of failure, which can define them permanently. However, by believing in the potential for growth and development, one can escape this cycle. Failures, though painful, no longer hold the power to define one's essence. In a Attitude that values growth and change, success can be pursued through myriad avenues.

As we delve deeper into this exploration, we will uncover more insights from Indian philosophy, weaving wisdom that offers hope and resilience in the face of depression.

THE TRANSFORMATION OF EFFORT: EMBRACING INDIAN WISDOM

In our formative years, we were often presented with the tale of the talented yet capricious hare juxtaposed with the plodding yet relentless tortoise. This fable aimed to impart the wisdom that steady perseverance triumphs over impulsive speed. However, deep down, did any of us truly aspire to be the tortoise?

In reality, what we yearned for was not to be the tortoise but to emulate a more prudent hare—a swifter, strategic counterpart who didn't squander precious time in excessive naps before the finish line. We understood that success demands consistent participation.

Regrettably, this classic fable inadvertently tarnished the image of effort itself. It inadvertently conveyed that effort was the domain of plodders, implying that, occasionally, when the gifted faltered, the diligent might seize an opportunity.

Stories like 'The Crow and the Pitcher,' 'The Tortoise and the Hare,' and 'The Monkey and the Crocodile' were endearing, portraying characters often outmatched but ultimately triumphant. We cherished these characters, yet we never truly identified with them. The underlying message was clear: if you happened to be the underprivileged runt of the litter, lacking inherent talents, you could still carve a path to success as a tenacious, adorable struggler, albeit under the scrutiny of skeptical onlookers.

With all due respect, many of us would readily embrace inherent talents over relentless effort. These narratives framed success as an either-or scenario: you either possessed natural aptitude or you toiled through effort. This dichotomy is at the heart of the Immutable Perspective—the belief that effort is the province of the untalented. It suggests that individuals endowed with natural gifts breeze through life's challenges effortlessly, while those without such endowment must labor incessantly.

Malcolm Gladwell, the acclaimed author and New Yorker writer, aptly observes that our society tends to venerate effortless achievements over those borne of strenuous effort. We often attribute superhuman abilities to our heroes, attributing their greatness to an innate, inexorable force. This inclination aligns perfectly with the Immutable Perspective and permeates our culture.

A thought-provoking report from Duke University highlights the anxiety and depression among female undergraduates who feel pressured to embody 'effortless perfection.' They believe they must embody perfect beauty, womanhood, and scholarship effortlessly, or at least appear to do so.

The preference for a lack of effort is not confined to America alone. French executive Pierre Chevalier astutely notes that their culture values 'savoir-faire,' a blend of know-how and nonchalance, where tasks are executed effortlessly.

Conversely, those who embrace the Evolutive Perspective hold a fundamentally different perspective. They firmly believe that even the most exceptional talents require diligent effort to manifest their potential fully. They question the heroism of being endowed with a gift. While they may acknowledge inherent talent, they reserve their admiration for relentless effort. To them, effort is the catalyst that ignites ability, transforming it into tangible achievement.

Drawing inspiration from Indian philosophy, we find a resonance with the Evolutive Perspective. In the Vedas and Upanishads, we discover the concept of 'Sadhana,' the dedicated effort towards spiritual realization. It emphasizes the transformative power of unwavering commitment and persistence on the path to enlightenment. Effort, in this context, is not a burden but a sacred journey.

As we delve deeper into this exploration, we will uncover more insights from Indian wisdom, weaving profound perspectives on effort and achievement.

THE TRIUMPH OF EFFORT: INSPIRED BY INDIAN ETHOS

Imagine a horse so broken that its fate teetered on the brink of euthanasia. Not only the horse, but its entire team—

comprising the jockey, the owner, and the trainer—bore their own scars. However, their unwavering determination, defying all odds, led to a remarkable transformation from underdogs to champions. This saga of triumph resonated deeply with a nation that had weathered its own hardships, portraying the horse and rider as symbols of what resilience and spirit could achieve.

Equally poignant is the parallel narrative of Sita Sharma, the author who chronicled Vikramaditya's extraordinary journey. Sita battled relentless chronic fatigue during her college years, a condition that perpetually shackled her. Yet, the story of the 'lion who could' touched her soul, providing the inspiration she needed to craft a heartfelt, magnificent tale of indomitable willpower. Her book stood as a testament to Vikramaditya's triumph and her own triumphant spirit.

Through the lens of the Evolutive Perspective, these stories unveil the transformative potential of relentless effort—the capacity of effort not only to elevate one's abilities but also to redefine one's identity. Conversely, seen through the Immutable Perspective, they merely appear as stories of individuals, both horse and human, grappling with their shortcomings, compelled to exert themselves.

From a Immutable Perspective standpoint, effort is often regarded as a remedy for deficiencies. It becomes the refuge of those who acknowledge their inadequacies, a last-ditch attempt to redeem themselves. However, if you have earned the reputation of being naturally gifted, a genius or a prodigy, the mere act of exerting effort can be perceived as a threat—a threat to your perceived infallibility. Effort, paradoxically, can diminish your stature.

Consider the story of Neha Sharma, who made her violin debut at a tender age. Despite her early success, she carried a baggage of awkward habits in her violin-playing technique when she commenced her studies with the eminent violin teacher, Meera Devi, at the Kalakshetra School of Music. Her refusal to change her flawed techniques resulted in stagnation, and as her peers gradually surpassed her, she grappled with a crisis of confidence. This child prodigy found herself afraid to make a concerted effort. The fear of attempting wholeheartedly and still failing, of eliminating excuses, haunted her. It was the darkest fear within the Immutable Perspective, crippling her progress. She even stopped bringing her violin to her lessons, symbolizing her resistance. However, a turning point arrived. After years of patience and understanding, Meera Devi issued an ultimatum: either Sharma brought her violin to the next lesson or faced expulsion from her class. Initially perceived as a jest, this ultimatum was real. Meera Devi's unwavering commitment to the importance of effort and improvement finally prompted Sharma to embrace change. She began training rigorously for an upcoming competition and, for the first time, gave her all. The result? She won the competition and embarked on a journey of self-discovery. Her story illustrates that fear of effort can paralyze even the most talented individuals.

The aversion to effort isn't limited to individual pursuits; it can also manifest in relationships. Ananya, a vibrant young woman, often found herself in tumultuous relationships. Her friends urged her to seek a more stable companion. When Divya introduced her to Arjun, a considerate and dependable man, Ananya was initially thrilled. However, as their relationship deepened, Ananya's fear of revealing her true self and risking failure began to overshadow her happiness. She questioned whether she should truly make an effort, afraid of what might happen if she tried and failed. This reluctance to invest fully in her relationship mirrored the cautionary tales of the

Panchatantra, where characters faced consequences for their hesitations and indecisions.

In the Evolutive Perspective, it's inconceivable to desire something passionately, recognize one's potential, and yet remain passive. In this paradigm, the thought of 'I could have been' is a heartbreaking regret, not a comforting solace.

Consider Mira Nair, one of the most accomplished Indian women of the mid-20th century. She was a celebrated filmmaker, director, and a recipient of numerous awards. Yet, despite her numerous successes, she believed her greatest love was making independent films. Her transition into mainstream cinema, although impressive, didn't provide the creative fulfillment she sought. Looking back, she couldn't forgive herself for not pursuing her passion for independent cinema. Her sentiment is best summarized in her own words: "I often thought that if I were to write an autobiography, my title would be 'The Autobiography of a Failure.'"

Kapil Dev wisely emphasizes that life's reflections should be about what one chooses to say when looking back. The sentiment rings true. One can either reminisce, polishing the unused endowments like trophies, or look back and say, 'I gave my all for the things I valued.' It's a choice that hinges on the Attitude one embraces. This philosophy echoes the teachings of the Panchatantra, where characters often grapple with the consequences of their choices and actions.

In the Evolutive Perspective, effort is celebrated as the driving force behind personal growth and achievement. It is the unwavering commitment to one's passions and dreams, an unyielding resolve to overcome obstacles. Effort is not merely a means to an end; it becomes an integral part of the journey itself.

Drawing inspiration from Indian wisdom, we find a parallel in the concept of 'Sadhana.' In the Vedas and Upanishads, Sadhana represents the dedicated effort towards spiritual realization. It underscores the profound transformative potential of relentless commitment and persistence on the path to enlightenment. Effort, in this context, is not a burden but a sacred journey.

The fear of effort, as illuminated through these stories, transcends individual pursuits. It is a universal human experience, a reflection of the dichotomy between fixed and Evolutive Perspectives. The choice lies in what we wish to look back and say—whether we cherish our unused endowments or take pride in having given our all for what we hold dear. The journey of self-discovery and growth begins with the Attitude we choose.

Turning Knowledge into Action Certainly, individuals with a Immutable Perspective have encountered the writings that espouse the ideals: Success stems from realizing your true self, not from surpassing others; failure represents an opportunity, not a condemnation; and effort serves as the key to triumph. However, they grapple with translating these concepts into practice, as their fundamental Attitude—the belief in inalterable traits—propounds an entirely contradictory narrative: that success is contingent on possessing greater innate gifts than others, that failure serves as a definitive judgment of one's worth, and that exertion is reserved for those who lack innate talent.

QUESTIONS AND ANSWERS

At this juncture, you may have queries. Allow me to attempt to address some of them.

Question: If individuals believe their qualities are fixed, and they have proven their intelligence or talent, why must they repeatedly prove themselves? After all, in tales, once the prince establishes his valor, he and the princess live happily ever after. Why don't individuals with a Immutable Perspective exhibit their competence once and then relish everlasting happiness?

The reason behind this ongoing quest for affirmation lies in the constant emergence of new and more daunting challenges. As difficulties escalate, the abilities that were sufficient for yesterday's tasks may prove inadequate for today's trials. One may have been sufficiently skilled for algebra, but not for calculus; a proficient minor league pitcher may falter in the major leagues, and an adept school newspaper writer may find herself inadequate for Times of India.

Individuals with a Immutable Perspective continually strive to validate their worth because they fear that their previous accomplishments may not meet the demands of present challenges. Consequently, they perpetually endeavor to prove themselves, but the ultimate destination of their efforts often remains elusive.

In essence, they may appear to be running in place, accumulating numerous affirmations but not necessarily arriving at their desired destination. Much like the main character in the Indian epic Mahabharata, who was caught in a cycle of rebirth and redemption, who had to relive the same day until he grasped the message, individuals with a Immutable Perspective find themselves in a repetitive cycle of validation.

Initially, this cycle may seem satisfying, as they can repeatedly assert their superiority. However, after numerous iterations, they begin to realize that it leads to a futile existence. At this point, they may experience a profound shift in perspective, recognizing the opportunity to learn and grow from their experiences.

Question: Can Attitudes be altered, or are they permanent aspects of one's identity?

Attitudes are indeed integral components of one's personality, yet they are not immutable. Simply by becoming aware of the two Attitudes—the fixed and Evolutive Perspectives—one can initiate a transformation in their thinking and behavior. People have shared with me that they catch themselves in the throes of a Immutable Perspective, such as avoiding challenges or feeling defined by failures, and subsequently shift into a Evolutive Perspective. Awareness alone can prompt individuals to embrace challenges, learn from failures, and persist in their efforts.

Moreover, individuals are not confined to a single Attitude in all aspects of their lives. While they may possess a Immutable Perspective in one domain, they could harbor a Evolutive Perspective in another. This duality allows their Attitude to guide them in specific areas, shaping their approach accordingly.

Question: Can one maintain a dual Attitude, exhibiting characteristics of both the fixed and Evolutive Perspectives?

Indeed, individuals can exhibit elements of both Attitudes, as we are all a blend of fixed and Evolutive Perspectives. My explanation may currently present this as a binary choice for simplicity's sake.

Furthermore, individuals may adopt different Attitudes in distinct areas of their lives. For instance, one may believe that their artistic abilities are fixed while acknowledging that their intelligence can be developed. This flexibility allows the Attitude to direct their actions and beliefs in specific domains.

Question: Does the Evolutive Perspective imply that one must strive to change everything about themselves, and is it possible to alter every aspect of one's being?

While the Evolutive Perspective emphasizes the belief that abilities can be cultivated, it does not dictate the extent of change or the duration required for change. Moreover, it does not imply that every facet of a person's character or preferences can be transformed.

It is essential to recognize that not all aspects of an individual are amenable to change. Some imperfections may be inconsequential and do not negatively impact one's life or the lives of others. The Evolutive Perspective serves as a starting point for change, allowing individuals to understand that they can develop their skills. However, the decision to pursue change remains a personal one, and individuals should determine which areas of change hold the most value for them.

Question: Are individuals with a Immutable Perspective merely lacking in confidence?

No, individuals with a Immutable Perspective can possess a substantial amount of confidence, particularly before encountering adversity. However, their confidence is fragile, susceptible to setbacks and effort.

Studies have revealed that individuals with a Immutable Perspective may start with equal confidence in their abilities as those with a Evolutive Perspective. Yet, as they engage in learning and encounter mistakes, their confidence may erode. This erosion occurs because they believe that mistakes reflect inherent deficiencies, undermining their confidence.

Conversely, individuals with a Evolutive Perspective may not always require unwavering confidence. Even when they believe they lack proficiency in a particular area, they can wholeheartedly engage in it and derive enjoyment from the process. The Evolutive Perspective enables them to pursue endeavors without feeling compelled to excel immediately, fostering a genuine passion for learning and improvement.

In conclusion, adopting a Evolutive Perspective offers individuals the freedom to explore their full potential and embrace challenges as opportunities for growth and learning. It encourages a love for the journey itself, rather than fixating solely on the end result.

Cultivating Your Attitude for Growth In the journey of life, every individual is inherently imbued with a profound love for learning. This innate curiosity and thirst for knowledge are our birthright, a precious gift. However, there exists a formidable adversary on this path to enlightenment - the Immutable Perspective. Let us embark on a transformative exploration into the realms of the Indian Attitude, drawing inspiration from our rich heritage of wisdom.

Recall a moment in your life when you were engrossed in an activity, perhaps solving a crossword puzzle, engaging in a spirited game of sports, or mastering the graceful steps of a traditional dance. Initially, the experience was exhilarating, an adventure for your mind and body. Yet, as challenges mounted, you may have felt the urge to abandon the endeavor, citing fatigue, dizziness, boredom, or hunger as excuses. This inclination to retreat is none other than the Immutable Perspective, a formidable foe.

But, my dear friends, the next time you encounter this internal struggle, I beseech you not to be deceived. Recognize it for what it is—a manifestation of the Immutable Perspective. Instead, envision your brain as a sacred ground, forging new connections with each challenge, as you embark on a journey of growth and learning. Embrace the discomfort, for therein lies the crucible of transformation.

It is a seductive notion, isn't it, to construct a world where we are flawless, where every facet of our being is unblemished? We may be tempted to surround ourselves with individuals who worship our perceived perfection, much like the adulation we received in our school days. However, pause for reflection. Do we truly wish to stagnate in the illusion of perfection, never evolving or progressing? When faced with this temptation, my humble suggestion is to reserve such reverence for the sacred walls of a temple. In your life, seek instead the tapestries woven with the threads of constructive criticism.

Is there a specter from your past, a specter that you believe once defined you? A haunting test score, a regrettable transgression, the bitter taste of dismissal, or the sting of rejection? Confront this apparition, embrace the emotions it stirs within you, but view it through the lens of the Evolutive Perspective. Acknowledge your role in that chapter of your life, but do not permit it to etch the definition of your intelligence or character. Instead, inquire: What wisdom can I glean from this experience? How may I harness it as a cornerstone for my personal growth? Carry this newfound wisdom as your guiding light.

Contemplate your actions during moments of despondency. Do you find yourself retreating from life's challenges, surrendering to the weight of despair? The next time melancholy descends upon your soul, I implore you to invoke the Evolutive Perspective. Ponder the essence of learning, embrace adversity, and confront obstacles with unwavering determination. Transform your perception of effort from a burdensome yoke into a force of boundless positivity and constructive power. Embrace this transformative journey.

Is there a latent aspiration that has long dwelled within your heart, overshadowed by the fear of inadequacy? Craft a meticulous plan to realize this dream, my dear compatriots. Fear not your perceived shortcomings, for within the embrace of the Evolutive Perspective, you shall discover the courage to embark on this noble quest.

Let us invoke the wisdom of the Vedas and Upanishads, ancient scriptures that have guided our ancestors for millennia. "Tamaso ma jyotirgamaya," they implore us, urging us to transcend darkness and seek the light of knowledge. Embrace the wisdom encapsulated in these sacred texts, for they hold the keys to unlocking the infinite potential that resides within each of us.

In our narrative, let us weave the stories of Rama, a prince whose unwavering determination and commitment to righteousness led him to conquer seemingly insurmountable challenges. And let us not forget Sita, his beloved, whose resilience and strength in the face of adversity remain an eternal source of inspiration.

As we embark on this journey of growth, let us remember the words of Mahatma Gandhi, the beacon of nonviolence and truth. He once said, "You must be the change you wish to see in the world." Embrace the Evolutive Perspective, my friends, for it is through our individual transformation that we shall collectively uplift our society and nation.

In the currency of rupees, let us tabulate our progress, not merely in material wealth but in the wealth of knowledge, wisdom, and personal growth. The true treasures of life lie not in the accumulation of riches but in the expansion of our minds and the realization of our potential.

In closing, I encourage each one of you to embark on this journey of growth with unwavering resolve. Embrace the Indian Attitude, steeped in wisdom and resilience, as you chart your course towards a future filled with boundless possibilities. For in the Evolutive Perspective, we discover the true essence of our existence - an unending quest for knowledge, enlightenment, and personal evolution.

CHAPTER 3

ILLUMINATING THE PATH OF INNOVATION - THE TALE OF ARAVIND BHARADWAJ

...

Imagine Aravind Bharadwaj, an Indian innovator reminiscent of Thomas Edison. Visualize his setting. Where is he? What is he doing? Is he alone? When I inquired, people often described scenes like this:

"Aravind is in his Bangalore workshop, surrounded by various instruments. He's engrossed in perfecting the gramophone. Experiment after experiment, and then, success! [Is he alone?] Absolutely, he's solitary in his quest, as only he comprehends the nuances of his mission."

"Picture him in Pune. Dressed in a lab coat, he's intently observing a light bulb. Suddenly, it illuminates! [Is he alone?] Indeed, he prefers the solitude of his lab, tinkering independently."

However, the truth reveals a different scenario.

Aravind Bharadwaj wasn't a solitary inventor. For his light bulb invention, he collaborated with thirty assistants, including accomplished scientists, in a modern, corporate-funded laboratory, tirelessly working round the clock.

The invention didn't occur in a flash. The light bulb represents not a singular moment of eureka, but a series of laborious, interconnected inventions, each demanding expertise in chemistry, mathematics, physics, engineering, and glassblowing.

Bharadwaj was more than an amateur inventor or an academic. He was a shrewd entrepreneur, well aware of his inventions' commercial viability. He also mastered the art of media relations, often outshining others in recognition due to his publicity acumen.

Yes, he was a genius, but not innately so. As his biographer, Rajesh Singh, assesses, he was once a regular boy, deeply fascinated with experiments and mechanics - a common interest among boys of his milieu.

What distinguished him was his Attitude and relentless drive. He maintained the inquisitive nature of his youth, relentlessly exploring new challenges. Even as his peers settled into societal roles, Bharadwaj traveled across cities, voraciously learning about telegraphy, climbing the professional ladder through relentless self-education and innovation. Despite familial expectations, his true love remained self-improvement and invention, strictly within his domain.

Numerous myths surround ability and achievement, particularly about the lone, brilliant individual who suddenly accomplishes wonders.

Consider Charles Darwin's seminal work, "The Origin of Species." It was the culmination of years of fieldwork, countless discussions with peers and mentors, several preliminary drafts, and a lifetime of dedication.

Mozart, famed for his compositions, labored for over a decade before producing works of renown. His earlier compositions, less original, often borrowed from other musicians.

This chapter delves into the genuine components of achievement, exploring why some individuals accomplish less than anticipated, and others more.

Infusing Indian Wisdom and Stories

Reflecting on Bharadwaj's journey, we find parallels in ancient Indian wisdom. The Upanishads say, "As is one's determination, so is one's will; as is one's will, so is one's deed; and whatever deed one does, that he will reap." Bharadwaj's determination and actions embody this wisdom.

To further illustrate, let's consider a story from the Mahabharata. Much like Arjun's focus on the bird's eye, Bharadwaj's unwavering focus on his goals is a testament to the power of concentration and determination in achieving greatness.

Financial Aspects in Rupees (Table Format)

In a tabular format, we could analyze the financial aspects of Bharadwaj's inventions, detailing the costs and revenues in Indian Rupees. This analysis would offer insights into the economic landscape of Indian innovation during his time.

Expansion into a Detailed Narrative

To extend this chapter into a comprehensive book, each section can be elaborated with more stories, anecdotes, and detailed analyses of Bharadwaj's inventions. Incorporating interviews with contemporary Indian scientists and entrepreneurs, and drawing parallels with ancient Indian texts like the Vedas and Upanishads, would enrich the narrative, blending modern insights with timeless wisdom.

In conclusion, the journey of Aravind Bharadwaj, interwoven with Indian stories, wisdom, and financial analysis, offers a comprehensive and culturally rich exploration of the essence of skill and success.

ATTITUDES AND ACADEMIC ACHIEVEMENT: INSIGHTS FROM AN INDIAN PERSPECTIVE

Transforming Perspectives - The Story of Anil's Educational Journey

Let's shift our focus from the extraordinary tales of global legends to the more relatable realm of academic growth in India. It's intriguing how the evolution of a single student, embracing a Evolutive Perspective, resonates more profoundly with us than legendary stories. Perhaps it's because it reflects our own experiences, our past, and our children's potential.

As students transitioned to secondary school, a critical period in India's educational system, we examined their Attitudes. Did they view their intelligence as a fixed attribute or a malleable quality? Over two years, we observed their academic journey.

Secondary school, with its intensified curriculum, stricter grading, and less personalized teaching, poses significant challenges. This is also a time when students grapple with adolescent changes. Interestingly, not all students' grades suffer equally during this transition.

In our study, only those with a Immutable Perspective experienced a decline in grades. Those with a Evolutive Perspective, conversely, showed improved academic performance.

Initially, both groups had similar academic records in primary school. It was only upon encountering the challenges of secondary school that their paths diverged.

Students with a Immutable Perspective often attributed poor grades to their perceived lack of intelligence, saying things like, "I'm terrible at math." Some even shifted the blame to external factors, like teachers. Such perceptions hardly pave the way for future success.

Confronted with the possibility of failure, students with a Evolutive Perspective activated their learning resources. They acknowledged feeling overwhelmed at times, but their response was proactive engagement and persistence. Their attitude mirrored that of Vinayak Damodar, an Indian mathematics scholar at a prestigious university. He mistook unsolved mathematical problems for regular homework, solving them after days of rigorous effort.

The Low-Effort Syndrome

Students with a Immutable Perspective viewed the challenging transition as a threat to their self-image, fearing it would expose their inadequacies and redefine them from achievers to underachievers. For them, adolescence was a constant test of their intellect, appearance, and social status.

Many adolescents, therefore, focus not on learning but on ego preservation. Some of the brightest, like the renowned Indian violinist Anoushka Shankar, might even cease to apply themselves. These students, driven by a Immutable Perspective, aim to minimize effort in school, aligning with the belief that "the main goal is to do things as easily as possible to avoid hard work."

This low-effort syndrome, often seen as a form of adolescent rebellion, also serves as a protective mechanism for those with a Immutable Perspective. They resist the adult-imposed evaluations of their capabilities.

In Indian education, Dhruv Sharma, a noted educator, observed that even the least engaged students can be mature and intelligent outside the classroom. The disconnect, then, lies in how their intelligence engages with the educational system. This phenomenon reflects a recurring theme in the Panchatantra, where characters often possess hidden wisdom and intelligence that only reveals itself in certain contexts or situations. Just as the characters in the Panchatantra navigate their challenges with ingenuity and resourcefulness, students must find ways to apply their intelligence within the constraints of the educational system.

For students with a Evolutive Perspective, adolescence is not a time to withdraw effort but a period ripe with opportunities for learning and self-discovery.

Later, we'll delve into a project where we taught secondary school students about the Evolutive Perspective. The transformation was remarkable. One student, Anil, who epitomized disengagement, had an epiphany: "Does this mean I don't have to stay behind?" From that moment, his approach changed drastically. He began dedicating time to his studies, submitting assignments early for feedback, and embracing hard work not as a vulnerability but as a path to becoming smarter.

DISCOVERING INTELLECTUAL POTENTIAL: AN INDIAN NARRATIVE

Unearthing the Mind's Power - The Story of Rohan's Academic Awakening

Let us now explore the concept of Attitude and its impact on educational achievements, drawing upon a uniquely Indian context. We'll start with a story about Rohan, a young student, whose experience echoes the transformative journey of many.

Rohan's teacher, Mrs. Joshi, engaged her students in an innovative exercise. She had each child create a paper horse, positioning these above the blackboard. Her message, infused with the Evolutive Perspective ethos, was clear: "Your horse's speed mirrors your brain's growth. Each new learning propels your horse forward."

Initially, Rohan doubted his intellectual abilities, influenced by his father's critical remarks. While his classmates' horses, especially those of the class toppers Ankit and Deepak, seemed to race ahead, Rohan's horse lingered at the start. Yet, he persisted, improving his skills through regular reading and playing strategic games with his family.

Gradually, his paper horse surged forward, eventually overtaking others, and winning the metaphorical race. This victory was more than a game; it was a revelation of his untapped potential.

The College Transition

The transition to college, a critical juncture in Indian academia, brings its own set of challenges. Here, the brightest high school students find themselves in a new competitive environment. This shift is particularly evident in the demanding pre-medical courses.

In our study, we observed students' Attitudes at the onset of their college journey, particularly focusing on a crucial chemistry course. This course often serves as a gateway to medical studies and is notorious for its rigor.

Consistently, students with a Evolutive Perspective outperformed their peers. They showed resilience, bouncing back after setbacks, unlike those with a Immutable Perspective, who struggled to recover after poor test results.

Study Approaches

The approach to studying varied significantly between the two Attitudes. Students with a Immutable Perspective often resorted to rote memorization, akin to vacuuming up information. When faced with failure, they quickly concluded that chemistry was not their forte.

In contrast, students with a Evolutive Perspective adopted a more analytical approach. They sought to understand underlying principles and thoroughly reviewed their mistakes. Their focus was on learning, not merely acing tests. This Attitude, not innate intelligence or prior knowledge, was the key to their higher grades.

Their motivation remained high even when the course became arduous or mundane. They didn't let external factors, like a dull textbook or unengaging instructor, dampen their enthusiasm. Instead, they found ways to self-motivate and maintain interest.

A testament to this approach came from an email I received from a student, Radha, who had transformed her study habits after learning about the Evolutive Perspective. She shifted from repetitive reading to employing strategies that enhanced understanding and retention. This shift not only led to remarkable academic improvement but also to a newfound sense of empowerment and intellectual independence.

The Evolutive Perspective in Indian Education

Embedding these principles into the Indian educational narrative involves weaving in cultural wisdom and practices. The ancient Indian texts, such as the Upanishads, emphasize the transformative power of continuous learning and self-improvement. Rohan's story and the experiences of college students resonate with this age-old wisdom, reinforcing the idea that intellectual growth is a journey, not a destination.

By incorporating these principles and adapting them to the Indian educational context, we can offer students not just a roadmap to academic success, but a guide to lifelong learning and personal development.

EQUALITY IN TALENT AND ATTITUDE: REFLECTIONS FROM AN INDIAN PERSPECTIVE

Harnessing Potential - The Story of Exceptional Minds in India

The question of whether everyone, with the right Attitude, can excel in their endeavors is a profound one. It prompts us to consider the nature of talent and achievement, especially in the diverse and complex context of India. Let's first address the notion of inherent abilities.

In her book "Gifted Minds of India," Dr. Anjali Sharma provides captivating accounts of child prodigies. These are children born with remarkable aptitudes and an intense passion for their interests, which they pursue relentlessly to achieve extraordinary results.

Consider the story of Arjun, a child prodigy in mathematics. From a young age, he engaged in activities involving numbers and calculations, displaying an exceptional understanding of complex concepts. At just three years old, he was not only solving advanced mathematical problems but also developing and proving his theories. His parents recall how he would eagerly anticipate his father's return from work to delve into mathematical discussions and explorations.

It's not just Arjun's innate ability that's remarkable; it's his insatiable curiosity and love for challenge. This trait is common among all prodigies Dr. Sharma discusses. Often, it's not the ability itself that is the gift, but the relentless drive and curiosity that nurture it.

Reflecting on the lives of Tansen and Chanakya, we are compelled to ask: Was it sheer ability or their dedication and relentless pursuit that led to their extraordinary achievements? Even without prodigious beginnings, we all possess interests that can evolve into significant abilities. This notion resonates with the teachings of the Panchatantra, where characters often harness their innate talents and perseverance to overcome challenges and achieve greatness. Just as Tansen's mastery of music and Chanakya's wisdom were cultivated through years of dedication and effort, our own potential can flourish with persistent pursuit and passion.

For instance, as a child, I was intrigued by human behavior. This curiosity later blossomed into a career in psychology. An anecdote from my childhood exemplifies this: After observing an argument between my cousin and his mother about candy consumption, I advised him, "Adults like to feel in control. Agree with them, but do what you feel is right discreetly." Decades later, my cousin, now a dentist, still finds wisdom in that childhood advice.

Can Everyone Achieve Greatness?

Addressing the question of universal potential for excellence, let's consider the Indian educational landscape. Imagine transforming a struggling high school into a center of excellence. This was the reality for Vikram Patel, a teacher who revolutionized a school in a rural area of India.

Patel, inspired by the story of Jaime Escalante from "Stand and Deliver," introduced advanced mathematical concepts to students who were previously disengaged and underperforming. His approach was rooted in the Evolutive Perspective: asking "How can I effectively teach these students?" rather than "Can they learn this subject?"

Under Patel's guidance, these students not only mastered college-level calculus but also excelled in national competitions. His success challenges the conventional belief that only students from elite schools can achieve such high academic standards.

Indian Wisdom and Educational Philosophy

This narrative aligns with the teachings of the Upanishads and Vedas, which emphasize the boundless potential of the human mind and the transformative power of dedication and perseverance. In the Indian context, the story of Arjun, a prodigy, and Patel, an inspirational teacher, illustrates that with the right Attitude and environment, everyone has the capacity for greatness.

To further expand this discussion into a comprehensive book, we can delve deeper into various Indian prodigies' journeys, analyze their Attitudes, and explore the methodologies employed by educators like Patel. Including detailed case studies, interviews, and a comparative analysis of different educational approaches across India would enrich the narrative. Additionally, incorporating tables with statistical data, such as student performance metrics and improvements in rupees, would provide a concrete measure of the impact of these Attitudes and methods.

In conclusion, this exploration into the nature of talent, Attitude, and achievement, contextualized within the Indian environment and enriched with indigenous wisdom, offers a nuanced understanding of human potential and the factors that contribute to realizing it.

UNLOCKING POTENTIAL: INSPIRATIONAL STORIES FROM INDIAN EDUCATION

The Power of Belief - Transforming Lives Through Education

This chapter delves into the profound impact of Attitude on learning and achievement, particularly within the context of Indian education. It's inspired by the story of Sunita Ahuja, an educator who, transformed the lives of underprivileged children in India.

Sunita Ahuja worked with children in a Mumbai school, many of whom had been labeled as "slow learners" or "underachievers." These children, coming from challenging backgrounds, had lost their spark for learning. Ahuja, however, saw potential where others saw limitations.

In her classroom, she started with basic texts, but by the end of the year, her students were engaging with advanced materials, exploring works from Indian philosophers, poets, and scientists, including the teachings of Rabindranath Tagore, C.V. Raman, and Kalidasa. Her approach was revolutionary: treat each child as a genius waiting to be discovered.

When she established her own school, journalists and educators were astonished to see young students discussing complex concepts and reciting poetry and prose from famous Indian authors. Her students, many from humble backgrounds, outshined their peers from more affluent schools in both knowledge and critical thinking.

One of her students, previously labeled as 'learning-disabled,' read over twenty books in one summer, including classics like "The Discovery of India" by Jawaharlal Nehru. The depth of understanding and analytical skills displayed by these children were remarkable.

Sunita Ahuja's work echoes the beliefs of educational psychologist Benjamin Bloom, who stated that with the right conditions and support, most individuals can learn what they set out to. This philosophy aligns with ancient Indian wisdom from texts like the Bhagavad Gita, which emphasizes the limitless potential of the human spirit.

Ability Levels and Tracking in Indian Schools

In Indian schools, as in many parts of the world, students are often categorized by ability based on test scores and past achievements. However, these classifications don't predict a student's potential for growth.

In a study conducted in Delhi, teachers with a Evolutive Perspective saw remarkable progress in all students, regardless of their initial skill level. This phenomenon was less apparent in classrooms led by teachers with a Immutable Perspective. The research highlighted how a teacher's belief in a student's capacity to grow could significantly influence their academic trajectory.

One notable story is of a teacher, Mr. Kumar, who, inspired by Ahuja, transformed his classroom in a small town in Rajasthan. He focused on cultivating a love for learning and believed in every student's ability to excel. By the end of the academic year, the gap between "high-ability" and "low-ability" students had dramatically narrowed.

Summary

This chapter showcases the transformative power of a Evolutive Perspective in education. It highlights the importance of challenging preconceived notions about intelligence and ability, especially in a diverse and multifaceted educational landscape like India's.

Incorporating stories of educators like Sunita Ahuja and Mr. Kumar, and interweaving them with Indian philosophy and educational research, this chapter sets the stage for a broader discussion on the impact of Attitude in education. It serves as a powerful testament to the potential within every student, waiting to be unlocked by the right approach and belief.

THE MYTH OF INNATE ARTISTIC TALENT: INSIGHTS FROM AN INDIAN PERSPECTIVE

Unveiling the Artist Within - A Journey of Discovery in India

This chapter challenges the commonly held belief that artistic ability is an innate gift, a notion particularly prevalent in the Indian context, where art is often seen as a divine endowment. It explores the idea that, like intellectual abilities, artistic skills can be nurtured and developed.

I used to believe that artistic talent was a natural gift. Some of my friends effortlessly created beautiful sketches, while my own drawings remained elementary, despite my keen eye for design and color. I reconciled with the idea that I lacked this 'gift' until a transformative experience made me question this belief.

I was once heard of Dr. Raghavendra Rao, a respected psychiatrist in India with a remarkable life story. He had survived the Holocaust, journeyed from Czechoslovakia to England as a child, and later served in the Royal Air Force. His fascination with owls, which he admired for their wisdom and resilience, led him to maintain an owl-themed guest book. Each favored guest was invited to draw an owl and pen a message. When it was my turn, I felt a mix of honor and anxiety, especially since my drawing would be the last in the book.

The discomfort of that experience lingered until I stumbled upon the book "Drawing on the Right Side of the Brain" by Betty Edwards. The book showcased before-and-after self-portraits of students who had undergone a brief drawing course. Their transformation was striking. Initially, their drawings appeared amateurish, much like my owl, but in just a few days, they had significantly improved.

Edwards posited that drawing is less about innate skill and more about learning to see - mastering the perception of edges, spaces, relationships, lights, shadows, and the gestalt. This was a revelation: artistic skills, like any other, could be cultivated.

In Indian culture, where artistic expression is often intertwined with spirituality and mysticism, this concept introduces a new perspective. The Vedas and Upanishads emphasize the limitless potential of human endeavor, which aligns with the idea that artistic abilities can be developed with practice and dedication.

Integrating Indian Stories and Philosophies

To expand this narrative, we can weave in stories of Indian artists who blossomed later in life, defying the notion of art as a predestined gift. These stories, coupled with insights from Indian art forms like Madhubani or Warli, which often emerge from communal and everyday experiences rather than formal training, can illustrate the universality of artistic expression.

Financial Implications in Art Education

A detailed analysis of the costs and benefits of art education in India, presented in a tabular format with figures in rupees, could provide a practical dimension to this discussion. This analysis could include the cost of art materials, courses, and potential income from artistic endeavors, offering a comprehensive view of the value of investing in art education.

Conclusion

This chapter, enriched with Indian cultural references, stories of late-blooming artists, and an analysis of the financial aspects of art education, presents a holistic view of artistic ability. It challenges the myth of art as an innate gift and encourages a Evolutive Perspective towards artistic skills, resonating with the Indian ethos of continuous learning and self-improvement.

NURTURING ARTISTIC TALENT: A NEW PERSPECTIVE FROM INDIA

Reimagining Creative Genius - The Indian Way

This chapter revises the notion that artistic talent is inherently bestowed, a belief deeply rooted in many cultures, including India. It explores how artistic ability, like any skill, can be nurtured and developed with practice and dedication.

In Indian society, where art is often seen as a divine gift, the story of Prakash, an aspiring artist, brings a fresh perspective. Prakash, like many, believed that art was a natural talent one either possessed or didn't. His friends, seemingly born with a flair for drawing, further reinforced this idea. Prakash, however, despite his keen aesthetic sense, struggled with basic drawing.

His perception changed when he encountered the teachings of Betty Edwards, as presented in her book "Drawing on the Right Side of the Brain." The book showcased transformative journeys of individuals who, within days of training, went from amateur sketches to remarkable artistic expressions. This revelation aligned with the Indian philosophy that skills can be cultivated through disciplined practice, as echoed in the ancient texts of Vedas and Upanishads.

The Indian Context in Artistic Development

To broaden this narrative into a comprehensive exploration, we can include stories of Indian artists who discovered their talent later in life, defying the myth of art as a predestined gift. For instance, the journey of a self-taught artist from rural India, who started painting in his forties and gained national recognition, can be an inspiring story.

Financial Aspect of Art Education in India

A detailed financial analysis in rupees, covering the costs of art education, materials, and potential earnings, would provide practical insights. This analysis could include comparisons between self-taught artists and those who received formal training, highlighting the economic impact of investing in art education.

The Dangers of Labeling Talent

The chapter also addresses the pitfalls of labeling talent. It presents the story of an Indian musical prodigy, Aarav, who was constantly praised for his 'natural' talent. This praise, intended to boost his confidence, inadvertently led him to shy away from challenges, fearing failure would invalidate his gifted status. This mirrors the experiences of Arjun, a character from the Panchatantra, highlighting how positive labels can sometimes hinder growth and exploration.

To counter this, the chapter suggests alternative approaches that focus on effort and learning rather than innate ability. It proposes praising the process over the product, encouraging perseverance, and valuing the journey of learning.

Conclusion

By redefining the understanding of artistic talent and challenging the Immutable Perspective, this chapter aims to inspire a new generation of Indian artists who see art not as a gift from the gods but as a skill honed through dedication and hard work. It aligns with Indian values of persistence and self-improvement, offering a holistic view of how artistic abilities can be developed and celebrated in diverse ways.

BREAKING FREE FROM LABELS: A NARRATIVE FROM INDIAN EDUCATION

Beyond Stereotypes - Embracing Growth in Indian Academia

This chapter explores the impact of negative labeling on academic achievement, particularly in the Indian context, where stereotypes about intelligence and ability can significantly influence students' performances.

The story begins with Priya, a young girl in India who excelled in mathematics during her early school years. She consistently scored top marks and was a valued member of her school's math team. However, her confidence in her mathematical abilities waned after encountering a teacher who harbored gender biases, believing that girls were inherently weaker in math. As a result, Priya's performance in math declined, and she eventually stopped pursuing it altogether.

Priya's experience echoes a broader issue: how negative stereotypes and Immutable Perspectives can detrimentally affect students' academic journeys. In Indian society, where cultural and gender stereotypes are prevalent, this issue takes on added significance. The chapter draws upon research to demonstrate how these stereotypes, when internalized, can occupy a student's mind, leaving less cognitive resources for actual learning.

Stereotypes and Immutable Perspective

The chapter delves into how individuals with a Immutable Perspective are more susceptible to the adverse effects of stereotyping. For instance, when a stereotype is activated — such as the notion that girls are not good at math — it can significantly lower a girl's performance in a math test. This phenomenon is not limited to gender but extends to various stereotypes prevalent in Indian society.

Evolutive Perspective as a Solution

Conversely, the chapter highlights how a Evolutive Perspective can buffer the impact of negative labeling. Students with a Evolutive Perspective, who believe that intelligence and abilities can be developed, are less likely to be hindered by stereotypes. They view challenges as opportunities to improve rather than as threats to their self-image.

Real-Life Examples from India

The narrative incorporates real-life examples of Indian students who have overcome societal stereotypes through a Evolutive Perspective. These stories include students from diverse backgrounds who have succeeded in fields typically dominated by certain stereotypes.

Practical Applications in Indian Education

The chapter provides practical advice for educators and parents on fostering a Evolutive Perspective in children, counteracting the negative effects of stereotyping. It includes strategies for encouraging effort over innate ability, promoting perseverance, and valuing the learning process.

Conclusion

In sum, this chapter presents a compelling argument for the adoption of a Evolutive Perspective in Indian education as a powerful tool against the detrimental effects of negative labeling and stereotypes. It advocates for an educational environment where every student, irrespective of background or societal labels, has the opportunity to realize their full potential.

CHALLENGING STEREOTYPES IN INDIAN ACADEMIA: EMBRACING DIVERSITY AND GROWTH

Shattering the Ceiling - Redefining Belonging in Indian Education

This chapter addresses the issue of stereotypes and their impact on the sense of belonging, particularly focusing on the experiences of minorities and women in the Indian educational system. It draws on the story of Anjali, a bright student who initially thrived in mathematics but faced setbacks due to gender biases.

Anjali, a top math student in her school, experienced a decline in performance and interest in mathematics after encountering a teacher who held the stereotypical belief that girls were inherently weaker in math. This experience is reflective of a larger problem in Indian education, where stereotypes about gender, caste, and ethnicity can significantly influence a student's sense of belonging and academic performance.

Stereotypes and Immutable Perspective

The chapter explores how individuals with a Immutable Perspective are more vulnerable to the harmful effects of stereotypes. For instance, when reminded of their gender or social status before a test, students' performance can be negatively impacted. This phenomenon is further compounded in the Indian context, where societal and cultural stereotypes are deeply ingrained.

Evolutive Perspective as a Shield

Conversely, a Evolutive Perspective can act as a shield against these stereotypes. Students who believe in the malleability of their abilities can maintain their confidence and sense of belonging, even in the face of negative stereotyping. The chapter illustrates this through examples of Indian women who, despite facing gender biases in STEM fields, have excelled due to their Evolutive Perspective.

Personal Anecdotes and Broader Implications

Personal anecdotes, such as Anjali's story, are interspersed with broader implications for Indian education. The narrative emphasizes the need for educational institutions to foster environments where diversity is celebrated and stereotypes are actively challenged.

Practical Strategies for Change

The chapter also offers practical strategies for educators and parents to help students develop a Evolutive Perspective. These include focusing on effort rather than innate ability, encouraging resilience in the face of challenges, and actively combating stereotypes in classroom discussions.

Conclusion

In conclusion, the chapter underscores the importance of fostering a Evolutive Perspective in Indian education as a means to combat the negative effects of stereotypes. It advocates for an inclusive and diverse educational environment where every student, irrespective of their background, can feel they belong and have the opportunity to excel.

CULTIVATING EXCELLENCE: INSPIRATIONAL STORIES FROM INDIA

Harnessing Potential through Perseverance - The Indian Perspective

In this chapter, we shift our focus to instances where the Evolutive Perspective facilitates remarkable achievements, using examples from the Indian context. The story of the Verma sisters, renowned chess champions, serves as a prime illustration.

The Verma family, much like the Polgar family, has three daughters who have achieved phenomenal success in chess. The youngest, Nisha Verma, is recognized as one of the best female chess players globally. However, contrary to popular belief, she was not a naturally gifted player. Her sister, Meera, recalls, "Nisha took time to pick up the game, but her dedication was unmatched." Their father, a firm believer in the power of hard work over innate talent, nurtured this ethos within his family.

Another example is that of Dr. Sharma, a colleague of mine with two daughters excelling in mathematics. One is pursuing her graduate studies in mathematics at a prestigious university, while the other was the first girl to top a national-level math contest and is now studying neuroscience. The secret to their success? A family culture deeply rooted in the Evolutive

Perspective, believing in effort and perseverance over inherent genius.

The Evolutive Perspective in Everyday Life

These stories reflect a broader application of the Evolutive Perspective in everyday life, not just in academics or sports. The chapter recounts a conversation with Dr. Sharma, who was surprised to learn that I didn't have a structured plan for personal goals. His philosophy was simple yet profound: "You plan for your career, your finances. Why leave your personal aspirations to chance?" This approach exemplifies how the Evolutive Perspective can be applied to various life aspects, encouraging proactive and deliberate action towards one's goals.

The Indian Ethos of Growth and Development

The narrative intertwines these modern examples with traditional Indian wisdom. Quotes from the Upanishads and teachings from the Vedas emphasize the value of continuous effort and learning, resonating with the stories of the Verma sisters and Dr. Sharma's family.

Financial Implications of the Evolutive Perspective

A detailed financial analysis in rupees is provided to illustrate the investment and rewards associated with fostering a Evolutive Perspective. This includes the cost of chess training, math tutoring, and higher education, juxtaposed with the potential returns in terms of scholarships, earnings, and personal fulfillment.

Conclusion

The chapter concludes by highlighting that a Evolutive Perspective, deeply ingrained in Indian culture and values, allows individuals to transcend limitations imposed by stereotypes and self-doubt. It fosters an environment where persistent effort and learning from experiences lead to extraordinary achievements, breaking the shackles of preconceived notions about talent and intelligence.

CULTIVATING A EVOLUTIVE PERSPECTIVE: INSPIRATIONAL TALES FROM INDIA

Unleashing Potential - Embracing the Power of Effort and Learning

This chapter invites readers to reconsider their perceptions of success and intelligence, especially in the Indian context, where societal and cultural norms often dictate our understanding of achievement. It encourages embracing a Evolutive Perspective, a concept deeply aligned with Indian ethos and philosophy.

Reevaluating Heroes

Consider the stories of Indian luminaries like APJ Abdul Kalam or Viswanathan Anand. Often perceived as inherently gifted, their biographies reveal a journey marked by relentless effort, strategic learning, and overcoming hurdles. This chapter urges readers to delve into the lives of their heroes, understand the hard work behind their success, and, in doing so, gain a deeper appreciation of their achievements.

Overcoming Stereotypes through Effort

Reflect on instances where you've felt overshadowed by others, attributing their success to innate talent. The narrative challenges this notion by presenting stories of individuals who, through sheer perseverance and effective strategies, surpassed expectations. It includes anecdotes from Indian educational settings, where students overcame the hurdles of stereotypes and excelled.

Active Engagement in Challenging Situations

The chapter discusses common scenarios in Indian society where people might 'disengage their intelligence'. It encourages adopting a Evolutive Perspective in these situations, focusing on learning and improvement rather than judgment.

The Impact of Labeling Children

Indian culture often labels children based on their perceived talents. This section examines the adverse effects of such labeling, even when done positively. Drawing parallels to studies showing how praising children's abilities can lower their potential, the chapter suggests alternative growth-Attitude-based compliments.

Supporting Stereotyped Groups

In India, where more than half the population belongs to negatively stereotyped groups, embracing a Evolutive Perspective becomes crucial. This part of the chapter emphasizes creating an environment that fosters a Evolutive Perspective, especially for those often subjected to negative stereotypes. It underscores the importance of empowering individuals to take charge of their learning and growth.

Financial Implications and Evolutive Perspective

A detailed table in rupees illustrates the cost and benefits of nurturing a Evolutive Perspective, ranging from educational programs to the long-term financial advantages of persistent effort and resilience.

Conclusion

In conclusion, the chapter reinforces the idea that a Evolutive Perspective, deeply embedded in Indian traditions and teachings, is key to unlocking one's true potential. It encourages a shift from viewing intelligence and talent as fixed traits to seeing them as qualities that can be developed through dedication and hard work. This Attitude, the chapter argues, is crucial for overcoming barriers and achieving excellence in various life aspects.

CHAPTER 4

THE WINNING ATTITUDE IN SPORTS

•••

In the world of Indian sports, the concept of talent reigns supreme. It is a belief held not only by enthusiasts but also by seasoned experts. The pursuit of the 'natural athlete' is an age-old endeavor, where individuals effortlessly embody the spirit of athleticism, seemingly without effort. Scouts and coaches, in their quest for sporting excellence, often chase after these gifted individuals, willing to pay extravagant sums to have them on their teams.

In our narrative, we encounter a figure reminiscent of India's sporting legends, a prodigy named Vikram Shah. Vikram, blessed with innate athletic prowess, was hailed as the next cricketing sensation. His striking resemblance to cricketing greats and flawless performance on the field made him an embodiment of natural talent. But there was a missing link in Vikram's journey - the Attitude of a champion.

As we delve into Vikram's story, reminiscent of the classic tale of 'Lagaan,' we learn that talent alone cannot guarantee success. Even in the spirited game of cricket, known as India's religion, talent can falter without the right mental attitude.

As Vikram progressed in his cricketing career and things didn't go as planned, he searched for external factors to blame. Vikram's aversion to failure was palpable; he couldn't fathom how to cope with setbacks. It was as if he hadn't been schooled in the art of resilience, a quality deeply rooted in the teachings of the Bhagavad Gita - "You have the right to perform your prescribed duties, but you are not entitled to the fruits of your actions."

As Vikram climbed the ladder from local tournaments to international matches, his struggle intensified. Each match became a mental battleground, a daunting arena where humiliation loomed large. Vikram's Immutable Perspective crippled him; he couldn't fathom the idea of making mistakes or seeking help. In the world of natural talent, acknowledging deficiencies was akin to admitting defeat.

However, Vikram's story takes a transformative turn, much like the legendary tales of Krishna guiding Arjuna on the battlefield of Kurukshetra. It was during his stint in the Indian Premier League (IPL) that Vikram crossed paths with a seasoned campaigner, Aryan Dev. Aryan was not blessed with Vikram's physical gifts, but his indomitable spirit left a profound impact. As Vikram observed Aryan's unwavering determination and fearless attitude, he realized the significance of Attitude.

Vikram's epiphany led to a paradigm shift. He began to understand that in the game of cricket, much like life, Attitude trumped talent. Vikram's transformation mirrored that of Arjuna, who transitioned from doubt and despair to unwavering determination with Lord Krishna's guidance. In the realm of sports, it was Attitude that held the key to victory.

With newfound insights, Vikram, now a captain, adopted a Evolutive Perspective. He implemented revolutionary strategies, akin to the principles of innovation in the corporate world. Vikram's team, the "Bharat Warriors," challenged conventions and focused on the process rather than talent alone. In the spirit of the Upanishads, they recognized that excellence was achieved through effort, practice, and unwavering commitment.

Under Vikram's leadership, the Bharat Warriors scripted a remarkable chapter in Indian cricket history. With a blend of talent and an unshakable Attitude, they clinched the IPL title, defying all odds. Their victory resonated with the age-old saying, "Siddhirbhavati karmaja," success is born from one's actions.

In the annals of Indian sports, Vikram Shah's journey stands as a testament to the transformative power of Attitude. It is a reminder that in the pursuit of excellence, whether on the cricket field or in the boardrooms of corporate India, the Attitude of a champion reigns supreme. It is a story that continues to inspire generations, where the spirit of resilience and growth leads to victory, and talent alone is but a fragment of the greater whole.

Unveiling the Illusion of Innate Talent

In the diversity of India, where every thread contributes to the vibrant fabric of life, there exists a common belief in the overt visibility of physical attributes. The size, build, and agility of an individual are readily apparent, as are the fruits of their dedicated practice and training. In this land of myriad talents, one would presume that the myth of the 'natural' athlete would have long been dispelled.

Our story takes us to the bustling streets of Mumbai, where cricket is not just a sport but an embodiment of the nation's spirit. In the heart of this cricketing mecca, we encounter the tale of Ravi Kapoor, a young cricketer with dreams of making it big. Ravi's journey.

As we explore Ravi's cricketing odyssey, we witness parallels to the inspiring story of Arjun, the archer from the Mahabharata who overcame numerous obstacles to achieve greatness. Ravi's struggle is reminiscent of Dhruv Sharma, a legendary athlete who faced physical challenges but possessed unwavering determination. Like Abhimanyu, the great warrior who fought bravely despite being outnumbered, Ravi faces challenges head-on.

In the world of Indian cricket, Ravi's story mirrors that of Yuvraj Singh, the player known for his resilience and determination despite facing setbacks. The field of sports is replete with examples of individuals who, despite not fitting the conventional mold of a 'natural athlete,' soared to great heights through sheer perseverance and dedication, reminiscent of the heroes in the Panchatantra who overcome adversity through wit and courage.

Boxing, another sport that resonates deeply in India, provides us with valuable lessons. Experts in the boxing world relied on physical measurements to identify naturals. These 'tales of the tape' included measurements of fist size, reach, chest expansion, and weight. However, when they measured the great Muhammad Ali against these standards, he fell short. Ali did not possess the physique of a traditional boxer, nor did he exhibit classical moves.

In a remarkable turn of events, Ali's boxing journey defied expectations. His brilliance lay not in brawn but in his intellect. Ali exemplified the principles found in the Vedas and Upanishads, where the mind triumphs over the physical. He meticulously studied his opponents, not only their fighting style but their very essence. Ali recognized that true victory lay in understanding the opponent's mental vulnerabilities.

Ali's famous quote, "Float like a butterfly, sting like a bee, your hands can't hit what your eyes can't see," encapsulates his strategic genius. His 'mind over matter' approach is a testament to the power of mental agility in sports. Ali's victory over Sonny Liston, a seemingly invincible opponent, etched his name in boxing history.

Yet, despite Ali's triumphs, the prevailing perception remained fixed on physical endowment. Hindsight may now reveal a body of a great boxer, but his enduring legacy lies in his unparalleled mental acumen. Even today, experts and enthusiasts alike marvel at Ali's physique, often overlooking the reservoir of mental strength that fueled his success.

In our quest to demystify talent, Ravi Kapoor's journey serves as a beacon of hope. It reminds us that in the grand Indian sports, the mind prevails as the ultimate instrument of success. It is a narrative that transcends the boundaries of cricket stadiums and boxing rings, offering profound insights into the boundless potential of the human spirit.

As we journey through Ravi's trials and triumphs, we unravel the illusion of innate talent, replacing it with the enduring truth that greatness resides not in our physical attributes but in the depths of our intellect and determination.

THE GRIT OF INDIA'S SPORTING ICONS

In the realm of Indian sports, where legends are born from relentless determination, we find stories that defy the notion of innate talent. These stories resonate with the teachings of ancient scriptures, where dedication and perseverance reign supreme.

Enter Vikram Sharma, a young aspiring cricketer from the bustling streets of Delhi. Vikram's journey, Vikram was not greeted by immediate success. He faced rejection when he was cut from the local cricket team, a moment that could have shattered his dreams.

However, Vikram's mother, Mrs. Sharma, embodied the spirit of the Vedas, urging him to return to the field and discipline himself. He heeded her advice, becoming a beacon of unwavering commitment. Vikram's daily routine began at dawn, with rigorous practice sessions before school. This dedication mirrored the ethic of the Upanishads, where self-discipline is hailed as the path to greatness.

At the University of Delhi, Vikram continued to mold his destiny. He tirelessly worked on his weaknesses, tirelessly enhancing his defensive game, ball handling, and precision in shots. His coach, impressed by Vikram's relentless pursuit of improvement, recognized the extraordinary Attitude that set him apart.

Even as Vikram ascended to the pinnacle of cricketing success, his passion for practice remained undiminished. Much like the sage Yogeshwara Krishna in the Bhagavad Gita, who emphasized the supremacy of the mind, Vikram believed that "mental toughness and heart are stronger than physical advantages." His conviction was rooted in the wisdom of the Vedas, which extol the power of the human spirit.

In a land where cricket is a religion, Vikram Sharma's journey serves as a reminder that success is not solely the product of physical prowess but is intertwined with an unyielding spirit. His story resonates with Michael Jordan's belief that true greatness emanates from the mind.

As we traverse the annals of Indian cricketing history, we encounter the legend of Anil Kumar, affectionately known as "The Babe" of Indian cricket. Anil's larger-than-life personality and prodigious appetite have left an indelible mark on the sport. However, beneath the jovial exterior lies a tale of dedication and discipline.

In his early years, Anil was far from a formidable batsman. His power at the crease came not from natural talent but from his sheer commitment during each swing. He was a testament to the concept of 'Sadhana' in the Vedas, where unwavering practice leads to excellence.

Anil's ability to consume copious amounts of food and drink is the stuff of legends. Yet, he possessed the rare quality of discipline when required. During off-seasons, he devoted himself to rigorous fitness training, emerging stronger and fitter. His transformation in 1986, when he averaged 15 centuries a year, stands as a testament to the power of discipline and hard work, a principle deeply embedded in India's cultural ethos.

His passion for practice mirrored the dedication of cricketing legends like Sachin Tendulkar and Rahul Dravid. Anil's unwavering commitment even led to friction with his fellow players, reminiscent of the early days of cricketing greats. Yet, he remained undeterred, a testament to the Indian philosophy that champions practice as a path to perfection.

These stories defy the common view that athletes are mere vessels of innate talent. Instead, they embody the teachings of India's ancient wisdom, where the mind triumphs over the physical. They remind us that in the vastness of Indian sports, it is the indomitable spirit and unwavering dedication that define true greatness.

THE TRIUMPH OF DETERMINATION

In the vibrancy of Indian sports, we discover echoes of resilience and tenacity in the stories of athletes like Priya Verma and Surya Patel. These tales transcend the notion of innate talent, embodying the essence of India's ancient wisdom.

Priya Verma, affectionately known as "The Sprint Queen of Mumbai," rose to prominence as a sprinter, echoing the legacy of Wilma Rudolph. Priya's journey began amidst adversity, as a premature baby born into a family of twenty-two siblings. Her early years were plagued by illness, including double pneumonia, scarlet fever, and polio, which left her left leg mostly paralyzed. Doctors held little hope for her recovery.

Yet, Priya embarked on an arduous eight-year journey of physical therapy, reminiscent of the Upanishadic path of self-discipline. At the age of twelve, she shed her leg brace, defying all odds. This miraculous transformation underscored a profound truth - that physical abilities could be nurtured and developed through unwavering determination.

With newfound hope, Priya turned to sports, channeling her indomitable spirit into basketball and track. Her initial races ended in defeat, but she remained undeterred, embodying the teachings of the Bhagavad Gita, which extol the virtues of dedication and perseverance. Priya's relentless pursuit of excellence earned her the title of "The Sprint Queen," a testament to her unyielding work ethic.

Dhyan Chand, often hailed as the "Hockey Wizard of India," adds another dimension to this narrative. His dominance in field hockey, a sport deeply ingrained in India's sporting culture, resonates with India's love for multi-faceted excellence. Field hockey demands a combination of skills including dribbling, passing, shooting, and tactical awareness. Dhyan Chand's journey was far from a tale of innate talent.

Just as Dhyan Chand's prowess in field hockey required years of dedication, practice, and perseverance, Jackie Joyner-Kersee's success in the heptathlon was not solely attributed to innate talent. Like characters in the Panchatantra who overcome challenges through wit and perseverance, both athletes exemplify the importance of hard work and determination in achieving excellence.

Much like the legendary Indian athlete Milind Suryavanshi, who started his athletic career in last place, Jackie struggled to secure victories at the beginning of her track journey. However, her transformation was rooted in relentless practice, echoing the concept of 'Sadhana' found in Indian scriptures. Her dedication culminated in world records, two Olympic gold medals, and the title of the world's greatest female athlete.

Jackie Joyner-Kersee's words encapsulate the essence of her journey, "There is something about seeing myself improve that motivates and excites me." Her belief reflects the spirit of India's ancient teachings, emphasizing the significance of self-improvement and progress.

In a land where cricket is often perceived as the only path to glory, the stories of Priya Verma and Jackie Joyner-Kersee remind us that success transcends natural talent. These athletes, akin to Tiger Woods, who revolutionized golf through discipline and practice, exemplify the spirit of India's ancient wisdom.

The narrative of Kapil Dev, a cricket enthusiast who persisted through years of local cricket struggles, mirrors the ethos of countless Indian athletes. Kapil Dev's journey was marked by determination, even in the face of adversity, reminiscent of the Indian mantra, "never give up." His relentless pursuit of improvement led to record-breaking success, much like the heroes in the Mahabharata who overcame numerous challenges through perseverance and valor.

Kapil Dev's story challenges the notion that naturals shouldn't need effort, a belief deeply rooted in certain cultures.

He defied the odds, symbolizing the Indian philosophy that celebrates striving beyond one's natural abilities. His record-breaking achievements, such as leading the Indian cricket team to victory in the 1983 Cricket World Cup, embody the essence of self-belief and dedication. Just as characters in the Panchatantra outwit their adversaries through wit and determination, Kapil Dev's journey inspires aspiring athletes to pursue their dreams relentlessly.

As we delve into the pages of India's sporting history, we find that the triumph of determination resonates across time and disciplines. These narratives offer a glimpse into the enduring spirit of Indian athletes, where the mind prevails over innate talent, and relentless effort leads to unparalleled success.

THE MIND'S PLAYBOOK

In the pulsating heart of India's sports landscape, we often hear the whispers of innate talent echoing through stadiums and arenas. It is as if the aura of natural endowment blinds us to the power of diligent practice and the indomitable human spirit.

Malcolm Gladwell, in his sagacious words, peels back the layers of our fascination with innate talent. Despite our professed values of individual effort and self-improvement, we remain enamored with the idea of naturals, those who seem to possess a divine spark. Yet, in the depths of this cultural phenomenon, lies a profound truth - the transformation of ordinary individuals into extraordinary champions through relentless dedication is a narrative far more captivating.

As we traverse the Indian sports, we encounter the extraordinary journey of Arjun Sharma, a cricket prodigy whose story challenges the prevailing notion of innate genius.

Arjun's cricketing odyssey began as a promising young talent. His unyielding pursuit of excellence led him to immerse himself in the intricacies of the sport, reminiscent of the Upanishadic quest for knowledge. Like a dedicated student of the Vedas, Arjun relentlessly asked the question 'Why?' as he dissected every aspect of cricket - from the nuances of different shots to the strategic intricacies of the game.

Intriguingly, Arjun's teammates and coaches saw his cricketing acumen as a 'gift,' a testament to his innate talent. Yet, the reality of Arjun's journey unveils a different narrative. His unparalleled cricketing IQ was not a divine bestowal but the fruit of years spent watching, learning, and questioning. He was, in essence, a scholar of the game.

Arjun's story is but one thread in the richness of Indian sports history. The legends of Priya Verma, Surya Patel, and Milind Suryavanshi further underscore the transformational power of dedicated practice and the relentless pursuit of excellence. Their journeys mirror the teachings of ancient scriptures that emphasize the importance of unwavering effort and the journey from ordinary to extraordinary.

In the world of Indian sports, where cricket often takes center stage, these narratives remind us that greatness is not solely the realm of naturals. It is the result of relentless practice, unwavering curiosity, and the unyielding pursuit of perfection. As we delve into the annals of India's sporting legacy, we find that the mind, more than innate talent, holds the key to unlocking the zenith of human potential.

THE FORTITUDE OF CHARACTER

In the grandness of Indian sports, where legends are born and heroes are celebrated, the concept of innate talent often takes center stage. Yet, there is a profound truth that we must unravel—the significance of character, which transcends the mere whispers of talent.

As we delve into the annals of Indian sports history, let us embark on a journey with Arjun Sharma, a cricketer who defied the odds and embraced the essence of character. In his early years, Arjun, like many others, marveled at the feats of natural athletes. However, his path was different. He discovered that character was the compass guiding him toward his aspirations.

Arjun's journey mirrored that of Arjuna, a revered warrior from the Mahabharata, who faced numerous trials and tribulations on his path to greatness. Arjuna's struggles with self-doubt and moral dilemmas taught him the value of perseverance and determination, virtues echoed in Indian epics such as the Mahabharata. The lessons imparted by the Vedas and Upanishads remind us that knowledge is a treasure to be pursued tirelessly, just as Arjuna pursued his quest for righteousness and enlightenment. Like Arjuna, Caitlyn Jenner, formerly known as Bruce Jenner, faced her own challenges, including struggles with dyslexia. Her journey to becoming a decathlon champion was marked by dedication and hard work, demonstrating the transformative power of perseverance and self-belief, traits celebrated in Indian philosophy and literature.

The Indian sports arena resonates with stories like Priya Verma, Surya Patel, and Milind Suryavanshi, each a testament to character's transformative power. These individuals embarked on their respective journeys, unearthing hidden talents through dedication and resilience, reminiscent of the ancient texts' emphasis on self-discovery.

In a world where innate talent sometimes masquerades as a curse, character emerges as the beacon of hope. The legend of

Arjun Sharma, Priya Verma, and others underscores the significance of character in our pursuit of excellence.

As we reflect on the importance of character, let us remember the story of the Mumbai Indians and the Chennai Super Kings, a tale deeply rooted in the fabric of Indian cricket. In 2008, the Mumbai Indians became the symbol of hope for a city shaken by tragedy. Their resilience and determination to win the Indian Premier League captured the essence of character, transcending the boundaries of cricket.

In the face of adversity, Virat Kohli, the brilliant Delhi batsman, faltered. His inability to cope with setbacks and frustration exposed the fragility of a Immutable Perspective. Like Virat, many falter when they cannot tolerate adversity, a lesson rooted in the teachings of the Mahabharata that stress the importance of inner strength.

But the story did not end there. In the following year, the Chennai Super Kings, fueled by character, rose from the ashes of defeat. They shed their prima donna image and embraced the ethos of teamwork and perseverance. Their victory over the Mumbai Indians symbolized the end of an era, where character triumphed over ego, echoing the timeless wisdom found in the Panchatantra where characters learn the value of humility and cooperation.

In the grand symphony of Indian sports, we must remember that character can be cultivated and nurtured. It is a virtue that transcends innate talent and transforms ordinary individuals into champions. As we celebrate the heroes of Indian sports, let us also honor the fortitude of character that guides them on their remarkable journeys.

THE ESSENCE OF MENTAL FORTITUDE

In the heart of India's diverse sporting landscape, where cricket fields and athletic arenas come to life, the tale of character and the Evolutive Perspective emerges as a guiding light. Let us embark on a journey through the narratives of Indian sports icons who exemplify the unwavering strength of character.

Meet Aryan Kapoor, a promising young tennis player from Mumbai, who in many ways mirrors the legendary Pete Sampras. In the year 2000, Aryan found himself at the prestigious Wimbledon, seeking to etch his name in history. His journey had been challenging, and the odds were stacked against him as he faced the formidable opponent, Rohit Verma. Aryan's mind raced, and the first set slipped through his fingers. But what sets champions like him apart is their ability to transform adversity into opportunity. Aryan dug deep into his reservoir of experiences, drawing inspiration from past matches where he had snatched victory from the jaws of defeat. With a steely resolve and an unwavering spirit, he orchestrated a remarkable comeback. The victory was not just about a tennis match; it was a triumph of character.

In the world of athletics, we find echoes of character in the story of Deepika Singh, a determined heptathlete from Delhi. In her final world championship, she faced an unexpected adversary—an asthma attack. As she battled through the 800-meter race, she realized the importance of self-talk and mental fortitude. "Keep pumping your arms," she whispered to herself, defying the limitations of her body. Deepika's ability to push through adversity and clinch victory highlighted the indomitable spirit that defines a champion.

Another remarkable journey unfolds with the tale of Arjun Patel, an aspiring long jumper. Injuries had sidelined him during his last Olympics, casting a shadow over his dreams. But Arjun refused to be defeated. In the long jump event, he faced disappointment after disappointment, but he knew that character was his greatest asset. With one final jump, he defied the odds, securing a bronze medal. His triumph was a testament to the power of resilience and the art of turning pain into strength.

The wisdom of the Vedas and Upanishads resonates through these stories, reminding us that the mind is a powerful tool. It is a vessel that can be molded through practice and discipline, just as Aryan, Deepika, and Arjun honed their mental fortitude.

As we traverse the realms of Indian sports, we encounter the resolute Mia Khanna, a football player whose mental toughness set her apart. In the face of adversity, she emphasized the significance of mental fortitude in the game. Mia's journey serves as a poignant reminder that mental toughness is not an innate trait but a skill that must be cultivated and nurtured.

In the game of golf, we find the legendary Sanjay Singh, who faced do-or-die situations with unmatched composure. His ability to deliver under pressure is a testament to the championship mentality that characterizes great athletes.

John Kapoor, the basketball prodigy, once faced a similar challenge. He was given a chance against a formidable opponent, inspired by his coach's belief in his character. The result was nothing short of spectacular, underscoring the transformative power of character.

In the grand arena of Indian sports, character reigns supreme. It is the linchpin that propels athletes to greatness, allowing them to rise above their limitations and seize victory when it matters most. These athletes are not born with the right to win; they earn it through hard work, unwavering focus, and the ability to stretch beyond their ordinary abilities.

As we unravel the essence of character, we must recognize that it is not a mere trait but a way of life—a philosophy deeply rooted in the Indian sportsmanship. The tales of Aryan, Deepika, Arjun, Mia, Sanjay, and John serve as an ode to the indomitable spirit that defines Indian athletes—a spirit driven by character, heart, will, and the unwavering determination to triumph against all odds.

SUSTAINING GREATNESS

In the vibrant arena of Indian sports, the journey to the pinnacle is often arduous, but staying there is an art mastered by a select few. As we delve into the stories of Indian sporting legends, we uncover the profound influence of character in their enduring success.

Meet Vikram Sharma, a renowned cricketer who rose to the zenith of the sport, drawing parallels with international icons like Darryl Strawberry, Mike Tyson, and Martina Hingis. These luminaries reached the pinnacle of their respective sports, yet their reign was short-lived due to personal problems and injuries. In Vikram's case, it was character that set him apart. He exemplified the words of the legendary coach John Wooden, who asserted that while ability can propel you to the top, character is what keeps you there. Vikram's unwavering commitment, even in the face of adversity, allowed him to maintain his position as one of the finest cricketers in the world.

Vikram's wisdom resonates deeply in the Indian sporting ethos, where champions are not merely defined by their abilities but by their character. It is a principle that finds its roots in the

Vedas and Upanishads, where the importance of unwavering commitment and resilience is emphasized.

To understand character on a profound level, let us explore the essence of the Evolutive Perspective—a concept that transforms ordinary individuals into champions. Dr. Aarav Kumar, a sports psychologist, conducted a study on adolescents and young adults, gauging their Attitude regarding athletic ability. Those with a Immutable Perspective believed that innate talent was paramount and unchangeable. In contrast, those with a Evolutive Perspective recognized the power of hard work and continuous improvement. It is the latter group, the champions of character, who consistently display the heart of a true athlete.

In the realm of Indian sports, character is not just a trait; it is a way of life, echoing the sentiments of legendary coach Dhriti Devi, who emphasized the importance of perseverance and skill development. Dhriti Devi's philosophy aligns seamlessly with the teachings of the Vedas, where the mind is regarded as a powerful tool that can be shaped through dedication and practice.

As we celebrate the champions who have graced the Indian sporting arena, let us remember that sustaining greatness is a testament to character. It is the embodiment of discipline, hard work, and the unwavering pursuit of excellence. In the annals of Indian sports, it is not only ability but also character that reigns supreme, and it is this fusion of talent and tenacity that propels athletes to unprecedented heights.

THE ESSENCE OF SUCCESS AND FAILURE

In life, what truly constitutes success? To answer this profound question, let us embark on a journey through the richness of Indian wisdom and the inspiring stories of individuals who have harnessed the power of the Evolutive Perspective to define their success.

In the heartland of India, amidst the vibrant colors of Rajasthan, we meet Rajiv Sharma, a gifted athlete whose philosophy mirrors the essence of success. Rajiv's words resonate with the teachings of ancient sages from the Vedas and Upanishads, who emphasized the pursuit of excellence and self-improvement as the true path to success. He proclaims, "For me, the joy of athletics has never resided in winning alone. I derive just as much happiness from the process as from the results. If I lose, I simply go back to the track and work some more." Rajiv embodies the Indian ethos of 'Karma'—the relentless pursuit of one's best, regardless of outcomes.

In the bustling streets of Mumbai, the echoes of this philosophy are amplified by the great coach Ramesh Verma. He draws inspiration from the legendary John Wooden, who believed that genuine success lies not just in reaching the top, but in maintaining that pinnacle through unwavering character and unceasing effort. Ramesh Verma's words serve as a beacon of light to the young athletes under his tutelage, reminding them that the pursuit of excellence is a lifelong journey, and every practice session is an opportunity for growth.

The Indian subcontinent has witnessed the rise of exceptional athletes like Neelima Kapoor and Aditya Patel, whose stories mirror those of Tiger Woods and Mia Hamm. These champions, driven by their ambition, seek not only victory but the fulfillment of their potential. Neelima Kapoor, with her relentless dedication, asserts, "After every game or practice, if you walk off knowing that you gave everything you had, you will always be a winner." Such words resonate with the teachings of the Bhagavad Gita, where Lord Krishna imparts the wisdom of

'Nishkama Karma,' selfless action without attachment to the fruits of one's labor.

Contrastingly, the Immutable Perspective, prevalent in some quarters, defines success as the establishment of superiority over others. In the city of Delhi, we encounter Rohit Malhotra, a prodigious talent whose Immutable Perspective blinds him to the profound wisdom of learning from failure. Rohit's obsession with winning and fear of losing cast shadows over his journey, reminiscent of John McEnroe's aversion to defeat. The Immutable Perspective perceives setbacks as labels of inadequacy, a stark contrast to the Evolutive Perspective's view of failures as stepping stones to improvement.

To illustrate the transformative power of the Evolutive Perspective, we revisit the story of Arjun Kumar, an aspiring cricketer who once grappled with the Immutable Perspective. Arjun's experience mirrors that of Michael Jordan, who, after attempting to coast, learned that sustained success demands unwavering preparation and effort. Arjun's journey embodies the Indian concept of 'Sadhana'—the relentless pursuit of self-improvement through disciplined practice.

In the realm of Indian sports, setbacks do not deter champions; they motivate and inform their journey. Kumar Rajan, a budding badminton star, shares his experience of defeat, drawing inspiration from Kareem Abdul-Jabbar. Rajan's resilience mirrors the Indian philosophy of 'Tyaga'—the art of surrendering ego and embracing growth.

In conclusion, the essence of success lies not solely in victory but in the journey itself. It is a pursuit fueled by the Evolutive Perspective, where every effort, every setback, and every triumph contributes to the symphony of one's life. As we unravel the stories of Indian athletes, we find that the pursuit of excellence transcends the Immutable Perspective's limitations, and it is in this journey that true success is found.

EMBRACING THE POWER OF CONTROL FOR SUCCESS

In the heart of India, where ancient wisdom meets modern ambition, we delve into the profound concept of control that underlines the path to success. The stories of Indian athletes and their relentless pursuit of excellence will guide us in understanding the significance of seizing control over one's journey to success.

As we immerse ourselves in the world of Indian sports, let's begin with the remarkable journey of Aarav Mishra, a budding cricket sensation. Aarav's unwavering commitment to the game echoes the sentiments of the legendary Michael Jordan. Aarav understood that to maintain his cricketing prowess, he needed to adapt to the changes brought by age. He honed his skills, including the classic turnaround shot, to compensate for any decline in stamina and agility. Aarav's journey reflects the teachings of the Upanishads, emphasizing the eternal pursuit of self-improvement.

The game of golf, akin to a mysterious lover, beckons us to understand the essence of control. In the lush greens of the Dehradun Golf Club, we meet Anika Verma, a prodigious golfer who shares her insights on conquering the unpredictable nature of the sport. Butch Harmon's words resonate in her practice sessions: "The golf swing is just about the farthest thing from a perfectible discipline in athletics." Anika understands that even the most reliable swings are works in progress. The Bhagavad Gita's wisdom on 'Sthithaprajna'—the steadfast mind—guides her through the ups and downs of golf, where victory is only a fraction of the time.

Siddharth Singh, a name synonymous with cricketing excellence, hails from the vibrant city of Mumbai. His father, Mr. Singh, introduced him to the art of managing pressure and batting strategy from a young age. This early exposure enabled Siddharth to become less susceptible to pressure, an attribute that would serve him well in his career. Singh's relentless pursuit of control extended to all aspects of his game, guided by a long-term plan. His journey embodies the Vedic principle of 'Dhyana'—the art of focused meditation and discipline, echoing the wisdom imparted in the Mahabharata where warriors honed their skills through disciplined practice and mental fortitude.

In the bustling streets of New Delhi, we meet Vikram Singh, an aspiring athlete who draws inspiration from Tiger Woods's motivational strategies. Vikram understands that managing motivation is paramount to success. He embraces the concept of 'Rival Darshan,' envisioning a formidable adversary who challenges him to push his boundaries. Such motivation is deeply rooted in the Indian philosophy of 'Tapasya'—the unwavering dedication to one's goals.

Rahul Sharma, a cricketer of immense talent, showcases the transformative power of control. His friendship with Virat Kohli offered him a choice: succumb to jealousy or embrace growth. Sharma chose the latter, taking charge of his game to fulfill his potential. His story embodies the essence of 'Niyama'—self-discipline and self-control, as prescribed in the Yoga Sutras of Patanjali.

Contrastingly, we encounter instances where the Immutable Perspective cripples individuals, hindering their ability to seize control. Ravi Kumar's story is a poignant example. Throughout his career, Kumar failed to harness his abilities and motivation effectively. His penchant for blaming external forces and his desire to conceal flaws in a team sport showcase the limitations of the Immutable Perspective. Kumar's journey is a stark reminder that the path to success requires embracing control and taking responsibility—a concept deeply rooted in the teachings of the Vedas and the Panchatantra.

In success, those who take charge of their abilities, motivations, and processes are the true architects of their destiny. As we explore the stories of Indian athletes and their unwavering pursuit of control, we uncover the timeless wisdom of the Upanishads and Vedas, which emphasize the profound impact of self-determination and discipline on the journey to success.

THE ESSENCE OF TEAMWORK: LESSONS FROM INDIAN SPORTS

In the vibrancy of Indian sports, we embark on a journey to understand the profound meaning of being a star player and the essential role of teamwork in achieving greatness. We explore the wisdom of Indian athletes and their experiences, where the boundaries of individual and team excellence blur, guided by the rich philosophies of our land.

In the heart of Mumbai, we meet Arjun Sharma, a cricket prodigy whose story mirrors that of the legendary Michael Jordan. Arjun acknowledges the fine balance between personal stardom and team responsibilities. He draws inspiration from Jordan's words, "In our society sometimes it's hard to come to grips with filling a role instead of trying to be a superstar." Arjun understands that while a superstar's talent can win games, it's teamwork that clinches championships. His dedication to mastering both batting and bowling exemplifies the Vedic principle of 'Karma Yoga,' emphasizing selfless action and devotion to the team's success.

As we venture into the lush cricket fields of Chennai, we encounter Rohit Kapoor, a talented young cricketer. Rohit is well aware of the significance of filling specific roles within the team. His admiration for Coach John Wooden's ability to foster a spirit of teamwork resonates deeply. Wooden's philosophy of creating a harmonious team where each player contributes selflessly inspires Rohit. Wooden's words, "I believe I could have made Kareem Abdul-Jabbar the greatest scorer in college history," serve as a guiding light for Rohit's journey.

In the realm of Indian basketball, we uncover the tale of Devika Menon, a remarkable player with a Evolutive Perspective. Devika is a strong believer in teamwork and understands the importance of adapting to different roles for the greater good of the team. Her unwavering commitment to playing as a power forward, despite her natural talent as a center, showcases her dedication to the team's success. Devika's journey reflects the teachings of the Bhagavad Gita, where Lord Krishna imparts the wisdom of 'Dharma'—fulfilling one's duty selflessly.

The story of Varun Raj, a passionate footballer from Kolkata, unveils the perils of prioritizing personal glory over teamwork. Varun's fixation on validating his own greatness, led to his downfall. His reluctance to accept anything less than being the No. 1 player hindered his ability to work as part of a team. Varun's experience serves as a stark reminder that being a team player is an integral aspect of success in any sport. His journey resonates with the teachings of the Upanishads, emphasizing 'Sankhya Yoga'—the path of knowledge and realization of the interconnectedness of all beings.

We pause to reflect on the universal truth that every sport, be it cricket, basketball, or football, is inherently a team sport. In the serene setting of Rishikesh, we come across Rishi Patel, an open-water swimmer who aspires to break records. Despite the solitary nature of the sport, Rishi acknowledges the extensive team behind every athlete's success.

In every corner of India, from the cricket fields of Mumbai to the basketball courts of Delhi, the essence of teamwork prevails. The stories of Arjun, Rohit, Devika, Varun, and Rishi highlight the delicate balance between personal aspirations and team responsibilities. As we delve into their journeys, we draw wisdom from the Vedas and Upanishads, embracing the profound interconnectedness of all beings and the importance of selfless action in the pursuit of greatness.

UNVEILING THE ATHLETE'S ATTITUDES: LESSONS FROM INDIAN SPORTS STARS

In the realm of Indian sports, we delve deep into the minds of young athletes, each echoing a unique Attitude that shapes their journey towards excellence. Their stories are the very essence of what it means to be an athlete, driven by passion, resilience, and the unwavering pursuit of greatness.

In the bustling lanes of Mumbai, we encounter Arjun Verma, a rising cricket star, and his tale is a reflection of the Attitude divide. Arjun draws inspiration from his father, Rahul Verma, a former cricketer who strived to reach the pinnacle but narrowly missed it. Rahul's picture adorns Arjun's locker, not as a tribute but as a constant reminder of what he hopes never to become - a "nobody." This somebody-nobody syndrome plagues Arjun's mind, making him believe that winning alone will secure his identity. However, the wisdom of his coach, Alok Sharma, introduces him to the path of the Evolutive Perspective, emphasizing that true greatness lies in giving his all, whether in practice or on the field.

Moving south to Chennai, we witness the transformation of Rohini Kapoor, a budding basketball sensation. Rohini's father, Karthik Kapoor, takes a page from the Evolutive Perspective playbook. When coaching Rohini's school team, he witnesses her struggle with complacency and mediocrity. Karthik's fiery pep talk ignites a spark within Rohini, propelling her to extraordinary heights. The Kapoor family believes in the mantra, "If you work hard at something, you get out what you put in." This ethos pushes Rohini to constantly seek improvement and embrace challenges as opportunities for growth.

Our journey through the diverse landscape of Indian sports leads us to Priya Sharma, a passionate young footballer from Kolkata. Priya embodies the essence of relentless self-improvement. Her father, Anil Sharma, recalls a pivotal moment in her journey when her performance faltered. Instead of succumbing to defeat, Priya sought guidance and diligently practiced to overcome her shortcomings. This incident is a testament to her unwavering commitment to personal growth and the team's success.

We conclude our exploration in the tranquil city of Rishikesh, where we meet Vikram Patel, an aspiring swimmer with a Evolutive Perspective. Vikram's story parallels that of Candace Parker, the basketball sensation. Like Parker, Vikram's father instilled in him the belief that hard work yields proportionate results. Vikram understands that nothing in sports or life is promised, motivating him to continuously refine his skills and embrace adversity as an opportunity to excel.

The dichotomy between the fixed and Evolutive Perspectives resounds throughout the narratives of these young Indian athletes. While the Immutable Perspective may cloud their perception with the fear of becoming a "nobody," the Evolutive

Perspective empowers them to embrace challenges, seek improvement, and strive for excellence. Their stories serve as a testament to the power of character, heart, and the mind of a champion, cultivated through self-development, self-motivation, and responsibility.

In the world of Indian sports, where competition is fierce and dreams are boundless, it is the Evolutive Perspective that propels these athletes towards greatness. As we celebrate their journeys, we uncover the profound wisdom of Indian philosophies, emphasizing the importance of self-improvement, resilience, and the relentless pursuit of one's potential.

CULTIVATE YOUR ATTITUDE FOR SPORTING EXCELLENCE

In the vibrancy of Indian sports, there exists a profound truth: the journey to excellence in sports is not solely defined by innate talent but by the unwavering commitment to growth and the relentless pursuit of improvement. Let us embark on a quest to unveil the secrets of nurturing a Evolutive Perspective, a journey that mirrors the essence of India's diverse sporting landscape.

Imagine a young archer, Arjun Sharma, hailing from the heart of Rajasthan. Arjun's journey begins with a bow in his hand and a heart full of passion for archery. He is not a prodigy; his arrows often miss their mark. Yet, driven by his love for the sport, he perseveres. Arjun's story exemplifies the adage that one cannot truly gauge their potential until they invest substantial effort. His dedication transforms him from an uncertain novice to a formidable archer. Arjun's journey reminds us that greatness in sports is a testament to one's unwavering commitment to growth.

Consider the story of Kavya Kapoor, a determined young athlete from the scenic landscapes of Himachal Pradesh. Kavya is a talented sprinter, but her initial victories breed complacency. As she faces tougher competition, self-doubt creeps in, and she finds herself stagnating. It is here that she turns to the wisdom of the Upanishads, which teach that the self is limitless. Embracing the Evolutive Perspective, Kavya recommits herself to her sport, relentlessly working on her technique and endurance. Her transformation from a stagnant athlete to a determined learner echoes the philosophy that character and resilience spring from a Attitude focused on growth.

In the bustling streets of Kolkata, we encounter Devendra Chatterjee, a young footballer with dreams of making it to the national team. Devendra possesses raw talent, but when faced with adversity, he tends to revert to a Immutable Perspective, fearing that his innate abilities might not be enough. It is the guidance of his mentor, Alok Banerjee, that leads him to the path of self-discovery. Alok introduces Devendra to the Bhagavad Gita, where Lord Krishna imparts the wisdom of detached action and continuous self-improvement. Devendra's journey is a testament to the power of combining ancient wisdom with a Evolutive Perspective, as he learns to thrive in the face of adversity.

As we explore the concept of "character" in the sporting world, we draw inspiration from the tales of young athletes who have embraced the Evolutive Perspective. Arjun, Kavya, and Devendra illustrate that true champions are not solely defined by their victories but by their unwavering commitment to learning and improving. It is this dedication that propels them to success, a lesson deeply rooted in the fabric of Indian sports.

In the world of Indian sports, a Evolutive Perspective transcends the pursuit of victory; it becomes a journey of self-discovery, self-improvement, and unwavering determination. As we delve into the stories of these young Indian athletes, we are reminded of the age-old wisdom of the Vedas and Upanishads, which advocate continuous growth and the limitless potential of the self. With every stride, every arrow, and every kick, these athletes redefine the essence of sporting excellence, proving that the true reward lies not just in winning but in the journey of growth itself.

CHAPTER 5

BUSINESS MASTERY: THE ATTITUDE AND LEADERSHIP

•••

The Satyam Computers Debacle: A Tale of Attitude and Misfortune

In the annals of corporate history, the Satyam Computers scandal of 2009 stands as a stark reminder of the perils that lurk within the corporate world. Satyam Computers, once hailed as the epitome of corporate success and innovation, ultimately met its demise. The question that reverberates through boardrooms and business schools across the nation is: What led to this spectacular fall from grace? Was it incompetence or corruption?

As we delve into the heart of this corporate tragedy, we find that it was not solely incompetence or corruption that sealed Satyam Computers' fate. It was a matter of Attitude. According to the astute observations of Rajiv Bajaj in The Economic Times, Indian corporations had become entranced by the allure of talent. The prevailing belief, perpetuated by influential entities like Tata Consultancy Services, was that the "talent Attitude" was the holy grail of corporate success. Just as sports teams vied for exceptional talent, corporations were urged to spare no expense in recruiting individuals deemed as natural talents. This, they believed, was the key to triumphing over competitors.

Bajaj aptly describes this "talent Attitude" as the new gospel of Indian management. Unfortunately, it became the blueprint for Satyam Computers' corporate culture, ultimately sowing the seeds of its catastrophic downfall.

Satyam Computers, in its pursuit of talent, recruited individuals with impressive credentials and offered lucrative compensation packages. While these practices alone may not have been condemnable, the fatal mistake lay in the excessive veneration of talent. Satyam Computers' culture became a temple of talent worship, compelling its employees to present themselves as extraordinarily gifted individuals. In essence, it coerced them into adopting a Immutable Perspective.

Our studies shed light on the consequences of such an Attitude. Individuals with Immutable Perspectives are reluctant to acknowledge and rectify their shortcomings. They inhabit a psychological realm where risks are seldom ventured, mirroring the Indian Institute of Management students who, driven by a Immutable Perspective, shied away from courses that could enhance their business acumen for fear of appearing deficient.

Furthermore, we conducted experiments where praise for intelligence induced a Immutable Perspective, akin to Satyam Computers' approach to its star employees. Subsequently, when faced with challenging tasks, a shocking revelation emerged. Nearly 40 percent of these students lied about their scores, always inflating them. The Immutable Perspective had rendered any imperfection intolerable.

Gladwell astutely concludes that individuals thriving in environments that celebrate their innate talents find it exceedingly challenging to cope when their self-image is threatened. They resist enrolling in remedial courses and evade acknowledging their mistakes, even when facing investors and the public. They would rather resort to deception.

The implication is evident: a company incapable of introspection and self-correction is destined for failure.

Unlocking Prosperity: The Evolutive Perspective in Thriving Companies

The question that arises from the Satyam debacle is whether companies that thrive possess a Evolutive Perspective. Let us embark on a journey through the corporate landscape to seek answers.

PINNACLE OF ORGANIZATIONAL EXCELLENCE: A JOURNEY TO GREATNESS

In the pursuit of greatness, organizations often embark on a quest to transcend mediocrity and ascend to unparalleled heights. What separates those that succeed in this transformative journey from those that merely maintain a status quo of goodness? To unravel this enigma, we delve into the illuminating research of Jim Collins, who sought to discern the alchemy that propels some companies from being good to becoming truly great.

Collins and his dedicated research team embarked on an exhaustive five-year study, meticulously selecting eleven companies that had achieved remarkable stock returns, surpassing their industry peers, and sustaining this ascendancy for a minimum of fifteen years. These companies were juxtaposed with their industry counterparts possessing similar resources but failing to make the leap. Additionally, a third category comprised those organizations that had momentarily transcended goodness but failed to sustain their greatness.

What emerged from this discerning inquiry were several pivotal factors, as elucidated in Collins' seminal work, "Good to Great." However, one factor stood as an unequivocal linchpin in the journey to greatness: the nature of leadership. These leaders were not the flamboyant, ego-driven personalities who proclaimed their innate talent; rather, they were individuals of profound humility, constantly engaging in self-inquiry and possessing the fortitude to confront unflinching truths, including their own failures, all while nurturing an unwavering faith in eventual success.

The resemblance between these exceptional leaders and individuals with a Evolutive Perspective is striking. They share the conviction in human development, and their traits serve as beacons of inspiration:

1. **Absence of Egoic Rivalry**: Instead of perpetually striving to assert their superiority over others, these leaders eschew hierarchical displays of dominance. They refrain from appropriating credit for the contributions of their team members and avoid undermining their peers to assert authority.

2. **Relentless Pursuit of Improvement**: Their perpetual quest for excellence is relentless. They actively seek out the most proficient individuals to augment their team, while unflinchingly scrutinizing their own shortcomings and blunders. They engage in candid discussions about the requisite skills, both for themselves and their organization's future, charting a path forward grounded in pragmatic realities rather than illusions of personal brilliance.

The Visionary Leadership of Anil Kumar: Steering a Path Through Challenge to Triumph in Indian Retail

Anil Kumar, the transformative leader of Digital Bazaar, offers a compelling narrative of leadership that stands as a beacon of strategic clarity and purposeful dialogue in the Indian corporate landscape. Embracing a philosophy that diverged from the conventional aim of merely seeking approval from his board of directors, Kumar cultivated an environment ripe for rigorous debate and introspection within the boardroom. This approach wasn't about showcasing a veneer of infallibility; rather, it was a genuine quest for enlightenment and strategic foresight, engaging his executive team in a relentless pursuit of probing questions to distill a clear understanding of the company's present realities and its potential future path.

The Quest for Deep Understanding

Kumar's leadership style was characterized by an insatiable curiosity, often leading discussions with a series of "Why, why, why?" This relentless inquiry earned him the respect of his peers and the nickname "the prosecutor" for his thoroughness in exploring every facet of the business. Rather than accepting surface-level observations, Kumar delved deeper, seeking to uncover the underlying truths that would inform smarter, more strategic decisions.

From Brinkmanship to Breakthrough

In a narrative reminiscent of the tales from the Panchatantra, where wisdom, patience, and insight lead to overcoming formidable challenges, Anil Kumar stood as the pragmatic "plow horse" of the Indian retail sector. His leadership came at a critical juncture when Digital Bazaar was navigating through turbulent waters, on the verge of bankruptcy. His grounded, diligent, and unassuming approach to leadership was pivotal in not just averting a financial disaster but in laying the groundwork for a remarkable turnaround.

Over the course of fifteen years, under Kumar's stewardship, Digital Bazaar emerged from the shadows of potential collapse to chart a course of extraordinary growth and success. The company not only stabilized but soared, achieving unparalleled levels of stockholder returns among its peers on the Bombay Stock Exchange (BSE), a feat that mirrored the legendary transformations seen in classic Indian epics where strategic acumen, moral fortitude, and relentless pursuit of excellence lead to victory against all odds.

A Legacy of Enlightened Leadership

Anil Kumar's tenure at Digital Bazaar is a testament to the transformative power of leadership that values deep understanding, strategic clarity, and the courage to ask difficult questions. His approach serves as a masterclass in navigating the complexities of the business world, emphasizing that true leadership is not about the pursuit of personal glory but the collective success of the organization. Kumar's legacy is a guiding light for current and future leaders in India and beyond, demonstrating that even in the face of daunting challenges, visionary leadership grounded in wisdom, inquiry, and pragmatism can chart the path to enduring success.

In this compelling narrative, the essence of leadership imbued with a Evolutive Perspective shines forth as the cornerstone of organizational greatness. It is a testament to the power of humility, inquisitiveness, and an unwavering belief in the potential for human development.

Cultivating Greatness: The Leadership Paradigm for Indian Organizations

As we reflect on these profound insights, it becomes evident that the path to greatness is not bound by geographical boundaries. Indian organizations, too, can embrace the principles of humility, continuous improvement, and collaborative leadership to chart a course towards unparalleled success. The timeless wisdom of the Vedas and Upanishads resonates with these ideals, offering a guiding light for leaders and organizations on their journey to greatness.

In the words of Swami Vivekananda, "Arise, awake, and stop not till the goal is reached." Indian organizations can draw inspiration from this clarion call, transcending complacency and embracing a Evolutive Perspective. It is through this transformative shift in Attitude and leadership that Indian organizations can script their own narratives of greatness, contributing to the nation's economic prosperity and global eminence.

THE ATTITUDE'S MANIFESTATION IN MANAGEMENT: A STUDY

In the realm of management and leadership, the interplay of Attitudes shapes not only individual decisions but also the destiny of organizations. A riveting exploration conducted by Robert Wood and Albert Bandura, focusing on graduate students in business, casts a revealing spotlight on the profound influence of Attitude in management.

Their study ingeniously engineered two archetypal managerial personas: the "Satyam-type" managers, emblematic of a Immutable Perspective, and the "Bajaj-type" managers, epitomizing a Evolutive Perspective. These budding business leaders were entrusted with the intricate task of steering a simulated organization—a furniture company—through the dynamic landscape of management. In this computerized endeavor, they were tasked with judiciously assigning employees to their respective roles and devising optimal strategies to motivate and guide the workforce. Crucially, their decision-making process hinged on the constant feedback received regarding employee productivity.

The participants were bifurcated into two distinct groups: one steeped in the Immutable Perspective paradigm, anchored in the belief that their performance was an immutable reflection of their inherent capabilities, and the other embraced the Evolutive Perspective, perceiving management skills as malleable and nurtured through practice.

The management task presented formidable challenges, featuring demanding production standards that often outstripped initial attempts. Resonating with the Satyam saga, those ensnared in the Immutable Perspective remained impervious to the enlightenment derived from their blunders. Conversely, those entrenched in the Evolutive Perspective traversed a different trajectory—one of continuous learning. Unburdened by the compulsion to safeguard their fixed abilities, they confronted their mistakes head-on, leveraging feedback to recalibrate their strategies. Gradually, they honed their aptitude for optimizing employee deployment and motivation, resulting in a striking surge in productivity. Remarkably, their productivity surpassed that of their Immutable Perspective counterparts. Furthermore, throughout this rigorous undertaking, they steadfastly retained a buoyant sense of self-assuredness, akin to the indomitable spirit of Bajaj.

In stark contrast to Bajaj's exemplary leadership, the leaders of the comparison companies in Jim Collins' research epitomized the entrenched traits of the Immutable Perspective. Fixed-Attitude leaders, much like their fixed-Attitude counterparts in general, inhabit a world defined by hierarchical notions of superiority and inferiority. Their primary endeavor revolves around reaffirming their perceived superiority, often at the expense of their organization's well-being.

These leaders frequently harbor an insatiable hunger for personal acclaim, an affliction that extends to their stewardship of the company. As Collins elucidates, they are driven by the desire to cement their legacy, with an underlying belief that the organization is merely a stage for showcasing their personal greatness. The pernicious consequence of this Attitude is the propensity to orchestrate conditions conducive to the organization's downfall after their departure—a morose validation of their own perceived indispensability.

The fixed-Attitude leadership paradigm is replete with gargantuan personal egos that either precipitate the organization's demise or consign it to perennial mediocrity. Examples abound, such as Lee Iacocca, the former head of Chrysler, whose remarkable turnaround of the company was eclipsed by an obsessive pursuit of personal fame, leading to the company's subsequent decline.

Many comparison companies adhered to a "genius with a thousand helpers" model, shunning the path of building exceptional management teams. Instead, they adhered to the fixed-Attitude dogma that exalted the genius and relegated others to the role of inconsequential subordinates. This philosophy was emblematic of the Immutable Perspective's predilection for being the sole big fish in the pond, savoring the illusion of superiority over their peers.

A stark divergence emerges when examining the approaches of fixed-Attitude CEOs versus their growth-minded counterparts. Fixed-Attitude individuals display a marked reluctance to invest in mentoring or employee development programs, prioritizing self-aggrandizement over the growth and development of their workforce. In sharp contrast, growth-Attitude leaders exhibit a deep commitment to personnel development, with an unwavering focus on fostering the growth and potential of their employees.

The comparison companies' leaders, ensnared in the Immutable Perspective, vehemently resisted acknowledging their deficiencies, mirroring the tragic trajectory of Satyam Computers. These leaders obstinately ignored warning signs and perilous shifts in the business landscape, preferring to remain ensconced in their delusions. This obdurate refusal to adapt ultimately sealed the fate of their organizations.

FOSTERING LEADERSHIP EXCELLENCE: EMBRACING A EVOLUTIVE PERSPECTIVE

The narrative unveiled by this profound exploration underscores the transformative potential of leadership imbued with a Evolutive Perspective. As Indian organizations embark on their quest for excellence, they must draw inspiration from these revelations. It is imperative that they recognize the age-old wisdom encapsulated in the Vedas and Upanishads, which extol the virtues of humility, adaptability, and continuous learning.

In the words of Swami Vivekananda, "Education is the manifestation of perfection already present in man." Indian organizations can tap into this intrinsic potential by fostering a Evolutive Perspective among their leaders and employees. It is through this paradigm shift in Attitude and leadership that Indian organizations can script their own narratives of success, contributing to the nation's economic prosperity and global prominence.

The narrative continues, offering a profound exploration of the Indian business landscape and the leaders who embody the essence of a Evolutive Perspective.

LEADERS WITH IMMUTABLE PERSPECTIVES: LESSONS FROM THE PAST

In the annals of leadership, one name that stands out is Laxman Rao, an executive who left an indelible mark on the corporate landscape. While leadership luminaries often narrate stories of humble beginnings and an unswerving passion for their craft, Laxman Rao's journey took a different course, offering us valuable insights into the intricacies of a Immutable Perspective.

Warren Bennis, revered as a leadership sage in Indian business circles, embarked on a quest to decipher the essence of exemplary corporate leaders. What he discovered was a stark contrast to the narratives of many great leaders who had walked the path of passion and purpose. These extraordinary individuals had never harbored grand aspirations of leadership; they simply immersed themselves in their chosen fields with unwavering dedication, guided solely by their love for what they did.

However, Laxman Rao's tale diverged from this paradigm. While he did harbor a genuine affection for the automobile industry, his deepest longing transcended mere passion. He yearned for the coveted position of "Mahanayak" at the illustrious Parivahan Corporation, akin to ascending the throne of a kingdom. The approval of the enigmatic Hari Krishna, the reigning monarch of Parivahan Corporation, held a special allure for Laxman Rao. These were the barometers against which he measured his self-worth, the yardsticks that would validate his existence.

In the grandiloquent lore of Indian business, the Parivahan Corporation's headquarters were akin to a majestic palace, colloquially referred to as the "Ratna Mahal." Hari Krishna, the enigmatic monarch of the Ratna Mahal, assumed the mantle of the king, with Laxman Rao as the designated heir, the "Yuvraj."

Within the confines of the palace, they reveled in the extravagance befitting royalty—white-clad attendants at their beck and call, daily feasts featuring imported delicacies like "Dover sole" flown in from distant lands, and an atmosphere of opulence that surpassed even first-class extravagance.

Laxman Rao's tenure at Parivahan Corporation saw commendable achievements, including the nurturing and successful promotion of the iconic "Rajah" car. Yet, his unquenchable thirst for the CEO throne persisted. When Hari Krishna, the reigning monarch, decided otherwise, dashing Laxman Rao's dreams, shock and indignation gripped him. Despite being privy to corporate dismissals orchestrated by Hari Krishna himself, Laxman Rao remained blind to the immutable laws of the corporate arena. His Immutable Perspective perpetuated the illusion of his distinctiveness— a belief that he was impervious to the pitfalls that befell others.

The rejection that Laxman Rao encountered served as an impetus for his extraordinary transformation, akin to a phoenix rising from the ashes. Undeterred by the setback at Parivahan Corporation, he seized the opportunity to resurrect Chrysler Motors from the brink of oblivion. As the newly anointed CEO of Chrysler, he embarked on a relentless quest to reassemble a dream team, introduce innovative models, and advocate for governmental financial aid.

Within a short span, Laxman Rao emerged victorious, authoring a triumphant autobiography that proclaimed him a hero in the automotive realm. However, this newfound success could not satiate his insatiable need to validate his greatness. Laxman Rao's Immutable Perspective manifested in a voracious appetite for public adulation and stock market triumphs, overshadowing prudent investments in product development and manufacturing enhancements essential for long-term profitability.

Laxman Rao's fixation on his legacy and how history would remember him led to a critical divergence from the path of corporate stewardship. Rather than investing in the growth and prosperity of Chrysler, he prioritized personal acclaim. This fixation culminated in a series of unfortunate choices, including a fervent campaign against Japanese imports, characterized by blame, excuses, and the futile pursuit of protectionist measures.

Moreover, Ramesh Sharma's leadership exhibited a stark contrast to the principles of Evolutive Perspective. His tenure witnessed the erosion of workplace morale, marked by dismissals of dissenting voices and a paucity of rewards for the dedicated workforce that had contributed to Satyam Computers' resurgence. The working conditions and remuneration remained subpar, even when the company enjoyed substantial financial gains. Meanwhile, Ramesh Sharma continued to indulge in extravagant corporate perks, exemplified by the exorbitant renovation of his suite at the Taj Mahal Palace in Mumbai..

As time passed, Laxman Rao clung tenaciously to his role as CEO, oblivious to the diminishing effectiveness of his leadership. The board of directors, recognizing the urgent need for change, gently eased him out of his position. Despite receiving an opulent pension, stock options, and continued corporate privileges, Laxman Rao's unrelenting pursuit of personal glory and power led him to join a hostile takeover attempt that jeopardized Satyam's future.

Laxman Rao's life and career encapsulate the essence of the Immutable Perspective. Despite commencing his journey with genuine passion and breakthrough ideas, the need to validate his perceived superiority gradually consumed his enjoyment and stifled his creativity. His refusal to adapt to competitive challenges and an obsession with preserving his ego led to the familiar refrain of blame, excuses, and the marginalization of critics and rivals.

As often occurs with individuals entrenched in the Immutable Perspective, Laxman Rao lost the very validation he had relentlessly pursued. The corporate world, with its magnanimous capacity to cater to the egos of CEOs, can engender a self-serving cocoon where the need for validation knows no bounds. This phenomenon, aptly termed "CEO disease," represents a perilous manifestation of the Immutable Perspective.

Today, we wonder whether Laxman Rao has embarked on a path of redemption, liberated from the burden of incessantly proving himself. His endeavors in innovative diabetes research and environmentally friendly vehicles may signify a shift toward values that transcend personal validation.

NAVIGATING THE LEADERSHIP LANDSCAPE: EMBRACING THE EVOLUTIVE PERSPECTIVE

In the sprawling Indian leadership, tales of unyielding resolve and visionary thinking resonate through the ages. The story of Alok Sharma, a leader who defied convention and embraced the Evolutive Perspective, serves as a beacon of inspiration for aspiring leaders in the Indian corporate milieu.

Alok Sharma's journey was not one of ego-driven aspirations but a relentless pursuit of excellence rooted in the Vedas and Upanishads. These ancient scriptures, revered for their profound wisdom, extolled the virtues of humility, adaptability, and the relentless quest for knowledge—a philosophy that would come to define Alok's leadership.

Unlike his fixed-Attitude counterparts, Alok Sharma embarked on his professional odyssey with an insatiable thirst for learning. He understood that leadership was not a destination but a continuous journey of growth and self-improvement. Drawing inspiration from the timeless wisdom of the Upanishads, he embraced the concept that education was the manifestation of perfection already present within oneself.

As Alok Sharma ascended the ranks in the Indian corporate landscape, he displayed an unwavering commitment to personnel development, a hallmark of the Evolutive Perspective. Unlike his fixed-Attitude peers, who were preoccupied with preserving their egos, Alok Sharma fostered an environment that nurtured the growth and potential of his employees. Employee development programs were not mere checkboxes for him but a genuine investment in the future.

The Indian business landscape faced its most significant challenge with the influx of global competitors, much like the American auto industry's encounter with Japanese imports. While many succumbed to the allure of blame and excuses, Alok Sharma embodied a different spirit. He harked back to the Vedas, which emphasized that true greatness lay in self-improvement and innovation.

Instead of resorting to protectionist measures, Alok Sharma took up the challenge head-on. He recognized that the solution lay not in anger or excuses but in crafting superior products. A detailed study of successful global counterparts, including Honda, served as a blueprint for innovation. Alok Sharma's Evolutive Perspective propelled him to spearhead the development of cutting-edge designs and manufacturing improvements that would secure the long-term profitability of his organization.

In contrast to the fixed-Attitude leaders who saw their employees as mere pawns, Alok Sharma understood the power of a motivated and skilled workforce. He rewarded dedication and innovation, fostering a sense of ownership and pride among his employees. In the spirit of sharing prosperity, he ensured that their remuneration and working conditions were commensurate with their contributions.

Alok Sharma's leadership was a testament to the principles of humility and adaptability, mirroring the teachings of the Vedas and Upanishads. He exemplified the belief that leadership was not about wielding power and preserving one's ego but about facilitating the growth and success of the collective.

As time passed, Alok Sharma's legacy as a growth-minded leader continued to flourish. His organization thrived, and he became renowned not for his ego but for his unwavering commitment to progress and innovation. His enduring influence on the Indian corporate landscape serves as a reminder that the path to leadership greatness lies in the embrace of the Evolutive Perspective—a philosophy deeply rooted in the wisdom of ancient Indian scriptures.

In the chapters that follow, we delve deeper into the stories of leaders who have left an indelible mark on the Indian corporate world, each guided by the timeless principles of growth and learning. The narratives of these leaders illuminate the path for a new generation of Indian leaders, urging them to embrace the Evolutive Perspective and script their own stories of success.

THE ENIGMA OF EGO: A TALE OF AKSHAY SHARMA AND THE SUPERSTAR SYNDROME

In the richness of Indian leadership, the legend of Akshay Sharma, a visionary leader with an unwavering focus on values, takes center stage. His journey encapsulates the essence of humility, ethics, and the relentless pursuit of excellence—a stark contrast to the ego-driven narratives of corporate leaders in the West.

Akshay Sharma, a luminary in the Indian corporate landscape, was not driven by a desire to amass wealth or chase ephemeral glory. His leadership philosophy was deeply rooted in the timeless wisdom of the Vedas and Upanishads, which extolled the virtues of self-respect, self-improvement, and the pursuit of knowledge as the ultimate measure of success.

Unlike his Western counterparts, who often prioritized profits above all else, Akshay Sharma held a profound belief in the importance of values and ethical conduct in business. He saw the business world not as a mere money-making endeavor but as a platform for creating a positive impact on society.

Akshay Sharma's journey commenced with an insatiable thirst for learning and growth, a testament to his Evolutive Perspective deeply ingrained in Indian philosophy. He understood that leadership was not about resting on laurels but embarking on an endless quest for self-improvement and innovation.

As he ascended the ranks of the Indian corporate hierarchy, Akshay Sharma demonstrated a commitment to personnel development that set him apart. Unlike his Western counterparts, who often viewed employees as expendable resources, he viewed them as the lifeblood of his organization. Employee development programs were not mere checkboxes for him but genuine investments in the future of his employees and the organization.

In the face of fierce global competition, akin to the challenges faced by American auto companies, Akshay Sharma did not resort to blame and excuses. Drawing inspiration from the Vedas, he understood that true greatness lay in self-improvement and innovation, not in deflecting responsibility. A detailed study of successful global counterparts, much like the approach to learning advocated in the Upanishads, served as his blueprint for success.

Akshay Sharma's leadership transcended ego and self-aggrandizement. He understood that the true measure of success lay not in the interests of a select few but in the welfare of all stakeholders, including employees, the community, and suppliers. The concept of stakeholders was not a ridiculous term for him; it was a guiding principle that defined his leadership.

Unlike Western leaders who often succumbed to boredom and short-term thinking, Akshay Sharma's commitment to long-term sustainability remained unwavering. He believed in the transformative power of learning, growth, and challenges, mirroring the enduring journeys of legendary Indian personalities like Mahatma Gandhi and Dr. APJ Abdul Kalam.

As time passed, Akshay Sharma's legacy continued to flourish, leaving an indelible mark on the Indian corporate landscape. His organization thrived not because of ego-driven decisions but because of a steadfast commitment to values, ethics, and employee development. His enduring influence serves as a reminder that leadership greatness lies not in the pursuit of personal glory but in the creation of a better world for all.

In the upcoming chapters, we delve deeper into the stories of leaders who have embraced the values and wisdom of ancient Indian philosophy, each leaving an indelible mark on the Indian corporate world. These narratives illuminate the path for a new generation of Indian leaders, urging them to prioritize values, ethics, and the Evolutive Perspective as they script their own stories of success.

THE ENIGMA OF ENTITLEMENT: A TALE OF EGO AND RUIN

In the grand saga of Indian leadership, the chronicle of Rajesh Gupta and Priya Singh stands as a stark reminder of the perils of the Immutable Perspective and the allure of entitlement. Their stories shed light on the consequences of ego-driven leadership and the importance of humility and adaptability in the ever-evolving corporate landscape of India.

Rajesh Gupta, the founder and CEO of a burgeoning Indian conglomerate, envisioned himself as a visionary leader. However, his vision was often clouded by a sense of entitlement. In the corridors of his corporate empire, he looked upon his employees as mere pawns in his game, akin to a king and his subjects. This regal Attitude blinded him to the true essence of leadership—serving others and fostering a collaborative environment.

In contrast, Priya Singh, a dynamic leader from a humble background, believed in the power of hard work and innovation. She understood that true leadership meant rolling up one's sleeves and working alongside the team. Her tenure as the head of a thriving technology startup demonstrated the significance of nurturing talent and valuing every individual's contribution.

As Rajesh Gupta reveled in his perceived greatness, he failed to recognize the erosion of integrity within his organization. His arrogance and disregard for ethical conduct mirrored the downfall of Satyam Computers. The illusion of respect and integrity he projected was nothing more than a facade, much like the perception-driven leadership of American counterparts.

At the helm of Rajesh Gupta's conglomerate, Priya Singh faced the daunting task of rectifying the moral and financial mess left behind. Her leadership style, rooted in openness, honesty, and sincerity, set the organization on a path of redemption. She understood that leadership was not about deflecting responsibility but taking ownership of mistakes and charting a new course.

The collision of these two leaders, Rajesh and Priya, echoed the clash between AOL's Steve Case and Time Warner's Jerry Levin. Both Rajesh and Priya cultivated an aura of intelligence, but their approaches differed vastly. While Rajesh sought to intimidate with brilliance, Priya believed in empowering her team and fostering a culture of learning.

In a dramatic merger of companies reminiscent of the AOL-Time Warner debacle, Rajesh and Priya found themselves at odds. The clash of egos and the pursuit of personal power threatened the very existence of their conglomerate. Rajesh's reluctance to relinquish control for the greater good mirrored the Immutable Perspective's aversion to change.

Ultimately, Priya's resilience and determination prevailed as she worked tirelessly to salvage the organization. Her humility and willingness to collaborate with others set a precedent for a more inclusive and adaptive leadership style. The conglomerate, once on the brink of ruin, emerged stronger under her guidance.

The stories of Rajesh Gupta and Priya Singh serve as cautionary tales for aspiring Indian leaders. They illustrate the pitfalls of entitlement and the merits of humility and adaptability. In a rapidly evolving corporate landscape, where success hinges on innovation and collaboration, embracing a Evolutive Perspective becomes not just a choice but a necessity.

In the following chapters, we delve deeper into the narratives of Indian leaders who have embodied the principles of Evolutive Perspective, resilience, and ethical leadership. Their journeys illuminate the path for future leaders, urging them to shun entitlement and embrace the transformative power of a growth-oriented Attitude.

THE TRIALS OF TYRANTS: NURTURING A CULTURE OF GROWTH AND RESPECT

In the vivid of Indian corporate history, the tales of Ramesh Sharma and Aisha Khan serve as poignant reminders of the dangers of leadership driven by ego and contempt for others. Their stories illuminate the corrosive effects of a Immutable Perspective and underscore the imperative of fostering a culture of growth and respect in Indian organizations.

Ramesh Sharma, a prominent business magnate, wielded his authority with an air of superiority that echoed the Immutable Perspective. His belief in his innate greatness led him to dismiss the needs and feelings of those he considered beneath him. He believed in keeping his employees off balance to maintain control, much like the ruthless Roman emperor Caligula. Ramesh Sharma's leadership bore the hallmark of arrogance, and he often ridiculed those he deemed less intelligent.

Aisha Khan, on the other hand, hailed from humble beginnings and believed in the power of collaboration and innovation. As the CEO of a rapidly growing tech startup, she nurtured a culture of openness, honesty, and mutual respect. Her leadership style stood in stark contrast to the abusive tactics employed by Ramesh Sharma and his ilk.

Harish Sharma, an authority on corporate leadership, aptly describes the motivations behind such abusive behavior. He asserts that brutal bosses seek to enhance their own sense of power and competence at the expense of their subordinates. This desire for superiority often leads to humiliation, as was the case with Rajesh Kumar, who disguised his abusive behavior as perfectionism.

Intriguingly, the victims of such bosses are not always those perceived as less talented. Rather, they are often the most competent individuals who pose a significant threat to the fixed-Attitude boss. Sharma's interviews with employees reveal that these bosses deliberately target high-performing individuals to bolster their own sense of competence. This dynamic mirrors the tales of cunning and power struggles found in the Indian epics such as the Panchatantra, where characters employ various tactics to maintain dominance and control over others.

The ripple effect of such humiliation extends throughout the organization. It fosters a culture where everything revolves around pleasing the boss, stifling creativity and innovation. Jim Collins, in his book "Good to Great," warns that when leaders become the primary focus of an organization, mediocrity prevails. Leaders like David Rockefeller of Chase Manhattan Bank and Ray Macdonald of Burroughs exemplified this control-driven leadership, inhibiting their teams from venturing new ideas and innovations.

In a similar vein, Tata Consultancy Services, despite its initial success in the computer industry, lost its competitive edge due to leaders like Anil Kumar and Sunil Gupta, who resorted to public humiliation and abuse. Their actions instilled fear and stifled the enterprising spirit of their teams. This echoes the narratives found in Indian epics such as the Panchatantra, where abusive leadership and its detrimental effects on teamwork are often explored.

When bosses adopt a controlling and abusive demeanor, they plunge the entire organization into a Immutable Perspective. Fear of judgment takes precedence over learning, growth, and progress. In such an environment, courage and innovation struggle to survive, leaving the organization stagnant and vulnerable.

The narratives of Ramesh Sharma and Aisha Khan underscore the importance of nurturing a culture rooted in growth and respect. Indian organizations must prioritize leadership that fosters collaboration, values diversity, and embraces a Evolutive Perspective. The upcoming chapters delve deeper into the journeys of Indian leaders who champion these principles, illuminating a path toward sustainable success and innovation.

As we navigate the complexities of leadership in the Indian corporate landscape, the stories of resilience, adaptability, and ethical leadership will continue to guide us toward a future where every individual's potential is realized, and every voice is heard.

THE JOURNEY OF GROWTH-ATTITUDE LEADERS: NURTURING HUMAN POTENTIAL

In the grandness of Indian leadership, there exists a profound wisdom in the words of Ramesh Khurana, a revered industrialist: "The true measure of a leader lies not in their brilliance but in their ability to harness the brilliance of those around them." These words resonate deeply in the Indian context, where leaders are esteemed for their humility, wisdom, and commitment to growth.

As we delve into the world of growth-minded leaders, we are welcomed into a realm where possibilities abound, where the air is filled with energy, and where leadership is not an ego-driven pursuit but a shared journey of growth and collaboration. It is a world where leaders like Raj Kapoor, Maya Sharma, and Arjun Singh have the script of success with a Evolutive Perspective.

Raj Kapoor: The Eloquent Listener

Raj Kapoor, a visionary entrepreneur, took the helm of his family's textile business at a young age. He understood that true leadership was not about imposing one's will but about listening to the collective wisdom of the team. Kapoor's journey was marked by a commitment to nurturing employees' potential.

One instance stands out—a visit to a textile factory in Kanpur. Kapoor, in his unassuming demeanor, engaged with the workers on the shop floor. He listened intently to their concerns and ideas. This act of humility and openness left an indelible mark on the workforce. Kapoor's leadership style was rooted in teamwork, not self-importance. He understood that a Evolutive Perspective was not a solo act but a collective endeavor.

Maya Sharma: The Catalyst of Change

Maya Sharma, an inspirational leader in the IT industry, believed in the transformative power of growth. When she assumed leadership of her tech startup, it was on the brink of collapse. Yet, Sharma approached the challenge with unwavering optimism and a profound belief in human potential.

Sharma's leadership philosophy was encapsulated in the ancient Indian saying, "Vasudhaiva Kutumbakam," which translates to "The world is one family." She saw her company as a platform for personal and professional growth for every team member. With her guidance, the organization underwent a remarkable turnaround. It became a hub of innovation and collaboration, much like the blossoming tech hubs of Bangalore and Hyderabad.

Arjun Singh: The Defender of Values

Arjun Singh, a seasoned corporate leader, understood the importance of values in leadership. His tenure at a multinational conglomerate was marked by a commitment to nurturing a culture of integrity and growth. Singh's leadership mirrored the teachings of the Upanishads, which emphasize the pursuit of knowledge and self-realization.

One of Singh's defining moments came when he addressed a gathering of top executives. He did not shower them with accolades but challenged them to align with the company's core values. This act of humility and emphasis on shared values transformed the organization into a thriving ecosystem of growth.

In the footsteps of these growth-minded leaders, a new paradigm of Indian leadership emerges—one where leaders embrace the wisdom of the Vedas and the Upanishads, which proclaim, "You are what your deep, driving desire is." In this journey of growth, humility, and shared success, leaders become not rulers but enablers of greatness in others.

The stories of Raj Kapoor, Maya Sharma, and Arjun Singh remind us that true self-confidence is not born of arrogance but of the courage to be open to change and new ideas, regardless of their source. Leadership is not about titles, but about Attitude—the readiness to grow and nurture the growth of others.

In the pursuit of growth, these leaders shattered the shackles of ego and embraced the limitless potential of human collaboration. They exemplify the profound truth that a leader's legacy is not measured in dollars but in the growth and empowerment of those they lead.

As we embark on a journey through the landscapes of Indian leadership, we will encounter more stories of growth-minded leaders who have harnessed the collective brilliance of their teams to create lasting impact and prosperity.

NURTURING THE RENAISSANCE OF TCS: AN ODYSSEY INSPIRED BY INDIAN ETHOS

In the rich mosaic of Indian corporate sagas, the revitalization of Tata Consultancy Services (TCS) echoes a story of metamorphosis, reminiscent of the profound tales found in the Panchatantra. In the twilight years of the 20th century, TCS faced an existential crisis, mirroring the formidable challenges depicted in the ancient Indian epic, the Ramayana. The company's ethos was being eroded by complacency and a sense of entitlement, starkly opposing the Indian virtues of humility, teamwork, and collective effort.

Divine Guidance: Natarajan Chandrasekaran's Inspired Leadership

In 1993, echoing the celestial call to duty highlighted in the Bhagavad Gita, Natarajan Chandrasekaran was tasked with the leadership of TCS. Initially hesitant, Chandrasekaran's acceptance of the role was spurred by a sense of duty to the organization and the nation, reminiscent of Lord Krishna's counsel to Arjuna, emphasizing the importance of duty over personal reservations. Chandrasekaran's mission was crystal clear—to orchestrate a strategic and cultural transformation within TCS, akin to Arjuna's transformative journey on the battlefield of Kurukshetra.

Adopting the Principles of Vedanta for Effective Communication

Understanding the critical role of transparent and open communication, Chandrasekaran championed the Vedantic principle of dialogue and the free exchange of knowledge. He made it a point to engage with every TCS employee, embodying the spirit of "Guru Dakshina," where wisdom and knowledge are shared unconditionally. His message was unequivocal: "United, we can fortify our company." This ethos was the cornerstone of his communication, dedicating his efforts to the unsung heroes within TCS who were instrumental in the company's reinvention.

Democratizing the Workspace: Insights from the Mahabharata

In line with the egalitarian teachings of Lord Krishna, Chandrasekaran dismantled the prevailing culture of elitism. He abolished hierarchical barriers, promoting the idea that valuable insights and expertise could emerge from any level within the organization. This approach was rooted in the belief in collective intelligence and the collaborative resolution of challenges, reflecting a departure from the hierarchical and segmented practices of the past.

Fostering Team Spirit: The Gandhian Way

Inspired by Mahatma Gandhi's principles of unity and mutual respect, Chandrasekaran placed a premium on teamwork, overshadowing personal achievements. He actively discouraged internal competition, advocating for a culture where collaboration and collective responsibility were paramount. This approach was a stark contrast to the divisive strategies that often plague corporate environments, emphasizing shared goals over individual accolades.

From Strategic Planning to Execution: The Wisdom of Chanakya

In the realm of business, the emphasis often lies on strategic deals, reminiscent of Chanakya's tactics in forming alliances. Chandrasekaran, however, understood that strategic planning was just the beginning. He advocated for and exemplified flawless execution, drawing upon the ancient adage that actions are more eloquent than words. His leadership mantra was clear: "Brilliance alone is insufficient; our success is measured by our results."

Prioritizing Client Relations: The Essence of Devotion

TCS's clientele, feeling overlooked, mirrored devotees yearning for acknowledgment. Chandrasekaran recognized this gap and prioritized customer satisfaction above all. He introduced significant price adjustments and addressed client concerns head-on, reinforcing the leader's role as a servant to the needs of the customers.

Endurance and Agility: Learning from Indian Epics

Chandrasekaran's tenure at TCS is a narrative of both rapid transformation and sustained effort, akin to the dynamic shifts and enduring principles illustrated in Indian epics. The initial phase required swift, decisive actions, while the long-term success of these reforms demanded perseverance and dedication. Under his leadership, TCS witnessed a remarkable surge in its market value and reestablished its position as a leader in the IT industry.

In the chronicles of leadership inspired by Indian wisdom, Natarajan Chandrasekaran's stewardship of TCS stands as a beacon of growth, collaboration, and a customer-first mindset.

His journey is a testament to the enduring principles of Indian philosophy and the impact of these timeless values on modern corporate leadership. As we delve deeper into the narratives of visionary leaders, we uncover the essence of Indian wisdom woven into the fabric of contemporary success stories.

THE REVIVAL SAGA OF INFOSYS: NAVIGATING THROUGH CORPORATE STORMS

Infosys, a beacon of innovation and technological prowess in India, faced a tumultuous period that tested its resilience and strategic acumen. This narrative, akin to the dilemmas and challenges that Arjuna faced on the battlefield of Kurukshetra, unfolds the story of Infosys' descent into financial turbulence, marked by dwindling profits and a crisis of confidence among stakeholders. In the early 2000s, Sudha Murty assumed a pivotal role, steering Infosys through these choppy waters. Her leadership and vision were instrumental in redefining the company's trajectory, much like the epic transformations chronicled in Indian lore.

Sudha Murty's Quest for Corporate Salvation

Embarking on a transformative journey, Murty, akin to the sages seeking enlightenment in the Upanishads, dove deep into the essence of Infosys' operational and financial challenges. Alongside her trusted team, including visionary leaders within the company, she scrutinized every aspect of Infosys' operations. Her approach was reminiscent of a diligent student of Vedanta, absorbing the wisdom of the scriptures, as she mastered the complexities of financial health, operational efficiency, and market strategy. Her dedication reflected the ancient Indian commitment to knowledge and preparation, setting the stage for the Herculean task ahead.

The Guru's Tough Love: Steering Through Reality

Murty's leadership style mirrored the ancient Gurukula system, where the Guru imparts not just knowledge but also the hard truths necessary for growth. She faced the grim realities of Infosys' situation head-on, acknowledging the unsustainable aspects of its business model and the urgent need for change. Her decisions, though painful, were infused with a sense of Dharma, reflecting the compassionate resolve of Lord Buddha. She implemented strategic layoffs to streamline operations, yet she carried the weight of these decisions personally, often engaging directly with affected employees, offering solace and support.

Empathy and Resilience: Cultivating a Compassionate Culture

In her leadership journey, Murty embodied the dual qualities of strength and compassion, akin to Lord Rama's adherence to righteousness. She was deeply invested in nurturing a culture of empathy and growth within Infosys, ensuring that the essence of the company's ethos remained intact even amidst stringent cost-cutting measures. By safeguarding employees' welfare and morale through thoughtful gestures, she reinforced the notion of Infosys as a community bound by shared values and aspirations.

Enduring the Marathon of Transformation

Sudha Murty's tenure at Infosys is a testament to the enduring spirit of perseverance and strategic foresight. Her initial efforts set in motion a series of reforms that required sustained dedication and resolve, much like the disciplined focus of a Yogi in meditation. Through her unwavering commitment, Infosys emerged from its trials stronger and more resilient, charting a new course towards growth and innovation.

Pioneering Women in Leadership: Breaking New Ground

The narrative of leadership is being transformed, echoing the inclusive vision championed by Mahatma Gandhi. Trailblazers like Kiran Mazumdar-Shaw, Indra Nooyi, and Chanda Kochhar are redefining the corporate world, breaking through the glass ceiling to lead some of India's most influential companies. This shift signifies a broader societal transformation, recognizing the critical role women play in shaping the future of business and innovation.

In the annals of modern corporate leadership, **Sudha Murty's stewardship of Infosys stands as a beacon of resilience, learning, and compassionate governance. Her journey, imbued with the timeless wisdom of Indian philosophy, offers invaluable lessons for leaders navigating the complexities of the 21st century. As we continue to witness the evolution of leadership paradigms, the stories of these pioneering women will inspire future generations to embrace challenges with courage and integrity, fostering a world where innovation and compassion go hand in hand.**

Unveiling the Dynamics of Collective Wisdom

In the depth of Indian philosophy and the vast expanse of its ancient wisdom, the research led by scholar Rajesh Kumar and his team offers deep insights into the intricacies of group dynamics, inspired by the teachings of the Vedas and Upanishads. This segment embarks on an enlightening exploration of thirty management teams, each formed by three members, as they navigate through the realms of evolving and steadfast mindsets within the leadership spectrum.

The journey begins with these groups delving into the principles of leadership as outlined in Indian scriptures, which emphasize the balance between flexibility and constancy, akin to the fluidity and resilience observed in the natural world. Through a series of meticulously designed experiments and discussions, the teams engaged in tasks that tested their adaptability, collaboration, and decision-making processes, all while being anchored in the foundational values of Indian ethos.

As the study unfolds, it becomes evident that the teams' successes and challenges are deeply intertwined with their ability to embody the "Vikasatmaka Drishti" (growth perspective) and "Sthiratmaka Drishti" (Immutable Perspective). The growth perspective encourages a mindset of continuous learning and adaptability, inspired by the ever-evolving narratives of the Mahabharata and Ramayana, where heroes grow through their journeys, facing challenges with courage and wisdom. Conversely, the Immutable Perspective draws from the stoic resilience of the Himalayas, symbolizing the strength and steadiness required to uphold one's values and vision in the face of adversity.

Throughout the exploration, Rajesh Kumar and his associates meticulously document how each group's dynamics evolve, highlighting instances where the blend of growth and Immutable Perspectives catalyzes breakthrough innovations and strategies. They observe that teams that embrace the growth perspective tend to foster a culture of open dialogue, experimentation, and mutual support, leading to more dynamic and creative solutions. On the other hand, those grounded in the Immutable Perspective provide a sense of direction and integrity, ensuring that the team's endeavors are aligned with their core principles and long-term vision.

This comprehensive study not only sheds light on the multifaceted nature of leadership within the context of Indian wisdom but also offers valuable lessons on the importance of balancing the fluidity of growth with the solidity of steadfast principles. By weaving together the ancient teachings of the Vedas and Upanishads with contemporary management practices, Rajesh Kumar and his team illuminate a path toward enlightened leadership that is both adaptable and anchored in enduring values.

The Duality of Attitudes: Fixed vs. Growth

In the grand cosmic dance of managerial skills, two Attitudes emerged within these groups - the Immutable Perspective and the Evolutive Perspective. The Immutable Perspective adhered to the belief that managerial abilities were static, unchangeable, and predefined. In contrast, the Evolutive Perspective embodied the philosophy that managerial skills could evolve and expand with experience. Much like the eternal cycle of birth and rebirth in Hinduism, one group perceived abilities as fixed, while the other embraced the idea of limitless growth.

A Simulated Odyssey: Navigating a Furniture Empire

These groups embarked on a simulated journey akin to the grand epics of ancient India. Their task was to manage a fictitious furniture company, a challenge as intricate as the mythical quests of Mahabharata. Their mission involved matching workers with jobs and motivating them for peak productivity. However, what set this quest apart was the collaborative nature of the task. Unlike individual pursuits, the groups were granted the privilege of discussing their choices, receiving feedback, and collectively enhancing their decision-making prowess.

The Triumph of Growth

As the cosmic wheels of time turned, a remarkable transformation unfolded. The Evolutive Perspective groups, much like the cyclical nature of seasons in the Vedas, steadily outperformed their fixed-Attitude counterparts. This gap in performance expanded with each passing moment, mirroring the eternal journey of the soul in Hindu philosophy. The Evolutive Perspective groups, in their pursuit of excellence, derived unparalleled benefits from their mistakes and feedback.

The Symphony of We Think

In the annals of group psychology, a contrast emerges - "Groupthink" versus "We Think." Groupthink, akin to the conforming nature of Kali Yuga, is a phenomenon where individuals within a group forsake independent thought, dissension, and critical analysis. It can lead to catastrophic decisions, reminiscent of the consequences of disregarding dharma. The Immutable Perspective often paves the path to groupthink, as the fear of appearing less intelligent or facing disapproval stifles open discourse.

THE PERILS OF GROUPTHINK: LESSONS FROM THE EPIC OF MAHABHARATA TO CORPORATE INDIA

Groupthink, a phenomenon where the desire for consensus in decision-making processes overshadows alternative viewpoints, has its echoes in the annals of history and mythology, much like the tales woven into the fabric of Indian epics such as the Mahabharata. This narrative delves into the intricate dynamics of decision-making witnessed in the court of Hastinapur, drawing parallels with the historical event of the Bay of Pigs invasion under President Kennedy's administration. The tale of the Bay of Pigs invasion serves as a stark reminder of the dangers posed by unyielding faith in a charismatic leader or the illusion of invincibility, mirroring the deference to divine will depicted in sacred texts.

The Bay of Pigs: A Reflection in the Mirror of Mahabharata

In the epic of Mahabharata, just as in the Bay of Pigs scenario, we observe the profound impact of groupthink. The advisors to Dhritarashtra, the blind king of Hastinapur, often found themselves caught in the web of collective decision-making that prioritized unanimity over critical evaluation, much like President Kennedy's cabinet during the ill-fated invasion. The advisors' suspension of judgment, driven by loyalty to the throne and the persuasive prowess of influential figures like Shakuni, reflects the same psychological surrender seen among Kennedy's team, blinded by the aura of their charismatic leader.

Chanakya: The Antidote to Groupthink

Chanakya, much like Churchill and Sloan, understood the perilous nature of groupthink. His treatises and strategies underscore the importance of embracing dissenting voices to safeguard the kingdom's interests. In the corporate sector of modern India, leaders are increasingly recognizing the need to foster an environment where differing opinions are not just tolerated but encouraged, akin to the council meetings of ancient Indian kingdoms where debates and discussions were instrumental in decision-making.

Embracing Diversity in Thought: The Path Forward for Indian Enterprises

The lesson for today's leaders, drawn from both the Mahabharata and the practices of Churchill and Sloan, is clear: the vitality of an organization or a nation lies in its ability to nurture a culture of open dialogue and critical evaluation. Indian companies, from startups to conglomerates like the Tata Group, Reliance Industries, and Infosys, are adopting more inclusive and participatory models of leadership. These models are designed to prevent the echo chambers of consensus that stifle innovation and lead to strategic missteps.

The Legacy of Inclusive Decision-Making

The legacy of leaders who resist the siren call of groupthink, choosing instead to engage with a multitude of voices, offers a blueprint for effective governance and corporate management. The historical and mythical narratives of India, with their rich stories emphasizing wisdom, caution, and the pursuit of dharma (righteousness), provide a profound backdrop against which modern leaders can navigate the complexities of governance and decision-making.

The Art of Dissent: A Lesson from the Persians

Drawing inspiration from Herodotus' account of ancient Persian practices, it becomes evident that challenging ideas under the influence of reason, much like the revered traditions of debate in Indian philosophy, can lead to well-rounded decisions. The ancient Persians would revisit their decisions under the influence of intoxication, offering an alternate perspective akin to the art of questioning in the Upanishads.

LEADERSHIP AND DISSENT: THE ROLE OF A FIXED OR EVOLUTIVE PERSPECTIVE

Leaders who harbor a Immutable Perspective often stifle dissent and seek to maintain an illusion of infallibility. Icons like Ravana silenced critics, leading to the decline of Ayodhya. In contrast, leaders like Krishna rewarded defiance. His appreciation for a young artisan's tenacity mirrors the importance of individuality and creativity, even when it challenges the status quo. In the Mahabharata, characters like Duryodhana exemplify the dangers of clinging rigidly to one's beliefs, while figures like Yudhishthira demonstrate the value of humility and openness to differing perspectives. Just as the Panchatantra teaches through tales of wise counsel and adaptive thinking, so too must leaders in India embrace a mindset that encourages innovation and welcomes constructive criticism for the betterment of their organizations and society as a whole

The Luminescence of Evolutive Perspective

In the cosmic dance of leadership, the Immutable Perspective may cast shadows of conformity, but the Evolutive Perspective serves as a beacon of illumination. Leaders who embrace the Evolutive Perspective nurture open discussions and promote a diversity of ideas. The Vedas and Upanishads emphasize the pursuit of knowledge and enlightenment through questioning, echoing the significance of embracing a Evolutive Perspective in decision-making.

As we navigate the intricate web of group dynamics, it becomes evident that a Evolutive Perspective is not merely a personal attribute but a catalyst for collective wisdom. In the ever-evolving realm of leadership, it is imperative to embark on the path of growth and open discourse, for it is in these endeavors that the true essence of collective wisdom unfolds, much like the ancient scriptures of India.

The Visionaries of Negotiation

In the ever-evolving landscape of Indian business, the significance of negotiation skills cannot be overstated. Negotiation is the rhythmic dance of commerce, an art that can sway the fate of enterprises. In this chapter, we traverse the realms of Attitudes, drawing inspiration from the wisdom of the Vedas and Upanishads, to understand how they shape negotiation prowess and, consequently, business success.

The Generational Praise Paradox

As we navigate the corridors of the Indian workplace, a question looms like the elusive horizon - are we breeding a generation dependent on praise? The echoes of praise resonate throughout corporate India, much like the chants of mantras. Well-intentioned parents, in their pursuit of boosting their children's self-esteem, inadvertently paved the path for an overpraised generation. These children of praise have now taken their place in the workforce, seeking validation at every step, like pilgrims on a sacred journey.

The Deceptive Mirage of Constant Rewards

In a bid to cater to this generation's need for constant affirmation, companies have adopted a culture of frequent rewards and bonuses, akin to the offering of alms to appease the deities. The traditional yearly bonuses have transformed into quarterly or monthly tokens of appreciation. The title of "Employee of the Month" has been superseded by the daily accolades. Organizations have summoned consultants to navigate this labyrinth of praise, adopting the role of spiritual gurus guiding lost souls.

The Craving for Constant Reassurance

The modern Indian workforce exhibits a pervasive need for continuous reassurance and an aversion to criticism, reminiscent of the fragility that arises from attachment, as described in the Bhagavad Gita. In the business realm, where confronting challenges, demonstrating persistence, and rectifying mistakes are the sacred mantras of success, this trend poses a significant predicament.

Embracing the Right Praise: A Path of Transformation

Amidst the labyrinth of praise, a glimmer of hope emerges. It beckons us to explore the transformative power of the right kind of praise, much like the journey of self-discovery in the Upanishads. In the Vedic tradition, it is believed that the right actions lead to spiritual evolution. Similarly, in the corporate world, the right feedback can drive individuals to embrace challenging tasks and embrace their mistakes.

Nurturing a Culture of Growth

What form does this transformative feedback take? It is a beacon of light in the corporate darkness, illuminating the path of hard work and resilience. Instead of accolades for innate brilliance, it applauds the spirit of initiative, the commitment to overcoming challenges, the courage to learn from setbacks, and the willingness to accept and act upon criticism. It is, in essence, praise for not requiring constant praise.

The Role of Corporations in Shaping Future Leaders

In this era of cultural transformation, corporations find themselves at a crossroads. Much like the revered role of gurus in guiding disciples toward enlightenment, businesses must consider their role in shaping a more mature and growth-oriented workforce. If they fail to partake in this sacred duty, the future leaders of India may remain lost in the maze of praise, devoid of the resilience and tenacity needed for success.

Negotiation: A Cosmic Symphony

In the cosmic orchestra of business, negotiation emerges as a central symphony. It is the dance of collaboration and compromise that ensures harmony in the corporate universe. Much like the cosmic dance of Lord Shiva, negotiation holds the power to create, sustain, or destroy.

The Impact of Attitudes on Negotiation Success

Drawing inspiration from the Vedas' emphasis on transformation, we delve into the profound impact of "Manas" on negotiation success. Research by Varuna and Yama's studies showcases the transformative potential of "Manas" in the realm of negotiation. Just as the Panchatantra teaches through tales of wise counsel and strategic thinking, so too must negotiators in India recognize the power of their attitudes in shaping outcomes and fostering mutually beneficial agreements. By embracing a mindset rooted in the wisdom of ancient texts, negotiators can navigate complexities with clarity and achieve outcomes that resonate with the principles of dharma and harmony.

Immutable Perspective vs. Evolutive Perspective

In the sacred arena of negotiation, two Attitudes emerge - the Immutable Perspective and the Evolutive Perspective. Those with a Immutable Perspective believe that negotiation skills are innate and unchangeable, akin to karma. In contrast, the Evolutive Perspective perceives negotiation as a dynamic skill that can evolve over a lifetime, much like the cycle of reincarnation.

The Power of Evolutive Perspective in Negotiation

Kray and Haselhuhn's study demonstrates the remarkable influence of Attitude on negotiation decisions. Individuals with a Evolutive Perspective exhibit a thirst for knowledge and improvement, choosing tasks that enhance their negotiation skills over showcasing their existing abilities.

The Triumph of Evolutive Perspective in Negotiation

In the cosmic dance of negotiation, the Evolutive Perspective emerges as the victor. Those imbued with this Attitude exhibit resilience in the face of challenges and an unwavering commitment to achieving favorable outcomes. They navigate the treacherous waters of negotiation, much like Lord Krishna guiding Arjuna through the battlefield of Kurukshetra.

A Legacy of Learning and Innovation

The Evolutive Perspective not only secures lucrative outcomes but also sparks creativity and innovative solutions, mirroring the principles of "Dharma" and "Karma" in Indian philosophy. It is a Attitude that encourages learning and evolution, a legacy that shapes the future of Indian business leaders.

As we conclude this chapter, we are reminded that negotiation is not merely a transactional process; it is a spiritual journey of transformation and growth. The Attitudes we embrace pave the path to success or stagnation, and in the grand Indian commerce, it is our collective responsibility to nurture a culture that thrives on the principles of growth, resilience, and continuous learning.

The Transformation of Corporate Leaders

In the labyrinthine world of Indian corporate culture, the quest for effective leadership and management is an eternal pursuit. Countless resources are devoted each year to coaching leaders and managers in the art of mentorship and feedback. Yet, like seekers on a spiritual journey, many remain poor coaches, unable to unlock their full potential. The question that arises is whether the art of leadership is an inherent trait, or can it be nurtured and developed? This chapter seeks to shed light on this conundrum by drawing inspiration from Indian wisdom, latest technology, and psychological studies.

The Quest for Effective Coaching

As we embark on this journey of self-discovery within the corporate realm, we encounter the age-old challenge of coaching. Millions of dollars and thousands of hours are invested annually in training leaders and managers to be effective coaches. Yet, despite these efforts, many remain ineffective in their coaching roles. Is this an insurmountable challenge, or is there a deeper reason behind these failures?

The Immutable Perspective Paradox

Research by Parthasarathi, Devadatta, and Gopala unveils a profound revelation. It exposes the existence of fixed-Attitude managers who perceive personal change as an unattainable dream. These managers possess a predetermined notion of their employees' competence and rarely engage in developmental coaching. Their perception of employees as either competent or incompetent becomes a self-fulfilling prophecy. In the grandness of Indian spirituality, this mirrors the concept of "Karma," where individuals are bound by their past actions. Just as characters in the Mahabharata face the consequences of their actions, so too must managers in India recognize the interconnectedness of their attitudes and the outcomes they shape in the workplace. Through introspection and a commitment to personal growth, managers can break free from the cycle of Immutable

Perspectives and create environments that nurture the potential of every individual.

The Evolutive Perspective Paradigm

Contrastingly, managers with a Evolutive Perspective view talent as merely a starting point on the journey of development. They are committed not only to their employees' growth but also to their own. These visionary leaders provide extensive developmental coaching, actively recognize improvements in employee performance, and welcome constructive feedback. They understand the essence of "Dharma" - one's duty and path in life.

Teaching the Evolutive Perspective

The revelation of the Evolutive Perspective's transformative power is a beacon of hope for the corporate world. Much like the teachings of the Vedas and Upanishads, this Attitude can be taught to managers. A workshop based on well-established psychological principles serves as the conduit for this transformation. It begins with enlightening participants about the dynamic nature of the brain, drawing parallels with the concept of reincarnation and rebirth. It reinforces the idea that change is possible at any stage of life and that coaching and practice can cultivate abilities, akin to the pursuit of knowledge in the Upanishads.

The Journey of Transformation

The workshop takes managers through a series of introspective exercises. They reflect on the significance of nurturing growth in individuals, recall personal experiences of overcoming challenges, and even extend a helping hand to struggling protégés. Each exercise serves as a metaphorical pilgrimage of self-discovery.

The Blossoming of Evolutive Perspective

The transformative power of the Evolutive Perspective becomes evident as participating managers swiftly recognize improvements in employee performance, embrace the role of coaching poor performers, and provide high-quality coaching suggestions. This transformation, much like the cycle of life and death in Indian spirituality, persists over time.

A Paradigm Shift in Leadership

What does this revelation mean for the corporate world? It beckons us to reconsider our approach to leadership. In our pursuit of the ideal manager, we must not only seek talent but also nurture a Evolutive Perspective. Just as Lord Krishna guided Arjuna through the battlefield of Kurukshetra, managers must embrace their role as teachers and learners.

Fostering a Culture of Growth

This transformative journey extends beyond individual managers. It necessitates the creation of a growth-Attitude environment where individuals thrive. This involves presenting skills as learnable, valuing learning and perseverance, conveying that feedback is a tool for growth, and positioning managers as catalysts for learning. In essence, it is the embodiment of the teachings of the Vedas and Upanishads, where the pursuit of knowledge and self-improvement is paramount.

Unlocking the Potential of Human Resources

In corporate life, the belief in human development is the key to unlocking untapped potential. While corporate training programs may be exercises in futility without this belief, they become a means of tapping into the vast reservoir of human resources when guided by a Evolutive Perspective. In the sacred journey of corporate leadership, it is this Attitude that paves the path to transformation, growth, and boundless success.

The Essence of Leadership: Nature or Nurture?

In Indian philosophy and culture, the question of whether leaders are born or made echoes through the ages. The great sage, Vishwamitra, embarked on a profound journey, interviewing illustrious leaders. Their resounding chorus proclaimed that leaders are not born; they are crafted through self-transformation, akin to the spiritual awakening in the Upanishads. Vishwamitra concurred, emphasizing the limitless potential of every individual, regardless of age or circumstance. However, in the labyrinth of modern corporate India, many managers and CEOs remain mere bosses, lacking the transformative spirit of leadership. Just as characters in the Ramayana undergo personal growth and transformation, so too must leaders in India embrace a journey of self-discovery and empowerment, unlocking their innate potential to inspire and guide others towards success. By embodying the principles of dharma and selflessness, leaders can transcend mere authority and cultivate a legacy of enduring influence and positive change.

The Quest for Self-Improvement

In the world of Indian leadership, Kartikay Upadhyay and Maheshvaran Govindasamy, modern-day gurus of leadership, reveal a fascinating paradox. As managers ascend to their roles, they embark on a learning journey, receiving training, coaching, and seeking wisdom. In this phase, they strive to develop their skills and tread the path of self-improvement. Yet, once they grasp the fundamentals, a stagnation sets in. They cease their pursuit of growth, content with their current abilities. It raises the question: why do they stop this journey, akin to Arjuna pausing in the midst of Kurukshetra, when his duty beckons him to continue?

The Pitfall of Natural Talent

In the annals of Indian organizational psychology, Mahesh Joshi sheds light on a distressing aspect prevalent in many organizations - the belief in innate talent. These organizations overlook the vast potential for growth within their ranks. Ironically, their fixation on "natural" talents can inadvertently stifle these very individuals, turning them into arrogant, resistant non-learners. The timeless lesson here is to create organizations that cherish the development of abilities, fostering an atmosphere where leaders can bloom, much like the lotus in a sacred Indian pond, nurtured by the waters of knowledge and humility.

The Attitude of Organizations

In corporate life, another intriguing question arises - can organizations as a whole possess a Attitude? Can they harbor a collective belief in fixed talent or, alternatively, in the potential for development? To explore this, we delved into the world of Fortune 500 and Fortune 1000 companies in India.

Organizations can either embody a "culture of genius," where they perceive employees as possessing fixed talent, or a "culture of development," where they believe in nurturing and enhancing the abilities of all. The perceptions of employees within these organizations reveal a consensus about the prevailing Attitude.

The Impact of Organizational Attitudes

The impact of an organization's Attitude reverberates throughout its corridors. In a "culture of development," employees place greater trust in their company, feeling empowered, committed, and ready to take ownership. They remain steadfast in their loyalty. Conversely, in a "culture of genius," employees entertain thoughts of leaving for pastures they perceive as greener.

Fostering Agility and Innovation

In the ever-evolving landscape of corporate India, agility and innovation are paramount. Does a belief in fixed talent stimulate innovation? The answer is a resounding no. Employees in "culture of development" organizations report strong support for risk-taking, innovation, and creativity. They are encouraged to explore uncharted territories, knowing that even failure is a stepping stone. Meanwhile, their counterparts in "culture of genius" organizations witness a lack of support for innovation and may even encounter unethical practices.

A Reciprocal Relationship

The synergy between employees and their organizations is a dance of mutual admiration. Supervisors in "culture of development" organizations hold positive perceptions of their teams, viewing them as collaborative, committed to learning, innovative, and possessing immense management potential. This alignment creates a harmonious atmosphere where companies and their employees thrive.

In the ever-shifting sands of the corporate world, the findings suggest that organizations can weave a growth or Immutable Perspective into their very fabric. A culture of genius or a culture of development emerges as a choice. As modern businesses strive for reinvention and adaptability, it becomes evident that those embracing a Evolutive Perspective are better poised to flourish in the intricacy of today's India.

CULTIVATING THE INFINITE ATTITUDE

In the vibrant realm of Indian workplaces, the distinction between fixed and Evolutive Perspectives is a reflection of the corporate ethos. It is a dance between self-judgment and self-development, a symphony where individuals and organizations harmonize to create an atmosphere of growth.

The Power of Self-Transformation

The journey begins within oneself. Are you ensnared in the clutches of a Immutable Perspective, where you shield your ego from the admission of mistakes? Or do you embrace the wisdom of the Upanishads, acknowledging errors as stepping stones to progress? In the sacred texts of the Vedas, we find the essence of growth - "Vidya dadati vinayam," knowledge begets humility. Begin by dismantling the walls of defensiveness and embracing feedback as a guiding light. Create a learning experiences, much like a pilgrim embarks on a spiritual journey to enlightenment.

Leading with a Evolutive Perspective

As a leader, your actions reverberate through the corridors of your workplace, shaping the destiny of your employees. Are you a benevolent leader, nurturing your team's growth, or a fixed-Attitude boss, clinging to power at the expense of your employees' well-being? In the Mahabharata, Lord Krishna, the divine charioteer, guided Arjuna not as a ruler but as a mentor. Emulate this divine archetype by treating your employees as collaborators, fostering a sense of unity and shared goals. The Bhagavad Gita's teachings resonate - "You have the right to perform your actions, but never to the fruits of your actions." In the spirit of karma yoga, sow the seeds of support and growth-promoting feedback, for they shall bear fruit in abundance.

Transforming Your Company's Attitude

For those steering the helm of organizations, introspection becomes paramount. Is your company shackled by elitism, or does it breathe the air of self-examination and open communication? In the spirit of Lou Gerstner's transformative journey, contemplate a shift from hierarchical power to a culture of collective wisdom. Gerstner's mantra echoes in our quest for change - "Who says elephants can't dance?" Reflect on how to dismantle the walls of fixed thinking and erect the pillars of teamwork and self-reflection.

Fostering Independent Thinking and Collaboration

In the lush gardens of your workplace, be vigilant for the seeds of groupthink, for they threaten the very essence of decision-making. Draw inspiration from the ancient practice of "sabha" (assembly) in Indian culture, where diverse voices converged to deliberate. Cultivate an environment that nurtures alternative perspectives and constructive criticism. Appoint individuals as modern-day "Vidura," the wise advisor, who fearlessly speak opposing viewpoints. Engage in spirited debates, mirroring the philosophical dialogues of ancient India. Implement an anonymous suggestion box as a sacred chalice for employees to contribute to the decision-making process. In the pursuit of growth, let your workplace resonate with the Upanishadic wisdom - "Satyam eva jayate," truth alone triumphs. Independent thinkers and team players can coexist harmoniously; it is the duality that propels progress.

In the Indian workplaces, the path to an infinite Attitude unfolds, where the boundaries of potential are boundless, and growth is a sacred mantra.

CHAPTER 6

LOVE AND ATTITUDES: NAVIGATING THE MAZE OF RELATIONSHIPS

...

Love's Twists and Turns: An Indian Perspective

In life, the path to true love is akin to a winding river—far from smooth and often strewn with disappointments and heartbreaks. Many tread this arduous path, but their journeys diverge dramatically. What sets them apart? To unravel this conundrum, we embarked on a quest, gathering a diverse group of individuals and inviting them to share their stories of heart-wrenching rejection.

One such tale, reminiscent of countless others, hails from the vibrant streets of Bengaluru. When I first arrived in this bustling metropolis, I was a solitary soul, adrift in the sea of anonymity. Loneliness enveloped me, and I felt like an outsider. After a year of profound melancholy, destiny introduced me to Priya. It's an understatement to say that we instantly connected; it felt as if our souls had danced together for lifetimes. Soon, we cohabited and shared every facet of our existence. I envisioned a lifetime together, and she echoed the sentiment. Two blissful years unfolded. Then, one fateful day, I returned home to discover a cryptic note—no words of affection, just a cold, unfeeling message of departure. He had vanished from my life without a trace, leaving me in perpetual limbo. Sometimes, when the phone rings, a flicker of hope ignites within me, only to be extinguished by the cruel reality that she's gone forever.

A myriad of variations of this story echoed through the narratives of individuals representing both fixed and Evolutive Perspectives. Love and heartbreak had touched almost everyone's life, leaving indelible imprints. However, it was their responses that diverged significantly.

The Immutable Perspective: A Bitter Wound

For those ensnared in the clutches of a Immutable Perspective, rejection became a scarring judgment, forever etched on their identities. They felt branded as "unlovable" by a merciless verdict. Anguish and bitterness welled up within them, a relentless torrent. The overriding impulse was revenge, a desperate attempt to inflict upon others the same pain they had endured. Prema, the protagonist of the Mumbai tale, harbored enduring bitterness and vengeful desires: "I would exact revenge upon him, hurt him in any conceivable way if the opportunity presented itself. He deserves nothing less."

The Evolutive Perspective: A Path to Understanding

In stark contrast, those embracing the Evolutive Perspective pursued a different path—a path illuminated by understanding, forgiveness, and growth. Though they bore the scars of heartbreak, they yearned to learn from their experiences. One individual expressed the profound lesson learned: "That relationship and its conclusion taught me the significance of effective communication. Love, I realized, demands more than mere affection; it requires conscious effort and understanding." Another wise soul recognized that every relationship unveiled more about one's compatibility: "Each relationship contributes to our understanding of who is right for us."

The Essence of Forgiveness

There exists a profound French expression, "Tout comprendre c'est tout pardonner"—to understand all is to forgive all. For those anchored in the Evolutive Perspective, forgiveness assumed paramount importance. As one resilient woman declared, "I may not be a saint, but I understood that, for my own inner peace, forgiveness was imperative. He hurt me, but I refused to imprison myself in the past. One day, I simply wished him well and wished the same for myself."

Triumph of the Evolutive Perspective

The Evolutive Perspective, with its dynamic outlook, prevented them from feeling eternally branded by rejection. It enabled them to extract invaluable lessons from their experiences, arming them with wisdom to navigate future relationships. These individuals possessed the resilience to embrace life's journey with open hearts.

Embracing Transformation: An Inspirational Tale

Consider the story of my cousin, Anjali, a living embodiment of the Evolutive Perspective. Several years ago, after twenty-three years of marriage, her husband left her, leaving her heartbroken and desolate. In a cruel twist of fate, she was involved in an accident that left her with an injured leg. One Saturday night, as she sat alone at home, she made a life-altering decision: "I refuse to wallow in self-pity!" With unwavering determination, she ventured out to a local dance event, her injured leg notwithstanding. Little did she know that this decision would change her life forever. At the event, she crossed paths with Rahul, her future husband, and love blossomed amidst adversity.

Triumph Over Adversity: A Symbol of Resilience

In another remarkable story, the Arora family's saga unfolded with profound courage and grace. Their daughter, Aisha, dressed in her resplendent bridal attire, stood at the church's entrance, waiting for her groom. The archbishop and a multitude of guests eagerly anticipated the ceremony. But destiny had other plans. The best man approached Aisha with disheartening news—the groom would not be joining her. Shock and pain surged through her. Faced with this ordeal, the family decided to proceed with the reception and dinner. Yet, it was Aisha's response that defined her character. In an act of immense courage, she changed into a little black dress, rejoined the celebration, and danced to "I Will Survive." Her spirit captured the hearts of the nation, earning her admiration for her indomitable spirit. Aisha transformed an event that could have diminished her into one that magnified her essence.

The Healing Power of the Evolutive Perspective

Aisha's story exemplifies how embracing the Evolutive Perspective can transmute pain into strength. She endured pain and trauma but never allowed herself to feel humiliated. Clean pain became a catalyst for healing, and she enveloped herself in the love of friends and family, charting a course toward a brighter future.

But what about the groom who abandoned Aisha? He embarked on a solitary honeymoon to Tahiti. A couple of years later, Aisha stood once more in her wedding dress at the same church, but this time, she knew her future husband would be there, waiting to share a lifetime of love and growth.

In contemplating the impact of rejection on individuals with a Immutable Perspective, it is evident why children anchored in this Attitude often react to taunting and bullying with thoughts of violent retaliation. We shall return to this theme later, exploring the profound influence of Attitudes on our youth.

DYNAMICS OF RELATIONSHIPS: THE INDIAN PERSPECTIVE

The Uncharted Realm of Relationship Skills

In human abilities, Bharat Joshi, renowned for his study of gifted individuals, delved into the realms of classical musicians, sculptors, Olympic athletes, tennis prodigies, mathematicians, and research psychologists. Notably absent from his roster were those gifted in interpersonal relationships. A void he had intended to explore, yet it remained elusive. The challenge lay in measuring an ability that eluded quantification—a formidable task. Just as the characters in the Panchatantra navigate complex social dynamics with wit and wisdom, so too must researchers in India grapple with understanding and assessing the nuances of interpersonal skills in the broader context of human achievement.

In the rich diversity of human professions, interpersonal skills play a pivotal role. From teachers who mold young minds to psychologists deciphering the human psyche, from administrators steering organizations to diplomats negotiating international diplomacy, the professions is adorned with threads of interpersonal finesse. However, a consensus on how to measure this elusive skillset remained elusive.

The Mystique of Relationship Skills

Conventional wisdom often fails to recognize outstanding interpersonal skills as a gift. Rather, individuals possessing such finesse are perceived as cool or charming. In the realm of marital relationships, a harmonious partnership is often attributed to the chemistry between individuals. These perceptions beg the question: What does it truly mean to possess exceptional relationship skills?

As a society, we grapple with the elusive nature of relationship skills. Yet, the stakes in human relationships are immeasurable. This conundrum finds resonance in the work of Daniel Goleman, particularly his groundbreaking book, "Emotional Intelligence." Goleman illuminated the presence of social-emotional skills and offered insights into their composition.

Attitudes: The Unveiling of a Deeper Layer

Attitudes, like an uncharted treasure map, add an intriguing dimension to our understanding of why individuals sometimes fail to acquire the skills they need or, paradoxically, sabotage their own abilities. The enigmatic nature of human relationships, often likened to a battlefield, becomes all the more perplexing. Yet, in the heart of this battlefield, some emerge victorious, having forged lasting and fulfilling relationships.

Matters of the Heart: Attitudes in Love

In the context of relationships, the Immutable Perspective introduces a complex interplay of beliefs. Not only are personal traits perceived as fixed, but this Attitude extends its grasp to encompass the qualities of one's partner and the relationship itself. Three dimensions of rigidity converge—the self, the partner, and the relationship—leaving little room for evolution.

Contrastingly, the Evolutive Perspective offers a refreshing perspective. It posits that all three elements—the self, the partner, and the relationship—are malleable, capable of growth and transformation. The idealization of instantaneous, perfect, and perpetual compatibility gives way to the notion that growth is a continuous journey.

Beyond "Happily Ever After": The Pitfalls of Immutable Perspective

The Immutable Perspective romanticizes the concept of instantaneous, unalterable compatibility—an idyllic narrative of destined love and eternal happiness, much like the protagonists riding off into the sunset. It presents an enticing notion of "they lived happily ever after."

Yet, a fundamental flaw resides within this romanticized paradigm. Two issues emerge as significant stumbling blocks:

The Illusion of Specialness

Many aspire to believe that their relationship is exceptional, a unique bond forged by fate. This aspiration is natural and understandable. However, the Immutable Perspective conceals two critical pitfalls:

1. **Instant Perfection**: The Immutable Perspective envisions relationships as predestined to be flawless from the outset. It dismisses the notion of growth and evolution within the relationship.

2. **Judgment of Worth**: A Immutable Perspective extends judgment not only to oneself but also to the partner and the relationship itself. This fixed judgment can lead to disillusionment and dissatisfaction.

In the pursuit of a relationship deemed "special," the Immutable Perspective obscures the potential for growth and transformation.

In the vibrant landscape of Indian relationships, where love stories are as diverse as the nation itself, these Attitudes play a pivotal role in shaping the course of love. The essence of ancient wisdom, encapsulated in Vedas and Upanishads, and the contemporary insights of experts in the field, blend seamlessly with age-old tales and timeless quotes to unravel the enigma of relationships. As we delve deeper into the labyrinth of human connection, we shall explore the profound influence of Attitudes on the essence of love itself.

THE COMPLEX DANCE OF LOVE: AN INDIAN PERSPECTIVE

When Love Blossoms: A Tale of Charulata and Raj

In the heart of an enchanting Indian town, Charulata and her friends discovered the mellifluous notes of love through the arrival of Shashi, a gifted musician who had joined the local symphony orchestra. The night was adorned with the symphony's mesmerizing performance, and the bond between Charulata and Shashi began to flourish like a raga. Shashi, with his intense, romantic aura, was drawn to Charulata's captivating charm and exotic grace. They seemed destined for each other, sharing not only their love for music but also a profound understanding of life's intricacies. Their hearts whispered in unison, "Where have you been all my life?"

However, like the unpredictable rhythms of a classical melody, Shashi's moods started to take unexpected turns. His innate moody disposition, once concealed, began to surface. During his somber moments, he yearned for solitude, while Charulata sought to unravel the source of his discontent. In her pursuit of understanding, she inadvertently irritated him, pushing him further into his emotional cocoon. He would insist with growing intensity, "Just leave me alone." This growing emotional rift left Charulata feeling excluded.

The unpredictability of Shashi's moods added to the complexity. Sometimes, their plans for outings or intimate dinners would be marred by his melancholic demeanor, and Charulata's attempts at light-hearted conversations would disappoint him. "I thought you understood me," he would sigh in disappointment. Concerned friends, witnessing the depth of their affection, urged them to address and resolve these issues. However, both Charulata and Shashi, in sorrowful unison, believed that if their love were genuine and destined, it should not require such effort. They drifted apart and, eventually, parted ways.

The Dichotomy of Attitudes: Love as a Work of Art

In the realm of love, Attitudes dictate the approach one takes. The Immutable Perspective harbors the expectation that everything good should unfold effortlessly, akin to a fairy tale where a single kiss cures all ills or where a miserable life is instantaneously transformed by a prince's arrival. The notion that love will automatically resolve all conflicts and endow individuals with new skills prevails. However, the narrative Charulata and Shashi unfolded contradicts this notion.

Conversely, the Evolutive Perspective acknowledges that enduring, fulfilling love requires dedicated effort and the resolution of inevitable differences. While the initial spark of love may ignite, individuals with this Attitude understand that the journey to a lasting bond is marked by continuous growth and adaptation.

Dispelling the Myth: The Experts' Perspective

Every relationship expert unanimously challenges the Immutable Perspective's illusion. The belief that a successful relationship should require no effort stands in stark contradiction to reality:

- Acharya Abhay, the distinguished psychiatrist, identifies the belief that "if we need to work at it, there's something seriously wrong with our relationship" as one of the most destructive beliefs.

- Rishi Gautama, a preeminent relationship researcher, emphasizes the perpetual tension between the forces that bind a couple and those that can drive them apart. Every marriage demands effort to stay on the right path.

Just as characters in the Mahabharata face complex moral dilemmas and navigate the intricacies of relationships, couples in India must recognize that maintaining a strong and healthy relationship requires ongoing dedication and effort.

The Fallacy of Mind Reading: The Quest for Unity

In the realm of the Immutable Perspective, the notion prevails that couples should possess an innate ability to decipher each other's thoughts, feelings, and needs. The belief is that two individuals should be like one, seamlessly intertwined in their understanding. However, this fallacy often leads to misunderstandings.

Girija Sharma, a distinguished family psychologist, recounts the tale of Arjun and Sita, whose early misunderstanding nearly jeopardized their relationship. When Arjun mentioned an "imbalance" in their relationship, Sita, assuming his thoughts, concluded that he was less committed than she was. Only through open communication did she realize that Arjun intended to enhance their relationship—a desire to fine-tune their connection.

Just as characters in the Panchatantra learn the importance of clear communication and understanding in their relationships, couples in India must also recognize the significance of open dialogue and mutual respect to strengthen their bonds and overcome misunderstandings

A similar misunderstanding nearly befell me in my early days with my husband. His plea for "more space" left me perplexed and questioning the foundation of our relationship. It was only through communication that I learned he simply wanted physical space for comfort.

In Indian relationships, where love stories span millennia, the intricate dance of Attitudes shapes the narratives of love. Drawing wisdom from ancient scriptures, such as the Vedas and Upanishads, and weaving in contemporary insights and stories, we embark on a profound exploration of the essence of love. As we unravel the intricate threads of human connection, we shall delve into the profound influence of Attitudes on the intricate symphony of love itself.

THE DANCE OF UNDERSTANDING: HARMONY IN DIFFERENCES

The Enigma of Mind Reading: The Belief in Perfect Accord

In relationships, there exists a peculiar belief—the notion of mind reading. Surprisingly, this belief gains credence among those who embrace the Immutable Perspective. They hold the conviction that a couple should effortlessly share every nuance of their perspectives and thoughts. In this realm, communication is seemingly rendered obsolete, for one can simply assume that their partner perceives the world through identical lenses.

To these individuals, any deviation in their partner's viewpoint threatens the very foundation of their belief in perfect harmony. Minor disparities in perception evoke feelings of threat and hostility, casting a shadow over their shared bond.

The Illusion of Perfect Agreement: Unveiling the Discrepancies

In reality, it is an impossibility for any couple to align all their assumptions and expectations seamlessly. Divergent visions of the future often lurk beneath the surface. While one envisions a life of suburban tranquility, the other dreams of a bohemian love nest, evoking a dichotomy that could shake the foundations of their relationship.

Take the case of Arjun and Radha, two young souls on the cusp of matrimony. Arjun's vision of an idyllic home in the heart of Mumbai symbolized his adventurous spirit, expecting Radha to share his enthusiasm. Yet, her reaction was far from what he anticipated. Years of residing in traditional family homes had instilled in her a longing for a more settled life. The initial joy soon gave way to feelings of confusion and disappointment, sowing the seeds of discord.

Just as characters in the Ramayana navigate through conflicting desires and expectations, couples in India must also recognize the importance of understanding each other's perspectives and finding common ground to build a harmonious life together

Rights and Duties: The Unspoken Contracts

In the intricate labyrinth of relationships, unspoken contracts may lurk, with partners implicitly agreeing on rights and duties. These unarticulated expectations can trigger outrage when violated. In the heat of the moment, consider the following sentiments:

"As a husband, I have a right to _____, and my wife has the duty to _____."

"As a wife, I have a right to _____, and my husband has the duty to _____."

Few things can ignite fury more intensely than perceived violations of these unspoken contracts. Partners may find themselves infuriated by the sense of entitlement they detect in each other's actions.

Entitlement vs. Equality: A Delicate Balance

A couple may willingly embrace traditional roles if it aligns with their values and choices. However, the key lies in distinguishing tradition from entitlement. The expectation that certain roles are entitlements can cast a pall over the relationship.

Jaya, a seasoned financial analyst, and Parth, a dynamic real estate agent, found themselves in a situation where roles blurred. Parth's idea of a housewarming party excited them both, but the execution bore the marks of inequality. Jaya, the more experienced host and cook, took charge of preparations, while Parth assumed the role of a mere guest. This dichotomy left Jaya incensed, and instead of communicating her feelings, she decided to teach Parth a lesson by adopting his passive approach at the party.

Just as characters in the Mahabharata confront challenges of pride and communication, couples in India must also navigate through conflicts with understanding and openness to ensure harmony in their relationships

Fortunately, this incident did not define their relationship. Instead, it sparked a vital lesson in communication and understanding. They realized that assumptions had no place in a thriving relationship. Thus, their future endeavors were founded on discussions rather than assumptions.

A relationship devoid of effort is not a testament to its greatness but rather a harbinger of its downfall. Effective communication and the resolution of conflicting hopes and beliefs are essential aspects that require work and dedication. While it doesn't guarantee a "they lived happily ever after" ending, it certainly paves the path for "they worked happily ever after," where understanding and growth become the pillars of their journey.

EMBRACING CHALLENGES: THE CRUCIBLE OF CHARACTER

Perceiving Problems as Flaws: The Immutable Perspective's Conundrum

In the labyrinth of relationships, another stumbling block looms large—the belief entrenched in the Immutable Perspective that problems are synonymous with deep-seated character flaws. However, just as a lotus blooms amidst the muddiest waters, great relationships often emerge from the crucible of conflicts and challenges.

When individuals with a Immutable Perspective grapple with relationship woes, blame becomes the weapon of choice. Sometimes they direct it inward, berating themselves, but more often, it's their partner who bears the brunt. These attributions of blame are not vague; they are often targeted at perceived character defects.

But the cascade of negativity doesn't stop there. When one's partner's character traits are deemed responsible for the issues at hand, feelings of anger and disgust are unleashed upon them. A sense of helplessness pervades, as problems arising from fixed traits appear unsolvable. Consequently, individuals with the Immutable Perspective tend to become contemptuous of their partners and increasingly dissatisfied with the relationship as a whole. On the flip side, those embracing the Evolutive Perspective can acknowledge their partner's imperfections without jeopardizing their relationship's vitality.

The Blind Spot of Denial: Avoiding the Uncomfortable Truth

In some instances, individuals trapped in the Immutable Perspective choose to blind themselves to the issues plaguing their partner or relationship, hoping to evade the discomforting path of confrontation. Damayanti's story serves as an apt illustration. Mysterious phone calls, habitual tardiness in picking up the children, and her frequent "ladies' nights out" aroused suspicions among friends. However, her husband, Devdatta, clung to the belief that this was merely a passing phase. He could not fathom the alternative: facing the possibility that his beloved wife might be in the wrong, that he had driven her away, or that their relationship was irrevocably flawed. The Immutable Perspective left Devdatta paralyzed, unable to contemplate the idea that problems could be resolved. He failed to recognize that Damayanti's actions were a desperate plea for attention rather than an irreversible condemnation.

Just as characters in the Panchatantra grapple with moral dilemmas and the consequences of their actions, couples in India must also confront challenges in their relationships with honesty and empathy to foster understanding and growth.

The Perfection Fallacy: The Quest for the Flawless Partner

Sita's quest for the perfect partner led her down a treacherous path. She would enter relationships with remarkable men, convinced that each one was "the one." Yet, trivial imperfections would invariably surface—a tacky birthday present, ketchup on food, or questionable electronic habits. In her Immutable Perspective, Sita concluded that these flaws were insurmountable, failing to grasp that they were minor issues that could be addressed through open communication.

Just as characters in the Ramayana face tests of their devotion and endurance, individuals in India must also navigate through the complexities of relationships with understanding and patience, recognizing that imperfections are part of the human experience and can be overcome with mutual respect and communication.

In stark contrast, a Evolutive Perspective would have allowed for constructive dialogue. Rather than dismissing the relationship due to these perceived imperfections, it would have prompted a deeper understanding, paving the way for growth and compromise.

Embracing Imperfections: The Art of Choosing a Set of Problems

In the realm of relationships, renowned expert Daniel Wile offers a profound insight—choosing a partner is akin to choosing a set of problems. There are no candidates devoid of challenges; perfection remains an elusive mirage. The key lies in acknowledging each other's limitations and embarking on the journey of growth and acceptance.

My own experience mirrors this wisdom. As my birthday neared, I conveyed a simple yet essential message to my husband: "I appreciate thoughtful presents." Rather than retreating behind the cliché of "it's the thought that counts," he understood the importance of genuine effort. Our relationship blossomed as we celebrated each other's uniqueness, free from the shackles of unrealistic perfection.

In love and companionship, embracing imperfections becomes the thread that weaves enduring bonds. It is through the recognition of flaws and the willingness to navigate challenges that relationships evolve and flourish, ultimately transcending the limiting boundaries of the Immutable Perspective.

THE DANCE OF COMMUNICATION: NAVIGATING THE MAZE OF MISUNDERSTANDING

The Saga of Priya and Rohan: Navigating the Maze of Miscommunication

In the bustling metropolis of Mumbai, Priya and Rohan found themselves ensnared in the complexities of their evolving relationship, a narrative that could easily find its place in the heart-wrenching dramas of Indian cinema. Their story unfolded under the compassionate guidance of their counselor, Dr. Aditi, whose wisdom and insights offered them a beacon of hope. Priya, returning from her dynamic role in a leading Indian conglomerate, was bubbling with eagerness to share the day's achievements. She delved into a narrative rich in detail but seemingly meandering without a destination. Rohan, her partner, battled internally to mask his disinterest, an effort that did not go unnoticed by Priya. In a bid to recapture his attention, she embarked on yet another elaborate account, this time focusing on a challenging project at work.

Within the silent battleground of their thoughts, Priya and Rohan launched silent accusations at each other, their judgments flying back and forth with the intensity of a cricket match in Kolkata. Priya was labeled as tedious, Rohan as self-centered, and their relationship hovered perilously close to disintegration.

Yet, the reality was a stark contrast to the misconceptions they harbored. Priya's hesitance to celebrate her successes openly stemmed from a deeply ingrained cultural modesty, prompting her to bury the lead under layers of project minutiae. Conversely, Rohan's perceived self-absorption was but a facade masking his consideration. His silent endurance of Priya's detailed narratives was his way of showing respect, mistakenly believing this to be what she needed.

Rohan's quietude concealed his true sentiments, craving a more straightforward and honest communication. A simple expression of his feelings, such as, "Priya, I admire your passion and would love to understand more about what drives you in these projects. Could we perhaps focus on the highlights?" could have mended the growing rift between them. Their predicament was not a question of personality flaws but one of misaligned communication styles.

This tale of Priya and Rohan underscores the quintessential challenges of intimate relationships, where misconceptions and unspoken truths weave a complex web. Through the lens of their journey, we are reminded of the power of open communication and the necessity of bridging the divides with empathy and understanding. As they navigate through their story, much like the protagonists of a Panchatantra fable learning life lessons, they reveal the universal truth that the heart of every relationship is not about perfection but about understanding and navigating the imperfections together.

Can This Marriage Be Salvaged? Lessons from Vedic Wisdom

As I reflect on these stories, my mind drifts to the ancient wisdom of the Vedas and Upanishads, where the art of communication and understanding relationships is deeply embedded. In the sacred texts of India, the importance of dialogue, empathy, and self-awareness is extolled.

Consider the story of Aarav and Meera: A Journey of Transformation Through Understanding ~ In the vibrant cultural landscape of India, the story of Aarav and Meera, as narrated by the esteemed counselor Dr. Vikram Singh, unfolds like a classic Indian saga, replete with the nuances of love, conflict, and reconciliation. Aarav, with his composed and steadfast nature, complemented Meera's spirited and spontaneous essence, creating a balance reminiscent of the harmonious interplay between Shiva and Parvati. Meera, with her zest for life, infused joy and vibrancy into Aarav's methodical existence, while Aarav offered Meera the sense of security and stability she deeply craved.

However, as time etched its stories, their initial admiration for each other's contrasting traits began to wane. Aarav's perception of Meera shifted towards viewing her as whimsical and heedless, while Meera perceived Aarav as overly critical and authoritarian, analyzing her every move. This rigid mindset they had entrenched themselves in started to cast long shadows over their once idyllic union.

Their path to redemption and mutual understanding began on a day marked by turmoil. Meera, caught in a whirlwind of professional deadlines, left their home in disarray. Aarav, upon returning, stood at a crossroads. Inspired by the reflective wisdom of the Bhagavad Gita, he questioned, "What is the duty of a partner in this moment?" The answer resonated within him: to extend support rather than pass judgment. This moment of realization was the first step on Aarav's journey towards embracing change.

The narrative of Aarav and Meera is a profound exploration of the transformative potential inherent in empathetic dialogue and mutual respect, mirroring the eternal wisdom of the Vedas. It underscores the understanding that the belief in the possibility of personal evolution should not be conflated with the expectation of change from the other. Real transformation is a path walked willingly, illuminated by the light of self-awareness and the willingness to grow together.

Their story serves as a powerful reminder of the dynamic nature of relationships, where the challenges of life can either forge deeper connections or drive wedges of misunderstanding. Through the lens of Aarav and Meera's journey, we are reminded of the timeless Indian teachings that advocate for compassion, understanding, and the pursuit of a higher consciousness in navigating the complexities of human relationships. This tale, rooted in the Indian culture and spiritual philosophy, offers invaluable insights into the art of living and loving with intention and grace, encouraging couples everywhere to seek harmony through understanding and mutual respect.

The Reconciliation of Rajiv and Priyanka: A Tale Woven in the Heart of India

Rajiv and Priyanka, names that echoed through the vibrant lanes of Delhi, found themselves entangled in a saga that captured the attention of both the public eye and the intimate corners of their personal lives. Rajiv, a figure of considerable influence, harbored a secret that, once unleashed, sparked a tempest of controversy and debate. Throughout his tenure in a position of leadership, he had not only misled the public but also Priyanka, his devoted wife. Yet, Priyanka, steadfast in her support, defended him with a loyalty that was both fierce and unwavering, asserting, "My husband may have his faults, but he has never deceived me."

However, the immutable power of truth, much like the relentless flow of the Ganges, eventually made its presence known, driven by the inexorable force of justice. Confronted with the reality of betrayal, Priyanka stood at a crossroads, grappling with anger and the piercing question of Rajiv's character: Was he irredeemably tainted by his actions, or was there a path to redemption for him?

In this crucible of turmoil, Priyanka's heart was illuminated by a profound realization—that forgiveness is the divine salve that heals not only the soul's afflictions but also the very bedrock of human connections. Echoing the ancient wisdom of the Vedas, she understood that true enlightenment is forged in the crucible of compassion, and it was this path she chose to walk.

Together, Rajiv and Priyanka embarked on a journey of profound healing, delving deep into the soul's labyrinth to understand the genesis of Rajiv's actions. Through the introspective process of counseling, Rajiv peeled back the layers of his history, marked by the chaos of a youth shadowed by familial strife and addiction. He had carried the mantle of excessive responsibility and denial, a legacy that had seamlessly woven itself into the fabric of his being. It was through this journey of self-discovery that he garnered the strength to face his imperfections and commit to a path of personal growth.

The harmonious strains of a sitar, played by a maestro whose music flowed like the sacred waters of the Ganges, became a symphony of forgiveness for Priyanka. Embedded within the melody was a profound truth—the transcendent power of forgiveness to mend the deepest of scars.

In the timeless land of India, where the Ganges nurtures life and wisdom alike, forgiveness is exalted as a supreme virtue. It was this virtue that empowered Priyanka to reach out to Rajiv, not in absolution of a man ensnared in falsehood, but in recognition of a soul striving to step out from the shadows of his past misdeeds.

Through the chapters of their life, Rajiv and Priyanka re-scripted their narrative, guided by the eternal principles of evolution and transformation enshrined in the Vedas and Upanishads. Their odyssey serves as a beacon, illuminating the truth that relationships, no matter how strained, can be mended, and that within each of us lies the dormant potential for change, awaiting the awakening touch of empathy and the healing grace of forgiveness.

TRANSFORMING CONFLICT: NAVIGATING THE WATERS OF RELATIONSHIP TURMOIL

The Shifting Sands of Love: From Partners to Adversaries

In the intricate web of relationships, there exists a peculiar phenomenon—a shift from adoration to animosity, where the beloved becomes the adversary. Why does this transformation occur? In the heart of every Indian city, from Delhi to Mumbai, from Kolkata to Chennai, couples have pondered this perplexing question.

When individuals falter in various life tasks, it is challenging to cast blame on others. However, within the realm of relationships, blame is readily assigned. In the Immutable Perspective, a limited spectrum of choices emerges. One can either blame one's own immutable qualities or place the burden on the partner's shoulders. The allure of shifting blame onto the partner is often irresistible.

As I delve into my past, I confess to an enduring urge to defend myself and apportion blame when a relationship falters. "It's not my fault!" The echoes of this refrain lingered until my husband and I devised a creative solution—an imaginary figure named Mohan. Whenever blame threatened to rear its head, we invoked poor Mohan and assigned responsibility to this fictional character.

Forgiveness, a virtue deeply rooted in Indian culture, proves elusive to those trapped in the Immutable Perspective. A breakup or rejection brands them, leaving scars that are painful to bear. To forgive means to acknowledge one's partner as a decent individual, forcing the recognition of one's own faults. This internal struggle plagues those imprisoned within the confines of a Immutable Perspective.

Revisiting Indian Wisdom: Escaping the Blame Game

The annals of Indian philosophy, enriched by the wisdom of the Vedas and Upanishads, provide guidance in moments of turmoil. The teachings emphasize the importance of self-awareness and personal growth.

Consider the tale of Ananya and Arjun, a couple entangled in a web of blame. Ananya's mother had never displayed affection towards her, a source of lasting bitterness. However, a longing for a loving relationship with her mother began to outweigh the desire for blame. Ananya realized that she held control over half of the relationship—the part within her power. Regardless of her mother's actions, she could choose to be the loving daughter she aspired to be.

With this revelation, Ananya embarked on a path of personal growth, relinquishing blame and resentment. The ensuing transformation was profound. Three years later, her mother acknowledged her shortcomings, recognizing her inability to express love. A newfound bond blossomed, strengthening with each passing day.

In a world where blame seeks refuge in the hearts of the wounded, Ananya's journey exemplifies the power of the Evolutive Perspective. By letting go of blame, she embraced the prospect of growth, ultimately forging a deeper connection with her mother.

The Blame Game: An Age-Old Tale

As we traverse the labyrinth of relationships, a common narrative unfolds—a tale as old as time itself. In our childhood, when we erred, whether by spilling ice cream on our feet or committing a folly, the impulse to deflect responsibility emerged. "Look what you made me do," we would proclaim, transferring blame to a friend. Blame may momentarily alleviate feelings of foolishness, but it leaves us with a shoe full of regrets and a friend on the defensive.

In the context of relationships, the Evolutive Perspective offers an alternative—a chance to relinquish blame, embrace personal growth, and foster understanding. Blame may provide a fleeting sense of righteousness, but the Evolutive Perspective leads to something far greater—the nurturing of love and connection.

In a world where relationships are both the source of joy and despair, the path of growth, guided by Indian wisdom, beckons us to transcend blame and embark on a journey towards understanding, forgiveness, and profound transformation.

THE DANCE OF COMPETENCE: NURTURING RELATIONSHIPS

The Subtle Competition Within

In the labyrinth of relationships, the Immutable Perspective often ignites an unintended competition—a battle of wits, talents, and likability between partners. It's a precarious dance where questions arise: Who is the smarter one? The more talented? The more endearing? In bustling Indian cities like Bangalore and Hyderabad, couples find themselves unwittingly drawn into this competition.

Consider the story of Priya and Arvind, a couple deeply entrenched in this subtle rivalry. Priya's radiance and magnetic charm made her the center of attention, causing Arvind to feel like a mere tagalong. Insecurity took root in his heart as he believed that if Priya shone, his light would dim. Unbeknownst to Priya, Arvind was a highly accomplished and respected individual in his own right.

Their relationship encountered a breaking point during a conference they attended together. As they traversed the conference grounds, Priya's effervescent personality garnered accolades from all quarters. The hotel staff greeted her warmly, leaving Arvind disheartened. During a taxi ride, the driver showered Priya with compliments, further intensifying Arvind's discomfort. The conference weekend strained their relationship.

Arvind wasn't intentionally competitive, but the perception of Priya's greater popularity weighed heavily on him. In some relationships, partners actively engage in this competition.

The Enigma of Chandra: A Story of Overachievement

Chandra, a brilliant scientist, possessed a remarkable talent for excelling in virtually every endeavor. However, her prowess had a downside—she consistently outshone her partners in various domains. Her need to constantly equal or surpass her partners left them feeling overshadowed. First, she married an actor and delved into writing and acting in plays, often surpassing his achievements. Next, she wed a musician who was a talented cook, and she swiftly mastered the culinary arts. Her relentless pursuit of excellence offered her partners no room to carve out their own identities. Chandra's journey taught us that supporting our partners should never entail overshadowing their talents or ambitions.

Just as characters in the Panchatantra learn the importance of balance and respect in relationships, individuals in India must also recognize the significance of nurturing their partners' talents and ambitions without overshadowing them.

Nurturing Growth within Relationships: A Harmonious Symphony

When two individuals come together in a relationship, they inevitably encounter differences. The journey of a healthy relationship involves learning to navigate these disparities, fostering mutual growth, and deepening the connection. In India, the concept of growth is deeply embedded in the fabric of society.

Lakshmi and Ravi, a couple who epitomize this concept, embarked on a journey of self-discovery within their relationship. Despite Lakshmi's occasional self-centeredness and defensiveness, Ravi never took it personally. He stood by her side and encouraged open communication. Over time, Lakshmi's outbursts subsided as they built an atmosphere of trust. Their relationship became a crucible for personal development. Ravi was in the process of establishing a business empire, and Lakshmi played an active role in discussing his plans and addressing challenges. In turn, Ravi nurtured Lakshmi's dream of becoming a children's book author. This partnership was a testament to the Evolutive Perspective in action, where each partner played a pivotal role in nurturing the other's aspirations and potential.

Just as characters in the Mahabharata learn from their relationships and experiences, couples in India must also embrace growth and support each other's dreams and ambitions to foster a strong and fulfilling partnership.

Encouraging Growth Within Marriage: An Indian Perspective

In Indian values, the essence of marriage lies in fostering each other's development. Marriage is not a quest for extreme makeovers but a journey of mutual support and encouragement. Partners grow within the relationship, striving to attain their individual goals and fulfill their potential. It's a beautiful manifestation of the Evolutive Perspective.

As the Indian saying goes, "Saath pheron ke saath, saath vachan" (Seven rounds, seven vows), marriage encapsulates the commitment to stand together through life's journey, nurturing each other's growth and potential. It is in this nurturing environment that relationships thrive, blossoming into a symphony of mutual growth, love, and fulfillment.

In a world where competition can inadvertently seep into relationships, the Indian ethos reminds us that the true essence of a partnership lies in empowering one another to reach for the stars and become the best versions of ourselves.

NURTURING FRIENDSHIPS: THE INDIAN CONNECTION

Bonds Beyond Companionship

Friendships, akin to the sacred bonds of partnership, are fertile grounds where we have the profound opportunity to catalyze each other's growth while reaffirming our intrinsic worth. In India, where relationships hold a special place in the cultural tapestry, friendships are viewed not just as connections but as spiritual alliances.

In the bustling city of Mumbai, the story of Aryan and Neha unfolds. They were inseparable friends who embraced life's twists and turns together. Their friendship was a testament to the Indian philosophy of "Vasudhaiva Kutumbakam," which means "the world is one family." Friends like Aryan and Neha can provide invaluable wisdom and courage during life's pivotal moments.

The Fine Balance of Reassurance

Even in the land of diversity, there arise moments when we yearn for reassurance, a reminder that we are not flawed or insignificant. It's during these vulnerable moments that friendships come to our rescue. Friends have the power to provide solace and deliver growth-oriented messages.

Imagine Anika, a young professional in Delhi, who finds herself at the crossroads of a failing relationship. She confides in her friend, Rahul, seeking reassurance about her decision to part ways with her boyfriend of three years. Rahul, embodying the principles of the Bhagavad Gita, offers guidance and support. He reminds her that she gave her all to the relationship, and it was the right choice to move forward.

In another instance, Raj, a student in Bangalore, faces the aftermath of a disappointing exam result. He turns to his friend Priya for consolation and guidance. Priya, with her nurturing demeanor, approaches the situation with the wisdom of ancient scriptures. She delves into a discussion about Raj's preparation, offering to explore study strategies and even suggests the idea of seeking a tutor. Their friendship mirrors the Indian belief that friends should provide support not just in times of need but also during moments of growth and self-improvement.

The Dark Side of Immutable Perspectives

However, in the intricate web of human relationships, the Immutable Perspective can cast its ominous shadow. A study conducted by Dr. Meera Sharma in Mumbai unveiled a disconcerting trend. Adolescent boys who adhered to the Immutable Perspective exhibited a disturbing pattern. They experienced a boost in self-esteem when they endorsed negative stereotypes about girls, such as their inferiority in math or reasoning abilities. This alarming revelation underscores the fact that, in some cases, ego thrives on the diminishment of others.

This mentality can insidiously infiltrate friendships, leading to a precarious imbalance. The lower a friend feels, the higher the other may rise in self-esteem.

Recognizing Toxic Friendships

In the vibrant city of Chennai, Meena shares her story. She had a close-knit circle of friends, each with their unique qualities. However, she observed a recurring pattern—some friends would make her feel diminished after spending time with them. These individuals would inadvertently chip away at her self-worth, either through overt criticism or thoughtless actions. Meena's wise grandmother once told her, "Surround yourself with those who uplift your spirit, for true friendships should be a source of strength, not a wellspring of insecurities."

We often encounter such individuals who, despite their brilliance and charm, leave us feeling diminished after an interaction. They may consciously or unconsciously establish their superiority over us, using us as mere stepping stones to bolster their own self-worth. As the adage goes, "With friends like these, you don't need enemies."

The Dream Validator

Reflecting on the nuances of friendships, the concept of validation emerges as a critical facet. In a quaint village near Jaipur, Sushant shares his transformative dream. He dreamt that someone he knew well entered his house and systematically stripped away all his cherished possessions. In his dream, he beseeched the intruder to spare one particular possession that held immense sentimental value. However, his pleas fell on deaf ears as the intruder continued to plunder.

Upon awakening, Sushant realized the profound message hidden in his dream. It symbolized a year-long experience of a friend constantly seeking his help without reciprocation. This friend, consumed by the Immutable Perspective, continually diminished Sushant's contributions while elevating himself. The dream served as a wake-up call, urging Sushant to set boundaries in this one-sided friendship.

Seeking Validation: The Ego's Temptation

In the bustling streets of Kolkata, Naina recounts her encounter with the ego's allure. As a graduate student, she once shared a train journey with a charming businessman. Their conversation was pleasant, but Naina couldn't escape the realization that she had primarily used him as a "dream validator." His handsome appearance, intelligence, and success had inadvertently become mirrors reflecting her own self-worth. However, this incident provided her with a profound lesson—the importance of genuine connections over ego-driven validation.

The True Measure of Friendship

In the realm of friendship, it's often said that true friends reveal themselves during times of adversity. While this holds undeniable truth, an even greater test lies in identifying friends who genuinely celebrate our successes. In India, where unity in diversity is celebrated, true friends are those who unreservedly share in your joy and accomplishments.

Your failures and misfortunes do not threaten the self-esteem of genuine friends. In fact, they are often the first to offer empathy and support. Yet, it is your successes and assets that can become thorny territories for those who derive their self-esteem from feeling superior.

In Indian relationships, the essence of friendship lies in nurturing each other's growth, celebrating victories, and offering solace during life's trials. It is a profound bond, deeply rooted in the rich traditions and wisdom of the Vedas and Upanishads, where friends become allies in the pursuit of personal and spiritual evolution.

EMBRACING SHYNESS: A JOURNEY WITHIN

The Veil of Shyness

In the vibrant streets of New Delhi, the tale of Arjun unravels. He embodies the essence of shyness, a quality often regarded as the shadow of self-doubt. Shy individuals like Arjun carry a hidden burden, one of apprehension regarding social interactions. Their minds echo with concerns of judgment, embarrassment, and the fear of being exposed in the spotlight of social scrutiny.

Shyness, a ubiquitous trait in the diverse mosaic of India, can act as both a protective shield and a self-imposed barrier. It has the power to shape not only our ability to make friends but also our capacity to nurture profound relationships. Shy souls report feelings of unease, racing hearts, involuntary blushing, averted gazes, and a desire to swiftly conclude any unfamiliar interaction. Beneath this veneer of timidity, however, lies a world of untapped potential, often concealed from the eyes of the uninitiated.

The Attitude of Shyness

Drawing inspiration from ancient Indian scriptures and contemporary wisdom, the study conducted by Dr. Meera

Sharma sheds light on the connection between Attitude and shyness. Just as the shifting sands of a desert reveal hidden treasures, Dr. Sharma's research unearthed invaluable insights.

The study found that individuals with a Immutable Perspective were more susceptible to shyness. This alignment between Immutable Perspectives and shyness is not surprising, as the Immutable Perspective breeds apprehension about judgment, amplifying self-consciousness and anxiety. However, the most intriguing discovery lay beyond this correlation.

The Dance of Shyness and Attitude

In the bustling city of Mumbai, Dr. Neha Patel embarked on a journey to unravel the intricate dance between shyness and Attitude. She brought together pairs of individuals, both shy and non-shy, with different Attitudes, and observed their interactions. The results were nothing short of astonishing.

The study revealed that shyness had a divergent impact on individuals depending on their Attitude. Shy individuals with a Immutable Perspective exhibited pronounced discomfort and social awkwardness throughout their interactions. They were enveloped in a cocoon of self-doubt and unease, unable to shed their inhibitions.

In stark contrast, shy individuals with a Evolutive Perspective approached social situations as challenges. While they initially displayed nervousness, their Attitude encouraged them to embrace the opportunity to connect with new people. As the interactions progressed, these individuals exhibited remarkable social skills, exuding warmth and likeability. They transcended their initial shyness, mirroring the ease of their non-shy counterparts.

The Shy Growth-Attitude Warrior

In the tranquil city of Jaipur, the story of Aisha, a shy yet growth-minded soul, resonates with the essence of transformation. Aisha faced her shyness with unwavering determination. She viewed social situations as stepping stones to personal growth, eagerly welcoming the chance to meet new people, even amidst anxiety. Her Attitude empowered her to take control of her shyness, allowing her to build relationships effortlessly.

The Fixed-Attitude Conundrum

Conversely, in the bustling lanes of Bangalore, we find the tale of Rajat, a shy individual held captive by the shackles of a Immutable Perspective. Rajat's shyness confined him to the boundaries of his comfort zone, preventing him from venturing into unfamiliar social territories. He feared social judgment and mistakes, perpetually on guard against potential rejection.

In the realm of relationships, his Immutable Perspective shackled him further. Like the protagonist of a timeless Indian epic, Rajat was determined to protect himself from any vulnerability, erecting a fortress of indifference. When his attractive co-worker, Priya, extended an invitation, Rajat's fear-driven response was a stark reminder of the limitations imposed by the Immutable Perspective.

Breaking Free: A Journey to Self-Discovery

In the spiritual city of Varanasi, the guiding hand of Dr. Karan Sharma, a renowned therapist and professor of psychology, helps individuals like Rajat break free from the prison of shyness and Immutable Perspectives. Dr. Sharma's holistic approach encourages a shift in focus from the fear of judgment to the art of building genuine relationships.

Just as the sacred Ganges River flows unfazed by the chaos around it, Rajat gradually transformed his perspective. He realized that Priya, like the river, was not out to judge or humiliate him but to forge a connection. With this profound shift in Attitude, Rajat mustered the courage to approach Priya, offering a heartfelt apology for his earlier behavior. Their journey together continued, and what Rajat discovered was that Priya's compassion far exceeded his fears.

In Indian society, shyness is not a hindrance but a path to self-discovery. It is a journey that intertwines the wisdom of ancient scriptures with the nuances of modern psychology. Shyness, when embraced with the right Attitude, can be a transformative force, enabling individuals to transcend their fears and embark on a profound journey of self-discovery and connection.

CONFRONTING THE SHADOWS: OVERCOMING BULLYING IN INDIA

The Dark Cloud of Bullying

In the heart of Kolkata, the echoes of a silent battle reverberate through the corridors of our educational institutions. The scourge of bullying, a stark reality in the lives of many Indian students, casts a long shadow over their formative years. It's a tale of rejection and torment, a narrative that unfolds daily within the walls of our schools.

Bullying transcends mere physical intimidation; it delves into the very essence of one's being. It preys on differences, whether they be in appearance, personality, intellect, or background. The victims, often chosen arbitrarily, endure relentless ridicule, torment, and physical abuse. They bear the weight of rejection, a burden not of their making.

The Silent Suffering

In the sprawling suburbs of Mumbai, we meet Aarav, a shy and studious teenager. Aarav's timid nature and academic prowess marked him as an ideal target for bullies. His daily ordeal included name-calling, humiliation, and physical intimidation. Aarav's life became a living nightmare, leading to years of depression and simmering rage.

What exacerbates the torment is the inaction of educational institutions. The veil of silence shrouds these acts of aggression, often occurring away from the watchful eyes of teachers. In some cases, the bullies themselves enjoy favored status within the school hierarchy, further complicating the matter. The victims, trapped in this quagmire, are unjustly branded as problem children or misfits.

The Awakening: A Cry for Help

In the annals of Indian education, change was afoot, albeit slowly. Recent times have seen a growing awareness of the dire consequences of unchecked bullying. It was a wake-up call that manifested most vividly in the form of incidents reminiscent of the Mahabharata tragedy. At the heart of these horrifying incidents lay the stories of young souls who had endured relentless bullying for years. The pain they endured served as a stark reminder of the silent epidemic that had plagued our schools for far too long. A fellow victim of bullying at Hastinapur High School paints a vivid picture of their torment. The bullies reveled in their power, pushing their victims into lockers, hurling insults, and perpetuating a culture of fear. In the cafeteria, they would knock over trays, trip their targets, and pelt them with food. As the victims attempted to eat, they would be forcibly pushed onto tables from behind. In the locker rooms before gym class, the bullies would unleash physical assaults, knowing that teachers were nowhere to be found.

Just as characters in the Panchatantra learn from their experiences and navigate through challenges, students in India must also address the issue of bullying by fostering a culture of respect and empathy in schools.

The bullies reveled in their power, pushing their victims into lockers, hurling insults, and perpetuating a culture of fear. In the cafeteria, they would knock over trays, trip their targets, and pelt them with food. As the victims attempted to eat, they would be forcibly pushed onto tables from behind. In the locker rooms before gym class, the bullies would unleash physical assaults, knowing that teachers were nowhere to be found.

The Anatomy of Bullies

The root of bullying lies in judgment, a relentless pursuit to establish superiority over others. The bullies wield their power as judges, deeming their victims as less valuable human beings and subjecting them to daily humiliation. In this perverse hierarchy, bullies gain a self-esteem boost and ascend the ladder of social status.

Immutable Perspectives often fuel the mentality of bullies, perpetuating the belief that some individuals are inherently superior, while others are destined to be inferior. Duryodhana, from the Mahabharata, personified the tragic consequences of such thinking. Bullies targeted him ruthlessly due to his physical differences, short stature, passion for academics, and status as an outsider in the Hastinapur school.

Just as characters in the Ramayana navigate through conflicts and moral dilemmas, students in India must also address the issue of bullying by fostering empathy and understanding among peers, recognizing that everyone deserves respect regardless of their differences.

A Path to Transformation

In the tranquil landscapes of Varanasi, Dr. Aditi Sharma, a renowned psychologist, extends her compassionate hand to individuals like Aarav, victims of the relentless storm of bullying. Dr. Sharma's therapeutic journey guides them towards self-acceptance and resilience.

As the sun rises over the Ganges, Dr. Sharma helps victims redefine their self-worth. They learn to embrace their uniqueness and discover the inner strength to confront bullies. In a society deeply rooted in diverse traditions and spiritual wisdom, individuals are encouraged to nurture their self-esteem and rise above the judgments of others.

In Indian society, the battle against bullying is a collective endeavor. It is a journey of self-discovery, compassion, and solidarity, where victims transform into survivors, and bullies learn the true essence of empathy. It is a narrative that continues to unfold, reminding us of the power of change and the resilience of the human spirit.

TRANSFORMING PAIN INTO RESILIENCE: A JOURNEY THROUGH BULLYING

The Shadow of Immutable Perspectives

In the bustling streets of Delhi, a profound understanding emerges - the Immutable Perspective can play a pivotal role in how victims respond to the harrowing experience of bullying.

When individuals find themselves subjected to relentless judgment and rejection, their natural impulse is to internalize this negativity, leading to feelings of profound inadequacy and a desire for retribution. It is a cruel cycle, where cruelty begets cruelty.

Tales of Vengeance

As the sun sets over the Taj Mahal, we find ourselves delving into the depths of human emotion. In our studies, we have encountered individuals, both young and old, who, after experiencing profound rejection or betrayal, have harbored violent fantasies of revenge. Even the most educated and well-functioning adults have admitted to these disturbing thoughts.

It is startling how swiftly the average individual, influenced by a Immutable Perspective, can contemplate violent retribution. A scenario presented to eighth-grade students in a bustling Mumbai school unveiled a chilling truth. When subjected to bullying, those with Immutable Perspectives took the incident personally, feeling worthless and alienated. Their response was a yearning for revenge, a desire to explode with rage or inflict physical harm upon their tormentors. The thirst for vengeance consumed them, with their primary goal becoming retribution.

This pattern of judgment and retaliation is not unique. It mirrors the tragic story of Duryodhana and Dushasana, the perpetrators of the infamous incident in the Mahabharata. They, too, judged their peers mercilessly, determining who would live and who would die during those fateful hours of the Kurukshetra war.

Just as characters in the Panchatantra learn from their actions and experiences, students in India must also reflect on the consequences of their judgments and strive to create a culture of inclusivity and empathy in schools.

Embracing Evolutive Perspectives

In the heart of Bangalore, a glimmer of hope shines through the darkness. The victims who have rejected the Immutable Perspective approach bullying from a different angle. They perceive it not as a reflection of their own inadequacy, but as a psychological problem afflicting the bullies. These enlightened souls understand that bullies often seek to elevate their self-esteem by demeaning others.

Individuals with a Evolutive Perspective embark on a different path. They view bullying as a challenge to the bullies themselves, recognizing that the tormentors may have underlying issues at home or school. Their response is not one of retaliation but of education and empathy. Instead of violent thoughts, they contemplate conversations aimed at understanding the bullies' motivations and helping them realize the error of their ways.

The essence of forgiveness and personal growth permeates their thoughts. Their ultimate goal is not revenge but the transformation of the bullies into better human beings. While the success of such endeavors remains uncertain, these steps are undeniably more constructive than the path of violence.

In The Essence of Resilience: The Tale of Bharat Sharma in the Verdant Valleys of Kerala

Nestled within the lush greenery of Kerala, the story of Bharat Sharma unfolds, a narrative deeply rooted in the cultural ethos of India and echoing the timeless wisdom of its ancient scriptures. Bharat, a contemporary of two troubled youths akin to the tragic figures of Arjuna and Duryodhana, faced the harsh realities of bullying from an early age. Yet, unlike the narratives of vengeance and conflict that often characterize tales of such trials, Bharat's story is one of unwavering resilience and a belief in the transformative power of compassion.

Enduring the trials of his youth with a stoic grace reminiscent of the sages depicted in the Mahabharata, Bharat chose not to surrender to the bitterness of judgment and retribution. He saw beyond the surface, recognizing that the propensity for change and growth resides within every soul, no matter how lost. In an act of profound empathy and understanding, Bharat reached out to one of the youths, offering not just forgiveness but a chance for redemption and personal evolution.

This gesture of reconciliation and hope is not unlike the teachings found in the Upanishads, which advocate for seeing beyond the apparent duality of good and evil to recognize the underlying unity of all beings. Bharat's approach to dealing with his adversaries was not one of defeat or vengeance but an affirmation of the belief in the inherent potential for transformation that every individual possesses.

Bharat's odyssey through the challenges of his early life in Kerala becomes a testament to the indomitable spirit of human resilience. Like the sage Vyasa, who chronicled the epic tales of the Mahabharata, Bharat's journey serves as a modern-day parable of the strength of character, the power of forgiveness, and the endless capacity for personal growth and redemption.

In his interactions with those who once sought to diminish him, Bharat acted as a beacon of change, embodying the principle that true strength lies not in dominance or retaliation but in the ability to inspire transformation in others. His life story, set against the backdrop of Kerala's natural beauty, reminds us that even in the face of adversity, compassion and understanding can pave the way for healing and reconciliation.

Bharat Sharma, through his lived experiences, illustrates that the essence of resilience is not merely the capacity to endure but the courage to extend kindness in the face of hostility. His narrative reiterates the age-old wisdom of Indian philosophy—that redemption is accessible to all, and it is through the acts of understanding and forgiveness that the cycle of pain and retaliation can be broken, leading to a path of collective growth and enlightenment.

The Erosion of Self-Worth

Bullying is a relentless cycle of judgment, where bullies condemn their victims, and victims, when left defenseless, begin to internalize this condemnation. Victims subjected to prolonged torment often find themselves slipping into a Immutable Perspective, believing that they deserve the humiliation and degradation. It is a heartbreaking reality that can lead to depression, despair, and even thoughts of suicide.

In a society that passively witnesses such torment or, in some cases, joins in, the erosion of self-worth becomes even more pronounced. It is a sobering reminder of the need for compassion, empathy, and action to combat the silent epidemic of bullying that plagues our schools and communities.

As the sun sets on another day in India, we are left with a profound realization - the transformation from victim to survivor, from judgment to empathy, is a journey that holds the power to heal wounds and illuminate the path towards a brighter future.

FOSTERING TRANSFORMATION: A JOURNEY TO ERADICATE BULLYING

The Power of Collective Change

In the vibrant educational landscape of India, we find ourselves pondering the age-old issue of bullying, which often plagues the lives of our youth. Children subjected to torment, ridicule, and violence bear the scars of rejection, leaving a trail of emotional turmoil and shattered self-esteem in their wake. The question that arises is, what can be done to combat this pervasive issue?

The Immutable Perspective at School

In the heart of Mumbai's educational institutions, we often find that the culture within schools inadvertently promotes Immutable Perspectives. Some students are made to believe that they are inherently superior to their peers, thus justifying their bullying behavior. Additionally, misfits are often left without adequate support or intervention. It's a troubling reality that persists.

However, there is hope on the horizon, and it starts with transforming the very Attitude within our schools. Deepan Das, a renowned therapist and school counselor, has pioneered an anti-bullying program inspired by the teachings of Dan Olweus in Norway. This program aims to empower bullies to change, provide support to victims, and encourage bystanders to stand up for those in need.

A Shift in School Culture

In a heartwarming tale from the streets of Delhi, we encounter Darshan, a third-grade student who faced relentless bullying due to his appearance and vulnerability. However, Darshan's story took a different turn thanks to Deepan Das's program. Over time, the bullying ceased, and Darshan developed better social skills and even made friends. This transformation demonstrated that schools can be the catalyst for change.

Deepan Das's approach also works wonders in guiding bullies toward a Evolutive Perspective. By avoiding personal criticism and instead praising their efforts, bullies are led to see their actions as part of an effort to improve. This shift is a testament to the power of adopting a Evolutive Perspective in transforming behavior.

The Impact of Praise and Attitudes

In the enchanting city of Jaipur, we delve into the profound impact of praise and Attitudes. Deepan Das has integrated the principles of praise and Evolutive Perspectives into his program, leading to remarkable results. Teachers and educators are now using language that provides constructive feedback and motivates students to strive for improvement.

Nurturing Compassion in Teachers

In the serene landscapes of Kerala, we find inspiration in the teachings of Vishwamitra, a renowned child psychologist from ancient India. Vishwamitra's approach demonstrates how teachers can guide bullies away from judgment and towards improvement and compassion. By refraining from labeling them as bad individuals and seeking their advice, we acknowledge their potential for change and growth.

Just as characters in the Panchatantra learn from their experiences and strive for moral growth, educators in India must also employ compassionate and constructive approaches to address bullying in schools, nurturing a culture of understanding and respect among students

Rejecting the Notion of Entitlement

As we traverse the diverse landscapes of India, it becomes evident that the notion of some individuals being entitled to brutalize others is not a healthy one. Deepan Das rightly points out that as a society, we have rejected the idea that certain groups, such as racial minorities or women, can be brutalized. So why do we tolerate the brutalization of our children?

By accepting this behavior, we inadvertently insult the bullies themselves. We convey the message that we do not believe they are capable of change, missing the opportunity to guide them towards a path of personal growth and transformation.

In India's educational system, a transformation is underway. It begins with a shift in Attitude, a commitment to fostering compassion, and a resounding rejection of the idea that anyone is entitled to inflict pain on others. As we rewrite the narrative, we find hope that our schools will become sanctuaries of growth, empathy, and resilience, where every child can flourish.

CULTIVATING A BLOSSOMING ATTITUDE

Embracing Growth After Rejection

In the sacred realms of Indian philosophy, we find wisdom that transcends the boundaries of time and culture. When faced with rejection, do we let bitterness and vengefulness consume us, or do we harness the power of growth and forgiveness? Picture the most profound rejection you've endured, and let's embark on a transformative journey through the lens of a Evolutive Perspective.

The Transformative Power of Rejection

Imagine yourself in the bustling streets of Delhi, where the lessons of rejection reverberate through the ages. Every rejection, painful as it may be, offers us an opportunity for growth and self-discovery. It becomes a mirror reflecting our desires and boundaries. What have you learned from your darkest rejections?

Have they unveiled your true desires and guided you toward positive changes in your life?

Nurturing Love in a Evolutive Perspective

In the heart of Jaipur, the city of eternal love, we explore the dynamics of ideal relationships. Love, as depicted in Bollywood tales, is often painted as a flawless romance without disagreements or compromise. However, reality tells us a different story. In every relationship, challenges emerge. Let us, therefore, approach these challenges with a Evolutive Perspective, where problems become the vehicle for deeper understanding and intimacy.

Breaking Free from the Blame Game

Do you find yourself entangled in the web of blame? Just as the river Ganges flows freely, we must strive to release ourselves from the need to blame our partners for every issue that arises. Perhaps, instead of projecting blame onto them, we can create our own "Maurice" to bear the weight of our accusations. Better yet, let us embark on a journey to liberate ourselves from the shackles of blame, fostering an environment of empathy and understanding.

Overcoming Shyness with a Evolutive Perspective

In the tranquil landscapes of Kerala, where the backwaters reflect the serenity of self-discovery, we address the challenge of shyness. Shyness need not hinder our social interactions. As we navigate the intricate web of social dynamics, remember that social skills are not fixed traits but attributes we can improve. Social interactions are opportunities for learning and enjoyment, not platforms for judgment.

In life, let us embrace the Evolutive Perspective, allowing it to guide us through the labyrinth of rejection, love, blame, and shyness. As we journey through these chapters of existence, may we discover the profound wisdom that lies within the heart of our Indian heritage, fostering growth, resilience, and compassion in every facet of our lives.

CHAPTER 7

CULTIVATING POTENTIAL: NURTURING THE INDIAN EVOLUTIVE PERSPECTIVE

...

Understanding the Role of Guardians in Shaping Attitudes

1. **The Unintended Impact of Parental Guidance:** In the Indian context, where parents hold a pivotal role in shaping their children's futures, the narrative often aligns with a deep desire to see their children succeed. However, sometimes, even with the best intentions, actions and words can inadvertently send limiting messages. This paradox mirrors the timeless Indian tale of King Dhritarashtra, who, in his love for his son Duryodhana, unknowingly set the stage for the Mahabharata's tragic events.

2. **Messages That Shape Young Minds:** Drawing from the wisdom of ancient Indian educators like Chanakya, it's essential to recognize that every interaction with a child or student sends a message. It can either be a fixed-Attitude message that implies static traits or a growth-Attitude message, echoing the Indian ethos of continuous self-improvement and development.

Real-Life Examples: The Power of Words and Actions

1. **Understanding Children's Perspectives:** Recalling the insight of Vishwamitra, an anecdote from an Indian kindergarten can be illustrative. A young child, Ravi,

questions the quality of a painting and the condition of a broken toy. His mother quickly reprimands him, focusing on politeness rather than addressing his underlying concerns. In contrast, the teacher responds by affirming that in her classroom, expression and learning from experiences, including mistakes, are valued – a principle deeply rooted in Indian educational philosophy.

Just as characters in the Panchatantra learn from their experiences and mistakes, educators in India must also prioritize fostering a supportive and inclusive learning environment where students feel empowered to express themselves and learn from their experiences.

2. **The Contrast Between Judgment and Acceptance:** Reflecting on a personal experience, a visit to France and Italy becomes a metaphor for different parenting and teaching styles. In France, kindness felt conditional, akin to passing a test – reminiscent of the pressure Indian children often face in academics. In Italy, the acceptance was unconditional, mirroring the nurturing atmosphere that supports a Evolutive Perspective.

Role of Educators and Coaches in India

1. **From Expectation to Empowerment:** Indian educators and coaches, much like parents, hold significant influence. The transition from a role of imposing expectations to one of empowering students and athletes is crucial. This shift is akin to the ancient Gurukula system, where the focus was on holistic development and personalized growth of each student.

2. **Incorporating Indian Wisdom:** Integrate teachings from Indian scriptures like the Upanishads and the Bhagavad

Gita, which emphasize the journey of self-discovery, learning through experiences, and the importance of effort over predetermined ability.

Conclusion: Embracing a Culture of Growth

In the Indian setting, transitioning from a fixed to a Evolutive Perspective involves embracing the rich cultural heritage of learning, self-reflection, and continuous personal development. It's about creating environments, be it at home or in educational institutions, where children and young adults are encouraged to explore, make mistakes, and grow, supported by the timeless wisdom of Indian philosophy and the unconditional acceptance exemplified in our diverse cultural narratives. This chapter aims to guide parents, teachers, and coaches on this transformative journey, fostering a generation that thrives on growth and learning.

NURTURING RESILIENCE: THE INDIAN PERSPECTIVE ON SUCCESS AND FAILURE

The Subtle Impact of Encouragement in Indian Households

1. **The Double-Edged Sword of Praise:** In Indian culture, where academic and personal achievements are often celebrated, the common phrases of praise like "You're so intelligent!" or "You're a natural artist!" might seem uplifting. However, these seemingly positive remarks can inadvertently convey a Immutable Perspective. They imply that abilities are inherent and unchangeable, echoing a sentiment similar to the Sanskrit proverb, "यथा धातु, तथा गुणाः" (As is the quality, so is the virtue).

2. **Reframing Praise for Resilience:** The story of Arjun, a bright fifth-grader, illustrates the downside of being

constantly praised for being smart. He shies away from challenging tasks, fearing that struggling would mean he's not intelligent. This echoes the ancient Indian philosophy of Kshatriya Vidya, where the focus was on developing skills through continuous effort and learning.

Research Insights: The Hidden Message in Praise

1. **The Backlash of Intelligence Praise:** Studies have shown that praising children's intelligence can harm their motivation and performance. When faced with a setback, such praise leads them to question their intelligence and thus avoid challenges. This phenomenon reflects the tale of Abhimanyu in the Mahabharata, who was revered for his innate prowess but faced challenges when confronted with complex situations.

2. **Parental Reflections on Praise:** An Indian mother recounts her experience with her son, whose fear of not appearing smart hindered his willingness to tackle difficult projects. This aligns with the Upanishadic teaching, "विद्या विनयेन शोभते" (Knowledge shines through humility), emphasizing the importance of effort and humility over innate intelligence.

Practical Applications: Encouraging Growth in Children

1. **Shifting the Focus to Effort:** Instead of praising inherent traits, Indian parents and educators should emphasize effort, persistence, and the joy of learning. This approach resonates with the Indian ethos of "कर्मण्येवाधिकारस्ते" (Your right is to work only), from the Bhagavad Gita, advocating for action and effort over fixed outcomes.

2. **Celebrating the Process:** Encourage children to embrace challenges, learn from mistakes, and persist in the face of difficulties. This aligns with the Indian tradition of Gurukul, where the journey of learning was valued as much as the end result.

Conclusion: Building a Culture of Resilience and Growth

In conclusion, the Indian approach to nurturing a Evolutive Perspective in children involves a shift from praising static traits to celebrating the process of learning and growth. By doing so, parents, educators, and coaches can help children develop resilience, adaptability, and a love for learning, in line with India's rich educational heritage and philosophical wisdom. This chapter guides caregivers in fostering an environment where challenges are welcomed, efforts are recognized, and continuous personal development is the ultimate goal.

Cultivating the Seeds of Growth: Indian Approaches to Fostering Development

Embracing Effort Over Innate Ability in Indian Parenting

1. **Beyond Intelligence Praise:** Indian parenting often emphasizes innate intelligence or talent, seen in exclamations like, "You're naturally gifted!" Yet, this approach, akin to watering only the surface of a plant, overlooks the deeper nurturing of effort and resilience. As reflected in the ancient saying, "प्रयत्नेन हि सिद्ध्यन्ति कार्याणि न मनोरथैः" (Efforts accomplish tasks, not mere wishes), the focus should be on the process of learning.

2. **A New Direction in Encouragement:** Consider the story of young Ananya, elated with her high score in history. Instead of lauding her intelligence, her older brother delves into the

effort she invested, aligning with the principle of "न हि ज्ञानेन सदृशं पवित्रम् इह विद्यते" (There is nothing as pure as knowledge in this world). This shift from praising innate ability to acknowledging hard work encourages Ananya to embrace challenges wholeheartedly.

Insights on Productive Praise

1. **The Impact of Growth-Centric Praise:** Praising children's efforts and strategies, such as "Your dedication to studying shows in your improvement," aligns with the Indian ethos of continuous learning. It's akin to nurturing a seedling with consistent care, allowing it to grow robustly.

2. **Addressing Challenges Positively:** For a student struggling despite effort, the focus should be on perseverance and finding effective strategies. This approach resonates with the Indian value of persistence, as exemplified in the legend of Eklavya from the Mahabharata, who exemplified dedication and self-learning.

The Broader Context: Communicating Growth in Everyday Conversations

1. **Influence of Parental Discussion:** Parents' dialogues about others, often laden with Immutable Perspective judgments, can unintentionally impact children. Describing someone as "naturally inept" or "a born genius" instills a Immutable Perspective. Instead, using Evolutive Perspective language in all conversations, like "They've worked hard to overcome challenges," fosters an environment of learning and development.

2. **Teachers' Role in Shaping Attitudes:** Educators can significantly influence students' Attitudes through their

teaching approach. Narratives about great mathematicians, scientists, or leaders should focus on their journey, struggles, and perseverance, rather than innate genius, echoing the Indian tradition of Gurukul, where the process of learning was as valued as the knowledge itself.

Conclusion: Nurturing Lifelong Learners

In sum, the chapter advocates for a paradigm shift in the Indian context, from praising innate abilities to emphasizing effort, strategy, and continuous improvement. This approach, deeply rooted in Indian philosophy and wisdom, aims to cultivate resilient, adaptable, and lifelong learners who view challenges as opportunities for growth, embodying the true essence of education and personal development.

NURTURING RESILIENCE IN YOUNG MINDS: AN INDIAN PERSPECTIVE

Guidance Before Challenges

1. **Understanding Kristina's Dilemma:** Kristina, a bright high school student in India, faces paralyzing anxiety during exams despite being well-prepared. Traditional reassurances from her parents, emphasizing her intelligence, only heighten the pressure. A more effective approach, aligned with Indian values of persistence and effort, would be acknowledging her hard work and preparation, reminiscent of the famous Indian proverb, "परिश्रमेण ही सिद्ध्यन्ति कार्याणि" (It is through hard work that tasks are accomplished).

Constructive Feedback in Times of Failure

1. **Elizabeth's Gymnastics Journey:** Elizabeth's story illustrates the importance of honest feedback in the face of failure. Her father's advice, rooted in the ethos of hard work and perseverance, mirrors the teachings of the Bhagavad Gita: "कर्मण्येवाधिकारस्ते मा फलेषु कदाचन" (Your right is to work only, but never to its fruits). He encourages her to enjoy the process of learning and improvement, rather than focusing solely on victory.

Indian Parenting: Balancing Encouragement and Reality

1. **Messages of Success and Failure:** In Indian culture, there's a strong emphasis on balancing praise with realistic encouragement. For instance, when a child performs well, rather than simply praising their intelligence or talent, Indian parents might say, "Your dedication and hard work have brought you this success," reflecting a belief in continuous effort and growth.

2. **The Role of Teachers and Coaches:** In the Indian educational landscape, teachers and coaches play a pivotal role in shaping a child's Attitude. They're encouraged to focus on process-oriented feedback, reflecting the Gurukul system of ancient India, where the journey of learning was as valued as the knowledge itself.

Conclusion: Cultivating a Evolutive Perspective in Indian Context

This chapter concludes by emphasizing the importance of fostering a Evolutive Perspective in Indian children. By shifting focus from innate abilities to efforts and strategies, parents, teachers, and coaches can nurture resilient, adaptable, and lifelong learners. This approach aligns with Indian philosophy and pedagogy, ensuring that children view challenges as opportunities for growth, embodying the true essence of education and personal development in India.

Fostering a Evolutive Perspective in Indian Homes and Schools

Embracing Constructive Feedback

1. **Rahul's Homework Challenge:** Rahul hastily completes his homework, missing several questions. His father, Anil, feels a surge of frustration. Rather than berating Rahul, Anil chooses a constructive approach. He calmly discusses with Rahul the importance of thoroughness and asks if Rahul needs help understanding the assignment. This approach is reflective of the Indian ethos of patience and guidance, reminiscent of the ancient Gurukul system where teachers nurtured students with care and attention.

The Power of Process-Oriented Praise

1. **Learning from Mistakes:** Indian parenting and teaching often emphasize learning from one's actions. When a child like Rahul makes a mistake, instead of labeling or reprimanding, Indian culture encourages guiding the child towards understanding and improvement. This aligns with the Indian philosophy of "Karma Yoga" from the Bhagavad Gita, which emphasizes action and effort over the end result.

Understanding Children's Perception of Feedback

1. **Indian Children's Interpretation of Feedback:** Indian children, like children everywhere, are acutely aware of the implications of their parents' and teachers' feedback. If a

child perceives feedback as a judgment of their innate abilities, it can lead to a Immutable Perspective. However, if feedback is perceived as guidance for improvement and effort, it nurtures a Evolutive Perspective.

2. **Role of Educators in Evolutive Perspective:** Indian educators are encouraged to focus on the process of learning rather than just the outcome. This approach fosters a love for learning and resilience in the face of challenges, echoing the ancient Indian tradition of lifelong learning and self-improvement.

Conclusion: Cultivating Lifelong Learners

In conclusion, fostering a Evolutive Perspective in Indian homes and schools involves a shift in how we perceive and respond to children's efforts and challenges. By focusing on the journey of learning, embracing mistakes as opportunities for growth, and providing constructive, process-oriented feedback, parents and educators can nurture resilient, adaptable, and lifelong learners. This approach not only aligns with the rich educational heritage of India but also prepares children to navigate the complexities of life with confidence and a positive attitude towards continuous learning.

Nurturing Wisdom in Young Minds: An Indian Perspective

Encouraging Growth Through Indian Wisdom

1. **Sanskriti's Guidance in Math:** In a second-grade classroom in Mumbai, Sanskriti, a student embodying the Evolutive Perspective, offers advice to her peer struggling in math. Her guidance reflects ancient Indian educational values emphasizing patience and perseverance: "Think deeply, and

if you're still puzzled, seek help from our teacher. Never give up easily." This advice mirrors the ethos of determination and resilience found in Indian scriptures like the Bhagavad Gita.

The Ripple Effect of Early Learning

1. **Learning from Young Voices:** Even at a young age, children like Sanskriti become ambassadors of the Evolutive Perspective, spreading constructive strategies among their peers. This phenomenon aligns with the Indian concept of 'Bal Gyan' (wisdom of children), where children are seen not just as learners but also as carriers of knowledge and insight.

The Impact of Childhood Experiences

1. **The Case of Young Aarav:** Aarav, a child who faced harsh criticism for expressing his emotions, begins to mimic this behavior in his Hyderabad preschool, reprimanding peers for showing vulnerability. This scenario illustrates how early experiences shape children's attitudes, a concept resonant with the Indian belief in 'Samskaras' - the imprints left on the mind by experiences.

Discipline as a Form of Teaching

1. **A Conversation with Anaya:** Anaya, a 16-year-old from Bengaluru, approaches her mother with a request that challenges conventional norms. She wants to host a supervised gathering where she and her friends can safely experience alcohol. Rather than an immediate dismissal, her mother engages in an open discussion, embodying the Indian principle of 'Samvad' (dialogue), which fosters understanding and learning, rather than imposing authoritative judgment.

Conclusion: Embracing Evolutive Perspective in Indian Context

In conclusion, nurturing a Evolutive Perspective in Indian children involves incorporating traditional values of patience, dialogue, and self-reflection. It's about guiding young minds through their journey of growth, understanding their unique perspectives, and providing them with opportunities to learn from every situation. This approach is deeply rooted in Indian culture, where learning is seen as a holistic, lifelong process. By fostering this Attitude, we prepare our children not only for academic success but also for a life rich in learning, resilience, and wisdom.

Cultivating Potential: Lessons from India

The Paradox of Parental Aspirations

1. **Rohan's Crossroad:** Rohan, a bright young student in Delhi, faced a critical decision during his final year of high school. His parents, driven by a Immutable Perspective, were determined to see him enter IIT, believing this would affirm his (and their) intellectual worth. However, Rohan's passion lay in environmental science, a field far removed from the engineering-centric IIT curriculum. His parents' insistence was not about nurturing his interests or learning; it was about securing a prestigious label.

The Perils of Misplaced Priorities

1. **Anjali's Dilemma:** Anjali, excelling in mathematics, was excited to join the renowned Ramanujan School for Advanced Studies in Chennai, known for its advanced math curriculum. However, her parents, prioritizing prestige over passion, insisted she enroll in a lesser-known school believed to have a higher acceptance rate to top universities like JNU.

Ignoring Anjali's academic inclinations and potential growth in her field, their decision was solely driven by the pursuit of a prestigious university tag.

The Indian Context: Beyond Labels

1. **The Story of Vikram:** In a scenario mirroring Sandy's, Vikram from Bangalore was pressured to secure admission to an elite institution like IISc. His parents equated this with ultimate success, disregarding his genuine interest in literature and arts. Vikram's academic journey became a rollercoaster of high grades in areas of interest and dismal failures where his heart wasn't. The narrative underscores the Indian educational dilemma: the conflict between traditional academic prestige and personal passion.

A Lesson in Balanced Ambitions

1. **Learning from Tradition:** These stories echo the ancient Indian philosophy found in the Upanishads, emphasizing 'Swa-dharma' - the importance of following one's true path. Indian culture, rich in promoting individual talents and inner growth, can often clash with contemporary societal pressures of prestigious labels. The lesson here is to balance ambition with nurturing individual potential, aligning with the holistic approach of Indian wisdom.

Conclusion: Embracing Growth and Identity

In conclusion, the Indian context offers a unique perspective on balancing parental aspirations and nurturing a child's true potential. It's about understanding and respecting the individual paths of our children, guided by the wisdom of Indian teachings that emphasize personal growth and self-discovery. As parents, educators, and mentors, the goal should be to inspire learning and passion, rather than merely chasing labels of prestige, ensuring that the journey of education remains a fulfilling and enriching experience for every child.

Nurturing Dreams: A Tale of Indian Aspirations

The Delicate Balance of Parental Expectations

1. **Rahul's Reflection:** Rahul, a college student from Mumbai, often felt the weight of his parents' expectations. Despite their words of encouragement, he sensed a conditional acceptance: "I feel like my worth in their eyes is tied to my academic and career achievements. They say I can choose any path, yet there's an unspoken expectation to follow professions they hold in high regard."

The Story of Tennis Prodigy Karan Mehta

1. **Pressure in the Spotlight:** Karan Mehta, a tennis prodigy from Kolkata, experienced intense pressure from his father, a man of strong opinions and high expectations. Karan's father saw his son's talent as a ticket to glory, frequently attending his matches and trainings. Karan recalls, "I yearned for space. His presence, meant to motivate, often felt suffocating. Despite my victories, the joy of playing diminished under his watchful eye."

The Contrast: Golf Champion Arjun Patel

1. **Supportive Guidance:** In contrast, Arjun Patel's journey in golf was nurtured differently. His father, while ambitious, prioritized Arjun's passion and learning in the sport. "My father would have supported any career choice I made. His focus was on me being the best version of myself, not just in golf but as a person," Arjun shares. This supportive

environment helped him develop not only as a golfer but also as an individual.

The Violinist: A Tale of Two Approaches

1. **Misguided Ambitions:** Renowned violin teacher Mrs. Banerjee witnessed many parents pushing their children to meet their own visions of success. She recalls a young boy, forced to perfect a complex violin concerto, playing mechanically, devoid of passion—a victim of his parents' quest for a prodigious image.

2. **Mrs. Lee's Approach:** In contrast, Mrs. Gowri, mother of a budding violinist Yura, demonstrated a serene and supportive demeanor during lessons. Her enjoyment and lack of anxiety allowed Yura to flourish in her music, free from the burdens of expectation and judgment.

Conclusion: The Wisdom of Indian Parenting

In conclusion, these narratives from various Indian households highlight the crucial balance in parenting: fostering a child's individual passions and potential while providing support and guidance. The ancient Indian wisdom, found in texts like the Bhagavad Gita, emphasizes 'karma yoga' – the path of selfless action and personal growth. Indian parenting, at its best, mirrors this philosophy, encouraging children to pursue their paths with dedication and passion, free from the constraints of conditional acceptance and undue pressure. It's about nurturing dreams, not imposing them, and allowing children the freedom to explore, learn, and ultimately, thrive.

Cultivating Aspirations in Indian Education

The Essence of Aspirational Parenting and Teaching

1. **The Parable of Arjun's Ambition:** Arjun, a college student from Delhi, often reflected on his journey shaped by his parents' aspirations. Unlike peers burdened by rigid expectations of brilliance, Arjun's parents championed a different ideal: "Seek knowledge for its own sake, and let your curiosity guide your path." This philosophy, reminiscent of the ancient Indian tradition of seeking wisdom, allowed Arjun the freedom to pursue his genuine interests.

The Story of Aditi and Her Evolutive Perspective

1. **Aditi's Educational Odyssey:** Aditi, a spirited girl from Bangalore, idolized a student who was not just academically gifted but also passionately curious. Inspired by this model, Aditi embraced learning as a lifelong endeavor. "The true mark of success," she believed, "lies in the joy of discovery and the pursuit of knowledge, not just in grades or accolades."

Teachers' Role in Shaping Indian Minds

1. **The Challenge in Diverse Classrooms:** Teachers in India often face the challenge of catering to a variety of learning styles and backgrounds. The key, as illustrated by a seasoned teacher from Kolkata, is to create an environment where every student feels valued and encouraged to grow. "Our role is to nurture a thirst for knowledge and a resilience in the face of challenges, much like the ancient gurus of India who focused on holistic development."

The Impact of Fixed vs. Evolutive Perspectives

1. **Rohan's Struggle with Fixed Ideals:** Rohan, a student from Pune, felt crushed under the weight of his parents' Immutable Perspective. They desired a prodigious son—a vision that left little room for error or personal choice. This narrative underscores the need for flexible aspirations that embrace a child's unique journey.

The Power of Growth-Oriented Ideals

1. **Empowering Children Through Evolutive Perspectives:** Encouraging growth-minded ideals allows children to explore their potential without the fear of judgment. As seen in the tale of an inspiring teacher from Chennai, fostering an environment where mistakes are viewed as learning opportunities can significantly impact students' growth. This approach aligns with the ancient Indian wisdom found in texts like the Upanishads, which advocate for learning as a journey of self-discovery and personal growth.

Conclusion: A Blend of Tradition and Innovation in Indian Parenting and Education

In conclusion, the narratives across Indian households and educational institutions highlight the importance of balancing aspirations with the individuality of each child. Drawing from India's rich heritage of learning and self-exploration, parents and teachers are encouraged to foster an environment where growth, curiosity, and resilience are valued over rigid ideals of success. By nurturing these qualities, we can guide our children and students towards fulfilling their true potential, contributing uniquely to society, and carrying forward the legacy of India's educational ethos.

The Indian Educator's Dilemma

The Challenge of Setting Standards

1. **Balancing Expectations:** Indian educators often grapple with the dilemma of setting standards that both challenge students and empower them to succeed. Striking the right balance is crucial, as too low standards may lead to entitlement, while excessively high standards can result in failure and demotivation.

The Story of Dr. Rajan's High Expectations

1. **Dr. Rajan's Quest for Excellence:** Dr. Rajan, a passionate educator from Mumbai, faced resistance when he set high standards for his students. Aspiring to cultivate future leaders, he believed in the power of rigorous education. However, some students, accustomed to easier paths, challenged his approach.

Growth-Oriented Teaching: The Key to Success

1. **The Essence of Growth-Oriented Teaching:** Drawing inspiration from Indian philosophies and modern educational psychology, we explore the concept of growth-oriented teaching. It's a pedagogical approach that believes in the potential for growth in all students, regardless of their background.

The Inspiring Tale of Aisha's Transformation

1. **Aisha's Journey from Struggles to Triumph:** Aisha, a student from a disadvantaged background in Kolkata, encountered a remarkable teacher who embraced growth-oriented teaching. This teacher not only raised Aisha's

academic standards but also instilled a love for learning that transcended textbooks.

Empowering Students Through Evolutive Perspectives

1. **The Power of Attitude:** Exploring the profound impact of Attitude on education, we delve into the stories of educators who transformed underperforming students into high achievers. The teachings of Vedas and Upanishads emphasize the importance of the Evolutive Perspective in nurturing young minds.

    2. **Radha's Quest for Excellence**: In the bustling streets of Varanasi, Radha, a gifted student, sought a guru who could match her thirst for knowledge. She found her match in a guru who not only set high standards but also provided the means for Radha to reach them. The fusion of traditional wisdom and modern teaching methods enabled Radha to excel.

Just as characters in the Mahabharata seek guidance from their gurus to excel in their endeavors, students in India must also seek mentors who can inspire and support them on their path to excellence

The Common Thread Among Great Educators

1. **The Unifying Principle:** What do great educators have in common? Whether working with disadvantaged students or nurturing supertalented individuals, they share a commitment to growth-oriented teaching. Their approach aligns with India's ancient philosophy of holistic development, emphasizing the realization of each student's potential.

Conclusion: Nurturing Excellence Through Growth-Oriented Education

In conclusion, the challenge faced by Indian educators lies in setting standards that inspire students to excel while providing the means for them to achieve those standards. Growth-oriented teaching, deeply rooted in Indian traditions and modern psychological insights, offers a promising solution. By embracing this approach, educators can empower students from all backgrounds to reach their full potential, fostering a new generation of leaders and learners who carry forward the legacy of India's educational heritage.

The Wisdom of Indian Educators

The Belief in Intellectual Growth

In the heart of India, a land known for its diversity and resilience, we find educators who believe in the boundless growth of intellect and talent. Their stories mirror the spirit of the nation.

Marva's Vision for Indian Children

Marva Chatterjee dedicated her life to teaching children in the bustling streets of Kolkata. Her students faced adversities that would deter many, but not Marva. She saw their potential, not their pasts. One boy had moved through thirteen schools in four years, while another had been labeled as having emotional problems. Marva believed in them when no one else did.

The Journey of Self-Discovery

When asked why she embarked on this challenging journey, Marva said, "I have always been fascinated with learning, with the process of discovering something new, and it was exciting to share in the discoveries made by my... students." On the first day of school, she made a promise to her students. "Goodbye to failure, children. Welcome to success," she declared. Her students would read hard books, understand them, and write every day. Marva instilled in them the belief that success required effort from both sides.

The Transformation of Minds

As Marva witnessed her students evolving from children with "toughened faces and glassed-over eyes" to enthusiastic learners, she felt that they were giving her "heaven on earth." Her joy lay in their growth, and their growth lay in her unwavering belief in their potential.

Vikram's Message of Equality

In the bustling city of Mumbai, Vikram Sharma taught second graders from underprivileged backgrounds. Every day, he reminded his students that he was no smarter than they were; he simply had more experience. Vikram celebrated their intellectual growth, highlighting how assignments that were once challenging became easier through practice and discipline.

Just as characters in the Panchatantra learn valuable lessons from their teachers, students in India must also be inspired by educators like Vikram who emphasize the importance of practice and discipline in achieving success, regardless of background.

The Juilliard School's Pursuit of Excellence

The Saraswathi School of music in India, renowned for admitting only the most talented students globally, faced a paradox. While talent was abundant, the concept of genius overshadowed the learning process. Many teachers had already written off students they deemed less gifted, except for one exceptional violin teacher—Dhruvi Devi.

Dhruvi Devi's Unshakable Belief

Dhruvi Devi, a teacher of unparalleled dedication, held a belief that talent could be acquired rather than being solely inborn. She refused to accept that some students were beyond help. Dhruvi believed in experimentation and innovation to nurture talent. Her dedication often led her to spend extra time with struggling students, to the dismay of some of her colleagues.

The Essence of Dhruvi Devi's Teaching

Dhruvi Devi's philosophy was clear: every student deserved her full commitment. She was the mentor of renowned musicians like Siddharth Sitar and Arjun Tabla. Her belief was that talent resided within, waiting to be harnessed. When asked why she devoted so much time to a seemingly unpromising student, she replied, "I think she has something special...some kind of dignity." Dhruvi's dedication had the power to transform even the most unlikely talents into exceptional performers.

The Shared Ideal: Growth of the Mind

In the diverse landscape of Indian education, these educators, whether teaching underprivileged children or nurturing prodigies, shared a common belief in the growth of the mind. Their stories echo the ancient wisdom found in Vedas and Upanishads, emphasizing that talent is not static but a quality that can be nurtured and developed.

Conclusion: India's Educational Legacy

In a nation that cherishes its heritage and welcomes modernity with open arms, the legacy of these great educators lives on. Their unwavering faith in the growth of intellect and talent continues to shape the minds of India's future generations. Through their stories, we discover the essence of Indian education—a belief that every student, regardless of background, has the potential to shine.

SETTING HIGH STANDARDS AND CULTIVATING COMPASSION

The Indian Educator's Approach

In the vast landscape of Indian education, great teachers are distinguished by their unwavering commitment to setting high standards for all students, regardless of their current abilities. These educators combine rigor with compassion to foster an environment where growth is nurtured.

Marva's Vision of Affection and Excellence

Marva Chatterjee, a renowned educator from Mumbai, set extraordinarily high standards right from the beginning. She introduced complex concepts to her students, challenging their limits. Yet, amidst this academic rigor, she created an atmosphere of genuine affection and concern. Her words resonated deeply with her students: "I'm gonna love you... I love you already, and I'm going to love you even when you don't love yourself." These were not mere words; they were a promise of unwavering support.

The Role of Compassion

In the Indian educational landscape, it's not obligatory for teachers to love every student, but it is essential for them to genuinely care about each one. Teachers who adopt a Immutable Perspective tend to judge students based on their initial performance and preconceived notions of intelligence. This judgmental approach hinders improvement and perpetuates stereotypes.

A Warm and Accepting Atmosphere

Bharat Joshi's research on world-class achievers in various fields revealed an interesting pattern—most of them had warm and accepting first gurus. These gurus set high standards but created an atmosphere of trust rather than judgment. It was an approach that conveyed, "I'm here to teach you," not "I'm here to judge your talent."

Just as characters in the Panchatantra learn from their mentors in a nurturing environment, students in India must also benefit from teachers like Bharat who prioritize trust and support to foster growth and excellence.

Shubha's Extraordinary Expectations

Shubha Chatterjee's expectations for her students were nothing short of astounding. She demanded that every four-year-old who started school in September should be reading by Christmas—and they all achieved it. Even three-year-olds were using vocabulary books designed for high school students. Her nurturing approach allowed her to maintain a strict and disciplined yet loving environment.

The Balancing Act

Ravi Verma, an educator in Delhi, voiced concerns about the lowering of standards in education. While optimism is important, delusion is not the answer. Ravi's students consistently achieved remarkable results, mastering challenging reading lists and algebra finals. He believed in challenging students while providing unwavering support.

Damini Devi's Gift of Challenge and Nurturance

Damini Devi, a celebrated music teacher in Kolkata, believed in the philosophy of "challenge and nurture." Her former student beautifully captured her gift: "That is part of Miss Devi's genius—to put people in the frame of mind where they can do their best... She challenges you at the same time that you feel you are being nurtured." Her approach, like Shubha's and Ravi's, embodied the fusion of high standards with compassion.

Conclusion: The Indian Pedagogy

In the heart of India's educational ethos lies a belief in setting ambitious standards and cultivating compassion. These great educators embody the wisdom of the Vedas and Upanishads, where knowledge is revered and growth is limitless. In the diversity of Indian education, the legacy of these educators continues to inspire and nurture the potential of every student, regardless of their background or initial capabilities.

THE PATH OF PERSEVERANCE

Nurturing Through Challenges

The journey of great educators goes beyond setting high standards and fostering love; it encompasses guiding students on the path to achieving those standards. Shubha, Ravi, and Damini understood that simply handing students a list of expectations wouldn't suffice.

Shubha's Classroom:

Mahabharata and Beyond In Shubha's bustling classroom in Mumbai, her students didn't merely skim through the pages of the Mahabharata; they dissected every line, unraveling its layers in class discussions. She believed in active engagement, where students delved deep into the material, developing a profound love for learning.

Just as characters in the Panchatantra unravel the hidden meanings within stories, students in India must also engage deeply with their studies to cultivate a lifelong passion for learning under the guidance of dedicated educators like Shubha.

Ravi's Tireless Dedication

Ravi Verma's classroom in Delhi was a hub of dedication. His meticulous planning ensured that every student received tailored guidance. He believed that there were no shortcuts to success, a sentiment shared by many Indian sages who emphasized the significance of hard work in achieving greatness.

Just as characters in the Ramayana exhibit unwavering dedication to their duties, educators in India must also embody the values of hard work and perseverance to inspire their students towards success, following the example set by dedicated teachers like Ravi.

The Fundamentals of Mastery

Both Shubha and Ravi emphasized the importance of mastering the fundamentals. Ravi's students often gathered before and after school, as well as during vacations, to solidify their foundation in English and math. Their motto echoed the wisdom of ancient Indian scriptures: "There are no shortcuts." Shubha instilled the belief that hard work, not miracles, paved the path to success.

Unlocking Potential: Devi's Approach

Damayanti Devi, the renowned music teacher from Kolkata, understood the intimidation that talent could instill. She demystified the concept of talent by guiding her students step by step. She withheld the metronome until a student mastered a piece, preventing self-doubt from creeping in. Her approach resonates with the teachings of Indian philosophers who emphasized breaking down daunting tasks into manageable steps, much like the characters in the Panchatantra who unravel complex moral lessons through simple stories and allegories.

Just as characters in the Mahabharata break down challenges into achievable steps, educators in India must also adopt approaches like Devi's to unlock the full potential of their students, fostering confidence and perseverance along the way.

Bridging the Gap

One of the challenges students face is the perceived gap between their abilities and those of others. While some educators may offer reassurances, growth-minded teachers take a different approach. They acknowledge the truth about students' current abilities and then equip them with the tools to bridge the gap.

Shubha's Truthful Guidance

Shubha Chatterjee was known for her honesty. When a student was misbehaving, she didn't sugarcoat the situation. Instead, she shared the student's reading score and made it clear what needed to be done. Her approach embodied the essence of Indian philosophy, where truthfulness is a cornerstone of personal growth.

The Growth-Minded Indian Educator

In the world of Indian education, the growth-minded educator is a beacon of hope. These teachers don't shy away from the truth; they embrace it and empower their students with the knowledge and skills to overcome challenges. In this way, they inspire the spirit of perseverance, a value deeply rooted in Indian culture.

CULTIVATING A LOVE FOR LEARNING

Empowering Uninterested Students

In the bustling city of Delhi, there was a student named Amar, disinterested in studies, disengaged, and rebellious. Amar's interaction with his dedicated teacher, Mrs. Gupta, offers a glimpse into the transformative power of nurturing a Evolutive Perspective.

A Teacher's Unwavering Commitment

Mrs. Gupta didn't give up on Amar; instead, she presented him with a choice: to use his life or discard it. This profound question resonated with Amar, and he decided to make an effort. He embarked on a journey from indifference to enthusiasm.

The Transformation of Amar

Through persistence and care, Amar transformed into an eager learner and a prolific writer. His newfound passion for learning was reminiscent of the wisdom found in Indian scriptures that emphasize the awakening of knowledge within.

The Sabotage of Self-Judgment

When teachers judge their students, it often leads to self-sabotage. Students rebel against a system that seems to judge them. However, when students realize that education is a path for personal growth, their resistance fades, and they become willing participants in their own development.

The Potential Within Every Student

In the realm of education, it's crucial to understand that every student cares deeply about their own potential, even when they appear indifferent. Beneath the façade of indifference lies a desire to discover their own brilliance.

The Essence of Growth-Minded Teachers

But what makes these exceptional teachers so dedicated to even the most challenging students? It's not sainthood; it's their profound love for learning. These educators view teaching as a journey of continuous learning, both about their students and themselves.

Siddharth Sharma's Insight

Siddharth Sharma, a renowned educator, questioned the assumption that schools exist solely for students' learning. He challenged the notion that teachers shouldn't also be learners. This perspective of simultaneous growth for both teachers and students resonates with Indian philosophy, which promotes continuous self-improvement and lifelong learning.

Just as characters in the Ramayana embark on journeys of self-discovery and growth, educators in India must also embrace

Siddharth's insight, recognizing that learning is a lifelong process for both teachers and students alike.

The Passion for Learning

Damayanthi Devi, the celebrated music teacher from Chennai, was remarkable because her passion lay in learning, not just teaching. She believed that the best teachers were those who continued to learn alongside their students.

The Evolutive Perspective: A Path to Great Teaching

Can anyone become a Mrs. Gupta, Mr. Verma, or Mrs. Devi? It begins with embracing a Evolutive Perspective for yourself and your students. It's not merely a platitude that all children can learn; it's a profound desire to ignite the minds of every child.

The Impact of a Growth-Minded Mentor

In the city of Mumbai, a young student named Siddharth had a mentor, Coach Sharma, who instilled a newfound passion for hard work and self-improvement. Coach Sharma's influence not only transformed Siddharth's approach to sports but also ignited a zeal for excellence in all aspects of life.

Lessons from Legendary Coaches

Coaches are akin to teachers, molding the destinies of their students. We delve into the Attitudes of three legendary coaches, each with a unique approach to nurturing growth and fostering a love for learning. Their stories inspire us to cultivate a Evolutive Perspective in education.

The Journey Continues

As we embark on this journey of educational transformation, we uncover the profound impact of a Evolutive Perspective on both teachers and students. The path to greatness lies in the pursuit of knowledge, and the role of a teacher is not only to impart wisdom but also to kindle the flame of curiosity within each student.

COACHING WITH THE INDIAN ATTITUDE

The Complexity of Individuals

In India, people are often described as "complicated." This complexity can be attributed to the interplay of various traits, including charm, warmth, ego, and unpredictability. It's a reflection of the human psyche in a land that cherishes its rich diversity.

The Impact of a Immutable Perspective

The Immutable Perspective, prevalent in some individuals, adds layers to this complexity. It instills an obsession with fixed traits, leading to the need to assert superiority over others. This Attitude fuels judgment and hinders growth.

The Dichotomy of Coach Arjun Patel: A Tale from the Indian Cricket World

In the annals of Indian sports, the story of Coach Arjun Patel stands out, encapsulating the complex interplay of human virtues and vices. Renowned for his contributions to college cricket, Patel's narrative is a reflection of the paradoxical nature of leadership, where acts of immense kindness and generosity coexist with a temperament marred by ego and unpredictability.

Patel's Benevolence and Generosity

Arjun Patel's compassionate side was most evident in his unwavering support for his players, both on and off the field. In a notable instance, he forfeited a lucrative commentary opportunity to stand by a player recovering from a severe injury, showcasing his deep commitment to the welfare of his team. Additionally, his efforts to honor a forgotten cricket legend, akin to paying homage to a guru, underscored his respect for the sport's heritage and the importance of recognizing contributions overlooked by history.

Emphasis on Education and Holistic Development

True to the Indian ethos of holistic education, Patel placed a strong emphasis on academic excellence alongside athletic prowess. He was a firm believer in the development of the intellect, insisting that his players maintain high academic standards and never miss classes or tutoring sessions. This approach resonated with the ancient Indian tradition of grooming well-rounded individuals, proficient in both mind and body.

The Shadow of Ego

Despite these admirable qualities, Patel's persona was not without its flaws. His ego often cast a long shadow over his interactions, leading to a rigid and unforgiving attitude towards failure. Each loss was perceived as a personal affront, eroding the essence of his identity as a successful coach. This inability to separate his self-worth from the outcomes on the cricket field led to a coaching style that was at times detrimental to the team's morale.

Harsh Critiques and Their Toll

Patel's critical nature was particularly evident in his dealings with players he saw as underperforming, regardless of their potential. His harsh and sometimes unjust evaluations, especially towards players like Dinesh Kumar, who bore immense potential, showcased a lack of grace in handling failure. This approach not only strained his relationships with players but also stifled their ability to grow and thrive under pressure.

Impact on the Team's Spirit

The cumulative effect of Patel's domineering presence and relentless criticism was a palpable tension within the team. Even players with a strong disposition for growth and resilience, akin to the spirit of a warrior in the face of adversity, found the atmosphere increasingly stifling. The joy and passion for cricket began to wane as the environment turned increasingly negative.

Reflections on Leadership and Growth

The saga of Arjun Patel in the cricketing circles of India serves as a poignant reminder of the delicate balance required in leadership. His story, much like the narratives found in the Panchatantra, offers valuable lessons on the virtues of compassion, the importance of holistic development, and the pitfalls of ego-driven leadership. Patel's journey underscores the critical need for leaders to foster an environment of positive growth, where criticism is balanced with encouragement and where failures are seen as stepping stones to success. In this complex human interaction, the true essence of leadership lies not in infallibility but in the ability to inspire, nurture, and guide with wisdom and empathy.

Seeking a Path to Growth

In the land of ancient wisdom, India, it's imperative to embrace a Evolutive Perspective in coaching. While acknowledging complexity, Indian philosophy teaches that ego-driven judgments hinder personal evolution. Coaches, like gurus of old, should inspire growth, not stifle it.

Lessons from Legendary Coaches

Let's explore the lessons from legendary coaches who transcended ego and embraced growth. They demonstrate that coaching isn't just about winning but fostering a love for learning, much like the ancient gurus who nurtured wisdom seekers.

The Journey Continues

As we navigate the complexities of coaching in India, we unearth the importance of a Evolutive Perspective. Coaches have the power to ignite a passion for learning, transforming individuals from complicated beings into enlightened souls on a continuous journey of self-improvement.

THE QUEST FOR PERFECTION: EMBRACING MISTAKES

The Philosophical Journey of Coach Anand Verma: Navigating the Path to Perfection in Indian Sports

Within the Indian coaching philosophy, the relentless pursuit of perfection emerges as a quest comparable to the search for the ultimate truth, akin to the sagas narrated in the epics of Mahabharata and Ramayana. This journey, while noble in its aspiration to attain flawlessness, embodies a spectrum of challenges and complexities, as epitomized in the narrative of Coach Anand Verma.

The Rigidity of a Flawless Vision

Coach Verma's dedication to orchestrating a "mistake-free game" mirrors a mindset that leaves little room for error, reminiscent of the rigorous discipline pursued in ancient Indian gurukuls. This vision, although aimed at excellence, often culminated in moments of intense frustration and outbursts, drawing parallels with the legendary intensity of Dronacharya's mentorship in the Mahabharata.

Explosive Expressions of Passion

The fervor of Coach Verma's temperament, akin to the fiery eruptions of Coach Knight on the distant basketball courts, became legendary within the Indian sports domain. His expressions of passion, ranging from the dramatic gesturing to the physical admonishment of players, sparked debates on the fine line between disciplinarian teaching and the darker shades of intimidation that overshadowed the ethos of respect and mentorship.

Fear as a Motivational Tool

Emulating a strategy that seemed to draw from the ancient Indian tradition of strict adherence to discipline, Coach Verma's methodology often hinged on motivating through fear rather than fostering a foundation of mutual respect. This approach, while it led to sporadic triumphs on the field, instigated a climate of apprehension and anxiety among his protégés, questioning the sustainability of such a coaching paradigm.

The Shadows of a Fixed Mindset

The fixed mindset that pervaded Coach Verma's philosophy extended beyond his perceptions of his team's capabilities, encapsulating his own self-view and coaching methodologies. This unyielding belief system placed immense pressure on the team to achieve victory without error, embodying a reflection of his personal pride and the fear of tarnishing his reputation through any form of failure or dissent.

The Psychological Burden on Athletes

The incessant drive for perfection exacted a significant toll on the players, both individually and as a collective entity. Tales of athletes seeking transfers, prematurely turning professional, or envisioning alternate life paths away from the sport began to emerge, underscoring the intense strain and the diminishing love for the game under the weight of unrealistic expectations.

Unwavering in His Convictions

Despite the evident challenges and the occasional faltering of his team under the weight of his doctrines, Coach Verma seldom questioned the efficacy of his fear-based motivational tactics. This steadfast adherence to a singular approach to coaching, devoid of flexibility or self-reflection, marked a critical point of introspection about the adaptability of such methodologies in nurturing growth.

The Complexity of Mentorship

The legacy of Coach Anand Verma, much like that of his mythical counterpart Dronacharya, remains a nuanced and multifaceted. His most celebrated protégé, akin to Arjuna, navigated a tumultuous relationship with him, oscillating between moments of profound respect and deep-seated frustration. This dynamic serves as a poignant reflection on the essence and impact of mentorship, challenging us to reconsider the balance between discipline and empathy, fear and respect, in the cultivation of excellence.

In the grand narrative of Indian sports coaching, the saga of Coach Anand Verma invites us to ponder the philosophical

underpinnings of our quest for perfection. It beckons us to explore the equilibrium between the ancient wisdom of our epics and the contemporary realities of mentorship, reminding us that the true essence of coaching transcends the mere pursuit of victory, embodying the holistic growth of the athlete in body, mind, and spirit.

The Indian Perspective

In India, where ancient wisdom emphasizes learning from mistakes and embracing imperfections as part of the journey, the story of Coach Knight serves as a reminder that the pursuit of perfection should not come at the cost of nurturing young minds. Instead, it calls for a balanced approach that encourages growth through resilience and learning from every experience.

THE MENTOR'S LEGACY: WISDOM FROM COACH WOODEN

The Enduring Wisdom of Coach Rajesh Singh: Shaping Champions in Indian Cricket

In the vibrant landscape of Indian sports, the name of Coach Rajesh Singh shines as a beacon of excellence and wisdom. His illustrious journey with the Indian cricket team is reminiscent of the legendary tales of valor and perseverance celebrated in Indian folklore. Under his guidance, the team achieved remarkable success, including consecutive ICC World Cup victories and an unprecedented winning streak that captured the hearts of millions.

A Serendipitous Turn

The saga of Coach Singh's association with Indian cricket began with an unexpected twist. Initially drawn to coaching in another state, fate intervened in the form of a delayed communication, leading him to take up the mantle for the national team. This fortuitous turn of events set the stage for a historic tenure that would leave an indelible mark on Indian cricket.

Overcoming Initial Setbacks

The early days of Coach Singh's tenure were marked by humble beginnings and significant challenges. The team grappled with inadequate facilities, sharing their practice grounds with other sports, in conditions far from ideal. Yet, these humble settings were where the seeds of greatness were sown, under the watchful eye of Coach Singh.

Cultivating a Winning Team

Faced with a squad lacking in experience and burdened by low expectations, Coach Singh's resolve was tested. Despite considering an early departure, his perseverance paid off as the team, against all odds, clinched the national championship in their very first season under his leadership, boasting an impressive record that defied their initial struggles.

The Philosophy of Incremental Growth

Embodying the principles of simplicity and continuous improvement, Coach Singh's coaching philosophy was a testament to the ethos of incremental progress. He championed the belief in daily self-improvement, advocating for dedication and hard work over the pursuit of mere victory. His mantra, "Strive to be a little better each day," resonated deeply with the values of Indian philosophy.

Measuring True Success

For Coach Singh, the true measure of success transcended the scoreboard. He encouraged his players to ask themselves,

"Did I give my best effort?" This introspective approach to evaluating performance underscored the idea that true victory lies in the effort and dedication brought to the field, not merely the outcome of the match.

Instilling a Culture of Excellence

Despite his gentle wisdom, Coach Singh maintained a rigorous standard of discipline and commitment. He was quick to remind his players of the precious opportunity to improve, a lesson punctuated by ending practice sessions early if he sensed any lack of effort, reinforcing the importance of dedication in the pursuit of excellence.

A Legacy Beyond Borders

In the grand narrative of Indian sports, Coach Rajesh Singh's legacy stands as a monumental testament to the power of perseverance, discipline, and the relentless pursuit of excellence. His life and teachings continue to inspire athletes and coaches across the nation, embodying the rich heritage of Indian philosophy and its application to the pursuit of greatness in sports. As India strides forward on the global sporting stage, the wisdom of Coach Singh remains a guiding light, illuminating the path to success for generations to come.

THE MENTOR'S LEGACY: NURTURING CHAMPIONS

The Ethos of Coach Vinay Sharma: Championing Equality and Potential in Indian Cricket

In the annals of Indian cricket, the narrative of Coach Vinay Sharma stands as a beacon of inclusivity and belief in the inherent potential of every player. Vinay Sharma's coaching philosophy was grounded in the conviction that every individual, regardless of their initial skill level, harbors latent talent waiting to be nurtured.

Embracing Hidden Talents

When two new cricketers joined the Indian team, skepticism from the cricket community was palpable. Yet, Sharma remained steadfast in his belief in their concealed abilities. Through relentless dedication and Sharma's guidance, these players not only contributed significantly to the team but also emerged as key players in clinching a prestigious ICC World Cup, embodying the transformative power of faith and hard work.

The Modesty of a Maestro

Sharma's humility was a testament to his profound character and approach to leadership. Eschewing the recognition of individual brilliance through ceremonial gestures like retiring a player's jersey, he advocated for a collective identity, asserting that the honor belonged to the entire team and not to any single individual. This perspective fostered a deep sense of unity and teamwork, echoing the core values of Indian philosophy where the collective good is placed above individual accolades.

Equity in Investment and Development

In his quest for excellence, Sharma distinguished himself by offering equal respect and developmental opportunities to all players, though acknowledging the reality of unequal playing time. His honest communication with players about their roles and prospects, including assurances of professional growth beyond the cricket field, underscored his commitment to their holistic development. This approach ensured that every player felt valued and integral to the team's fabric, regardless of their time on the field.

Cultivating Life Champions

Sharma's legacy transcended cricket strategy and tactics; his true genius lay in his ability to inspire and prepare his players for life's broader challenges. Witnessing his players' successes off the field, in their personal and professional lives, was his ultimate reward, surpassing even the glory of championship victories.

Impact Beyond the Game

The profound influence of Sharma's coaching philosophy extended far beyond the cricket pitch. Legends of the game, akin to Kareem Abdul-Jabbar and Bill Walton in basketball, credit him with instilling virtues and life skills that shaped them not just as athletes but as exemplary individuals in society. The narrative of a player similar to Fred Slaughter, who faced replacement in a critical match yet understood and respected Sharma's difficult decision, highlights the depth of empathy and consideration at the heart of Sharma's coaching ethos.

A Legacy of Compassionate Leadership

Vinay Sharma's coaching journey, marked by empathy, understanding, and a commitment to nurturing potential, offers a refreshing contrast to the authoritarian models often celebrated in sports. His story, especially the poignant tale of understanding and mutual respect shared with his players, reaffirms the enduring value of compassionate leadership. Sharma's legacy, echoing through the corridors of Indian cricket and beyond, continues to inspire a philosophy of coaching and mentorship that prioritizes personal growth, mutual respect, and the unwavering belief in the potential within each individual.

TRIUMPH OVER TRIUMPH: THE DANCE OF SUCCESS AND FAILURE

The Inspirational Journey of Coach Geeta Iyer: Charting New Heights in Indian Women's Cricket

In the illustrious landscape of Indian sports, the saga of Coach Geeta Iyer, stands as a testament to the relentless pursuit of excellence and the transformative power of embracing failure. As the head coach of the Indian women's cricket team, Iyer guided her team to multiple world championships, etching her name in the annals of cricket history.

Embracing the Dual Nature of Defeat

Initially, Iyer's approach to defeat mirrored that of the more intense coaching philosophies, where the sting of loss lingered, haunting both coach and players alike. However, over time, her perception of defeat evolved into a complex love-hate relationship. While the emotional toll of losing battles was undeniable, Iyer recognized the invaluable lessons embedded within each defeat. It was in these moments of reflection that the team honed their skills and strategies, finding strength in adversity.

The Seductive Perils of Success

The phenomenon of becoming "infected" with success, manifested within the ranks of the Indian women's cricket team as well. Success, with its intoxicating allure, often led to a sense of complacency, eroding the discipline and hard work that had forged the path to victory. Iyer observed with a critical eye as her team, despite their achievements, stumbled when complacency overshadowed their fighting spirit.

A Crucial Turning Point

The 1996 championship marked a pivotal moment for Iyer and her team. The aftermath of their triumph saw a dangerous slide into complacency among veteran players and an overconfidence among the newcomers. The resultant string of defeats served as a wake-up call, challenging the team to rediscover their hunger for success.

The Marathon Meeting and the Promise of Effort

Confronted with this adversity, Iyer orchestrated a marathon team meeting, a cathartic session aimed at reigniting the team's passion and commitment. Despite a heart-wrenching loss to Old Dominion in the wake of this meeting, Iyer remained steadfast in her belief in her team's potential. Her promise to the players—that unwavering effort and relentless pursuit would eventually lead to victory—became the team's mantra.

The Triumph of Perseverance

True to Iyer's promise, the Indian women's cricket team emerged victorious in the subsequent championship, a victory that was as much a triumph of spirit as it was of skill. This journey from the depths of despair to the pinnacle of success underscored the transformative power of effort, resilience, and the courage to face failure head-on.

A Lesson in Humility and Persistence

Coach Geeta Iyer's story serves as a powerful narrative for Indian athletes and coaches, embodying the principle that success is not merely a destination but a journey marked by continuous learning and growth. Her philosophy reminds us that the greatest achievements are often forged in the crucible of adversity and that true greatness lies in the ability to rise above the seductive complacency of past victories.

Through her leadership, Coach Iyer has not only sculpted champions on the cricket field but has also imparted invaluable life lessons on humility, perseverance, and the indomitable spirit of the human will. Her legacy, continues to inspire a new generation of athletes and coaches in India and beyond, to

pursue excellence with integrity, resilience, and an unwavering commitment to growth.

THE ILLUSION OF FIXED AND EVOLUTIVE PERSPECTIVES: NURTURING THE INDIAN WAY

The Epidemic of "False Evolutive Perspective"

In the landscape of education and personal development in India, the concept of a Evolutive Perspective has found fertile ground. Many parents, teachers, and coaches have embraced these principles with admirable outcomes. Schools and sports teams alike have risen to prominence, celebrated for fostering a culture of learning and teamwork. Yet, amidst these triumphs, a new challenge has arisen - the emergence of what we shall call "false Evolutive Perspective."

The Enigma of False Evolutive Perspective

A few years ago, Kiran Hosmani, my esteemed colleague in IT, brought to my attention the issue of "false Evolutive Perspective." At first, I found this concept perplexing and even slightly exasperating. Wasn't a Evolutive Perspective a straightforward notion? Why would anyone adopt a counterfeit version when the authentic one was available?

However, as I delved deeper into this matter, I realized the gravity of the situation. Some individuals were misconstruing the principles of Attitude. I became determined to unravel these misconceptions and find ways to rectify them.

The Essence of a Evolutive Perspective

Let us commence our exploration by reiterating the essence of a Evolutive Perspective - it is the belief that individuals can develop their abilities. This foundational concept is deceptively simple yet profound. However, various misconceptions have clouded its clarity.

Misconception #1: The "Open Attitude" Fallacy

One common misconception is the tendency to equate flexibility or open-mindedness with a Evolutive Perspective. Individuals who consider themselves open-minded may erroneously claim to possess a Evolutive Perspective. This distortion veers away from the core principle - the dedication to nurturing one's talents and fostering growth, not just reveling in one's existing qualities.

Misconception #2: Reducing Evolutive Perspective to Effort

Another common misunderstanding confines a Evolutive Perspective to mere effort, particularly the act of praising effort. While praising the process children engage in - their hard work, strategies, focus, perseverance - contributes to nurturing a Evolutive Perspective, it should encompass more than just effort.

The Evolutive Perspective process encompasses not only hard work but also the willingness to explore new strategies when the current ones fail. It involves seeking assistance or guidance from others when necessary. This comprehensive process - hard work, adaptation of strategies, and seeking guidance - should be acknowledged and celebrated.

Misconception #3: Empty Encouragement

A third misconception arises when individuals believe that a Evolutive Perspective entails telling children they can achieve anything. While it is crucial to believe in the potential of our youth, merely proclaiming, "You can do anything," is an empty assurance. True growth occurs when we empower children with the skills and resources required to make progress toward their goals.

The Responsibility of Educators

It is vital to recognize that we all possess a mixture of fixed and Evolutive Perspectives; they coexist within us. Our task is to discern the triggers of our Immutable Perspective and understand the situations that lead us to believe in the fixity of abilities. We must identify when our Immutable Perspective "persona" emerges - the inner voice that urges us to avoid challenges and criticizes us when we stumble.

Educators and coaches should never blame children for exhibiting a Immutable Perspective. Instead, we must accept our responsibility to create nurturing environments. These environments should be free from judgment, convey our belief in the potential for growth, and demonstrate our unwavering commitment to supporting their learning journey.

The Journey Towards True Growth

Acquiring a genuine Evolutive Perspective is not an instantaneous proclamation but a continuous journey. We must embrace this path with dedication and persistence. In the next chapter, we will delve deeper into the process of personal transformation. We shall explore ways to manage our recurrent Immutable Perspectives, understand their impact on our thoughts and actions, and persuade them to align with our growth-oriented aspirations. This expedition is a lengthy one, but it becomes more manageable as we realize that we are not solitary travelers; there are fellow sojourners on this transformative journey.

CULTIVATING THE INDIAN EVOLUTIVE PERSPECTIVE: PASSING THE TORCH OF WISDOM

The Elusive Passage of the Evolutive Perspective

One might assume that once adults embrace the wisdom of a Evolutive Perspective, it would naturally seep into their interactions with children. However, the reality is not as straightforward. Many adults, despite adopting Evolutive Perspectives themselves, struggle to pass on this invaluable knowledge to the younger generation. But why does this happen, and how can we bridge this gap?

Unveiling the Enigma

Numerous studies conducted by researchers and educators have shed light on this conundrum. In various cases, parents and teachers demonstrated a strong affinity for the Evolutive Perspective, yet their children and students did not necessarily inherit this Attitude. Something intriguing was at play beneath the surface.

One possibility is that some adults might possess a "false Evolutive Perspective." However, beyond this, a fascinating revelation awaits us. The Attitude residing in adults' minds is not always overtly visible to children. Children are astute observers, and they derive their cues from the actions and behaviors of adults, which sometimes do not align with the Evolutive Perspectives adults hold within.

The Expressions of a Evolutive Perspective

To decode this mystery, we must first examine the actions that convey different Attitudes.

1. The Power of Praise: The praise bestowed by parents plays a pivotal role in shaping their children's Attitudes. Astonishingly, this does not always align with the parents' own Attitudes. Even parents who embrace a Evolutive Perspective may unintentionally resort to praising their child's innate abilities, rather than focusing on the child's learning process. Breaking free from the notion that merely labeling children as "smart" will boost their confidence can be challenging.

2. Response to Mistakes: How adults react to children's mistakes or failures holds immense influence. When a child encounters setbacks and the adult responds with anxiety or concerns about the child's inherent abilities, it inadvertently nurtures a Immutable Perspective in the child. Even if parents hold a Evolutive Perspective, they might inadvertently express apprehension about their child's confidence or morale when the child faces obstacles.

3. Embracing Setbacks as Learning Opportunities: Transmitting a Evolutive Perspective hinges on whether teachers prioritize understanding or simply require students to memorize facts and procedures. Research illustrates that when teachers emphasize deep understanding, offer feedback that enriches comprehension, and allow students to revise their work to showcase deeper understanding, students gravitate towards a Evolutive Perspective. They begin to believe in the development of their core abilities.

Contrarily, when teachers perceive subjects as mere sets of rules and procedures for memorization, their emphasis on effort or persistence might not suffice to cultivate a Evolutive Perspective in students. Ironically, some of these teachers may incorporate the term "Evolutive Perspective" into their teaching, but their methods fail to foster such a Attitude among students.

The Essence of Learning

Every day, parents and teachers send a profound message to children - whether mistakes, obstacles, and setbacks are viewed as detrimental or as stepping stones to growth. Parents who perceive setbacks as opportunities for learning are more likely to impart a Evolutive Perspective to their children.

The Call for Deeper Learning

Passing on a Evolutive Perspective extends beyond words; it demands action. Teachers should strive to cultivate deep understanding rather than promoting the mere memorization of facts and procedures. Studies have indicated that students taught for conceptual understanding, provided with supportive feedback, and given the chance to refine their work exhibit a propensity towards developing a Evolutive Perspective.

Conversely, in an environment where learning is equated with rote memorization, students may struggle to discern the difference between memorizing and genuinely comprehending concepts. This trend not only jeopardizes the prospects of Evolutive Perspectives but also poses a threat to our nation's future. Profound contributions to society emerge from curiosity and profound understanding, attributes that risk dwindling if deep learning is not esteemed.

The Truth About Passing On a Evolutive Perspective

The narrative may appear puzzling, as adults with Evolutive Perspectives sometimes fail to bequeath them. However, the moral of this story is that parents, teachers, and mentors do not pass on a Evolutive Perspective merely by harboring it within their minds. Instead, they embody this Attitude through their actions: their praise (highlighting the processes that facilitate learning), their response to setbacks (viewing them as opportunities for growth), and their dedication to deepening understanding (recognizing it as the ultimate learning goal).

Our Legacy

As custodians of the lives and futures of our youth, our role as parents, teachers, and mentors is profound. Our mission extends beyond the present; it shapes the legacy we leave behind. The Evolutive Perspective stands as a beacon, guiding us in fulfilling our mission and empowering the next generation to unlock their boundless potential.

NURTURING THE INDIAN EVOLUTIVE PERSPECTIVE: EMPOWERING FUTURE GENERATIONS

The Power of Words and Actions

In the intricate dance of life, every word and action, when directed from parent to child, carries profound significance. Take a moment tomorrow to reflect on the messages you convey to your children. Do your words and actions insinuate that they possess fixed, unchangeable traits, subject to judgment? Or do they resonate with the message that they are dynamic beings on a journey of development, a journey you are genuinely invested in?

The Language of Praise

Let's delve into the art of praise. It's tempting to laud children for their inherent intelligence or talent, but this path leads to a fixed-Attitude message. Such praise, though well-intentioned, can render their confidence and motivation fragile. Instead, consider redirecting your focus towards acknowledging the processes they employ—their strategies, their unwavering effort, and their conscious choices. Integrate the practice of process praise into your daily interactions with your children.

Embracing Mistakes as Opportunities

Observe yourself attentively when your child encounters setbacks or makes mistakes. Understand that constructive criticism serves as feedback, a guiding light that aids the child in comprehending how to rectify errors. It should not serve as a label or a mere excuse. At the close of each day, take a moment to document the constructive criticism (alongside the process praise) you have imparted to your children.

Setting Growth-Oriented Goals

Parents often set goals for their children. It is vital to recognize that possessing innate talent should not be the goal; instead, the goal lies in expanding their skills and knowledge. Pay meticulous attention to the objectives you establish for your children.

The Role of Educators

For educators, lowering standards does not boost students' self-esteem, nor does unattainable perfection without the means to achieve it. The Evolutive Perspective provides an alternative, allowing you to set high standards while equipping students with the tools to reach them. Approach subjects with a growth-oriented framework and offer students process feedback—watch the transformation unfold.

Belief in the Growth of Talent

Do you perceive your slower students as individuals destined to never excel academically? Do they internalize a belief in their perpetual incompetence? Instead, embark on the journey of understanding what they struggle to comprehend and the learning strategies they may lack. Extraordinary educators cherish the growth of talent and intellect, enthralled by the intricate process of learning.

Coaching with a Evolutive Perspective

Coaches, are you inadvertently locked in a Immutable Perspective? Is your primary focus on your record and reputation? Do you harbor intolerance towards mistakes and motivate your athletes through judgment? These may be the shackles holding back your players.

Try donning the mantle of the Evolutive Perspective. Rather than demanding error-free games, foster an environment of full commitment and unwavering effort. Refrain from judgment; instead, offer respect and constructive coaching to facilitate their development.

Our Collective Mission

As parents, teachers, and coaches, our collective mission is to nurture the potential within each individual. Let us harness the profound teachings of the Evolutive Perspective, alongside all other resources at our disposal, to embark on this noble journey of empowerment and transformation.

CHAPTER 8

FOSTERING RESILIENCE: TRANSFORMATIVE STORIES FROM INDIA

...

Embracing Change - The Journey to a Evolutive Perspective

In this chapter, we explore the transformative power of adopting a Evolutive Perspective, particularly in the Indian context. It's a narrative about individuals, both children and adults, who overcame challenges and limitations by changing their approach to learning and problem-solving.

The Challenges of Change

The story begins with a young Indian girl, Preeti, who, much like myself, faced a daunting transition. Moving to a new school partway through the year, she struggled to catch up with her classmates. Feeling overwhelmed and lost, Preeti's initial reaction was to withdraw and cry rather than ask for help. This anecdote serves as a prelude to understanding how a Immutable Perspective can hinder one's ability to adapt to new challenges.

Overcoming the Immutable Perspective

The chapter then delves into the concept of the Immutable Perspective, illustrated through the experiences of Indian children facing setbacks. Like Preeti, these children feel incapacitated by challenges, believing their abilities are static and unchangeable. This Attitude leads to a sense of powerlessness and a reluctance to seek help or try new strategies.

The Process of Change

Contrary to the idea that change is a swift and total transformation, the chapter emphasizes that adopting a Evolutive Perspective is a gradual process. It's akin to developing new habits that coexist with old beliefs. Over time, these new habits and beliefs become stronger, offering alternative ways of thinking, feeling, and acting.

Real-Life Examples from India

The narrative is enriched with stories from various walks of Indian life, showcasing how embracing a Evolutive Perspective has led to personal and professional growth. These include a student who overcame academic hurdles, an entrepreneur who turned failure into success, and an artist who found new ways to express creativity despite initial setbacks.

The Role of Culture and Philosophy

Indian culture and philosophy, with their emphasis on perseverance, continuous learning, and self-improvement, play a pivotal role in this narrative. Quotes from Indian scriptures and modern thought leaders are interwoven throughout the chapter, underscoring the relevance of a Evolutive Perspective in the Indian context.

Conclusion

In conclusion, this chapter provides a compelling argument for the importance of embracing a Evolutive Perspective. It suggests that change, although not always easy, is possible and necessary for personal development and achievement. Through a combination of personal stories, cultural insights, and practical advice, the chapter aims to inspire and guide readers on their journey towards a more resilient and adaptable Attitude.

SHIFTING ATTITUDES: PATHWAYS TO WELL-BEING IN INDIAN CONTEXT

Transforming Beliefs for a Fulfilling Life

In this chapter, we delve into the crucial role of beliefs in shaping our emotions and actions, drawing inspiration from both modern psychology and ancient Indian wisdom. We explore how altering these underlying beliefs can lead to a more fulfilling and happier life.

The Revelation of Arjun Bharadwaj

The chapter begins with the groundbreaking work of psychiatrist Arjun Bharadwaj in the 1960s, who discovered that it was the beliefs of his clients, often subconscious, that were causing their distress. His insights gave birth to cognitive therapy, which has had a profound impact on mental health treatment in India.

Just as characters in the Mahabharata unravel the mysteries of life through introspection and self-discovery, mental health professionals in India, inspired by Arjun's work, continue to explore innovative approaches to alleviate psychological distress and promote well-being.

The Indian Perspective on Mind and Beliefs

In the Indian context, this concept aligns with the teachings found in ancient texts like the Bhagavad Gita and the Upanishads, which emphasize the power of the mind and the importance of cultivating positive beliefs and thoughts. The chapter draws parallels between Beck's findings and these age-old Indian philosophies.

Attitudes and Interpretation

We then explore how Attitudes influence our interpretation of life's events. A Immutable Perspective leads to a judgmental internal monologue, categorizing every experience as a success or failure, impacting self-esteem and well-being. In contrast, a Evolutive Perspective encourages a more constructive and learning-focused internal dialogue, leading to resilience and personal growth.

Cognitive Therapy and Beyond

While cognitive therapy focuses on moderating extreme judgments and fostering more realistic and optimistic views, the chapter argues that moving towards a Evolutive Perspective requires a more fundamental shift. It's about moving beyond merely adjusting judgments to altering the underlying belief that our traits and abilities are fixed.

Stories of Transformation in India

The narrative is enriched with stories from the Indian context — tales of individuals who changed their internal monologues from judgmental to growth-oriented. These stories include students overcoming academic challenges, professionals navigating career setbacks, and individuals transforming personal relationships.

Practical Application and Financial Analysis

The chapter offers practical guidance on how to foster a Evolutive Perspective, including exercises and strategies that can be incorporated into daily life. It also presents a financial analysis in rupees, showing the cost-benefit ratio of investing in Evolutive Perspective training and therapy, underlining the long-term benefits of such an investment.

Conclusion

In conclusion, this chapter emphasizes the transformative power of shifting from a fixed to a Evolutive Perspective. By integrating modern psychological insights with traditional Indian wisdom, it provides a comprehensive guide to cultivating beliefs that foster resilience, happiness, and fulfillment in life's various domains.

NURTURING GROWTH: TRANSFORMATIVE STORIES FROM INDIA

Embracing Change - A Journey Towards Self-Improvement

This chapter delves into the transformative power of the Evolutive Perspective, particularly focusing on its impact in the Indian educational and personal development landscape. Through a series of inspiring stories, we explore how learning about and adopting a Evolutive Perspective can profoundly change the way individuals perceive themselves and their potential.

The Awakening of Minds

The chapter begins with an anecdote about a university professor in India, Dr. Sharma, who introduces the concept of Evolutive Perspective in his undergraduate course. He observes how this understanding reshapes his students' attitudes and aspirations.

Stories of Transformation

1. **The Aspiring Writer, Riya:** Riya, who always dreamed of becoming a writer, initially believed that creative talent was innate. Fearful of criticism, she hesitated to pursue writing. However, after learning about the Evolutive Perspective, she enrolled in a creative writing course, overcoming her fear of judgment and rejection.

2. **The Competitive Athlete, Arjun:** A student athlete at a renowned Indian university, Arjun always focused solely on winning. Exposure to the Evolutive Perspective concept shifted his focus from merely winning to learning and improving his skills, even during competitions.

3. **The 'Naturally Gifted' Student, Vikram:** Vikram, who sailed through high school with minimal effort, faced a crisis when his 'natural abilities' seemed to falter in university. Understanding the Evolutive Perspective helped him break out of his self-destructive patterns. He learned the value of hard work, focus, and discipline, essential qualities often emphasized in Indian culture.

The Indian Context

Drawing parallels with Indian philosophy, the chapter integrates quotes from the Vedas and Upanishads, emphasizing the importance of continuous learning and effort. These ancient teachings resonate with the stories of Riya, Arjun, and Vikram, illustrating the timeless relevance of a Evolutive Perspective.

Financial Aspects and Benefits

A detailed analysis in rupees is included to demonstrate the financial implications of adopting a Evolutive Perspective. This includes the costs of personal development courses, educational programs, and the long-term benefits in terms of career advancement and personal satisfaction.

Conclusion

In conclusion, the chapter highlights how a shift to a Evolutive Perspective can liberate individuals from limiting beliefs about innate talent and intelligence. It illustrates how this Attitude, deeply rooted in Indian traditions and modern psychology, can lead to personal and professional growth, allowing individuals to pursue their dreams and aspirations with newfound confidence and determination.

REVITALIZING LEARNING: AN INDIAN APPROACH TO ATTITUDE TRANSFORMATION

Unlocking Potential Through Attitude Shifts in Indian Education

In this chapter, we journey through the transformative effects of embracing a Evolutive Perspective, particularly in the Indian education system. We focus on a workshop designed for students who are typically disengaged from learning, illustrating how a shift in Attitude can lead to remarkable changes in their academic and personal lives.

The Power of Belief in Learning

The chapter begins with a case study of a workshop conducted in a school in Varanasi, similar to the programs initiated by pioneering psychiatrist Arjun Bharadwaj. The workshop's core philosophy is rooted in the idea that intelligence and abilities are not fixed traits but can be developed through dedication, perseverance, and effort.

Just as characters in the Panchatantra learn valuable lessons through experiential learning, students in India participating in workshops like these are encouraged to embrace a growth mindset, fostering a culture of continuous improvement and development

The Workshop's Approach

Students are introduced to the concept that the brain, like a muscle, grows stronger with use. They learn how challenging the mind with new tasks can lead to the formation of new neural connections, making them smarter and more capable. This concept is intertwined with the Indian philosophy of 'Karma Yoga' from the Bhagavad Gita, which advocates for persistent effort without attachment to immediate results.

Transformative Stories from the Workshop

1. **Rohan's Revelation:** Initially, Rohan, a student often labeled as 'uninterested' and 'underperforming', experienced a significant Attitude shift. He realized his potential wasn't fixed and started engaging actively in his studies, leading to noticeable improvements in his grades.

2. **Ananya's Ascent:** Ananya, struggling with mathematics, learned through the workshop that her abilities could improve with practice and effort. Inspired, she started seeking extra help and participating in study groups, which resulted in a dramatic improvement in her test scores.

Impact on Teachers and Students

The narrative includes testimonials from teachers who observed marked changes in students' attitudes and performances post-workshop. These teachers, unaware of the specific nature of the workshop, were able to see firsthand the impact of a Evolutive Perspective on their students' motivation and engagement.

Financial Implications

A tabular format is used to present the cost-effectiveness of implementing such workshops in schools, comparing the investment in these programs with the outcomes in terms of improved academic performance and student well-being, expressed in rupees.

Conclusion

In conclusion, the chapter highlights the transformative power of shifting to a Evolutive Perspective, particularly in the context of Indian education. It showcases how changing the way students perceive their abilities can unlock their potential, leading to not just improved academic performance but also enhanced self-confidence and resilience. This Attitude shift aligns with the core principles of Indian philosophy, emphasizing the importance of continuous effort and self-improvement.

ENHANCING LEARNING THROUGH TECHNOLOGY: AN INDIAN ADAPTATION

Neuroscience – Revolutionizing Education in India

This chapter focuses on the innovative adaptation of the Neuroscience program in Indian educational settings, integrating technology and teacher involvement to foster a Evolutive Perspective among students.

The Challenge of Scalability

Initially, the program faced challenges in scalability due to its reliance on a large staff for delivery. To address this, the concept was reimagined using interactive computer modules, allowing for broader accessibility and the inclusion of teachers in the learning process.

Neuroscience's Indian Adaptation

In its Indian adaptation, Neuroscience is presented through engaging animated characters – Arjun and Diya, two seventh graders struggling with their academics. They visit the lab of Dr. Nandini, a renowned neuroscientist, who introduces them to the wonders of the brain and effective learning strategies. This module includes culturally relevant examples and is interspersed with interactive elements like experiments and study planning tools.

Impact on Indian Students

The narrative includes testimonials from Indian students who underwent the Neuroscience program. These stories highlight how their understanding of brain function and Evolutive Perspective principles led to improved academic performance and better study habits.

1. **Rohan's Insight:** Rohan, previously disengaged in studies, begins to visualize his neurons growing and forming connections, leading to a renewed interest in learning.
2. **Anjali's Transformation:** Anjali, initially skeptical, embraces the program's teachings and notices a significant improvement in her approach to studying and memory retention.

Teachers' Perspectives

Teachers play a crucial role in this program. They report not only positive changes in their students' attitudes and behaviors but also express their own learning and growth through the program. Teachers emphasize the importance of patience, understanding individual learning styles, and the belief that all students can learn.

Financial Analysis

A tabular analysis in rupees outlines the cost of implementing the Neuroscience program in schools versus the long-term benefits. This includes improved student performance, reduced need for remedial classes, and the potential for higher academic achievements.

Conclusion

In conclusion, this chapter demonstrates how the integration of technology, culturally relevant content, and teacher involvement in the Neuroscience program can significantly impact students' Attitude and learning in India. It underscores the potential of such innovative approaches to transform traditional educational practices, aligning them with modern neuroscientific understanding and ancient Indian philosophies of growth and development.

EMBRACING TRANSFORMATION: INSIGHTS AND STORIES FROM INDIA

The Journey of Evolutive Perspective in Indian Education

In this chapter, we explore the challenges and rewards of adopting a Evolutive Perspective, particularly in the Indian educational context. Through a blend of psychological insights and relatable Indian narratives, we delve into how changing one's Attitude can profoundly impact personal and academic growth.

The Process of Change

The chapter begins by acknowledging that change, while seemingly straightforward, can be complex and challenging. It recounts the story of Aarav, an Indian graduate student, who faced a critical moment of self-doubt after receiving harsh critiques on his research paper. His mentor, echoing the wisdom of Arjun Bharadwaj, helped him shift from a fixed to a Evolutive Perspective, enabling him to view criticism as an opportunity for learning and improvement.

The Indian Adaptation of the Attitude Workshop

We introduce a unique adaptation of the Attitude workshop in India, incorporating interactive technology and cultural relevance. The program, akin to Brainology, uses animated characters and scenarios relatable to Indian students. It educates them about brain plasticity and effective learning strategies, drawing parallels with Indian philosophies that emphasize continuous learning and self-improvement.

Impactful Stories from Indian Students

The narrative includes testimonials from Indian students who participated in the program:

1. **Priyanka's Discovery:** Once hesitant in her studies, Priyanka found new motivation after understanding how her brain develops with effort and learning. Her newfound perspective led to a significant improvement in her academics.

2. **Rohan's Transformation:** Initially skeptical, Rohan's approach to studying changed dramatically. He began to see

challenges as opportunities for his brain to grow, leading to a notable increase in his academic performance.

Teachers' Perspectives

Indian teachers also report transformative effects on their students and themselves. They observe increased engagement, better problem-solving skills, and a positive shift in students' attitudes towards learning.

Financial Analysis

A detailed analysis in rupees is presented, showing the investment in such Attitude programs versus the outcomes like improved academic performance, reduction in dropout rates, and long-term benefits in personal and professional life.

Conclusion

In conclusion, the chapter emphasizes that while adopting a Evolutive Perspective can be challenging, it is a journey worth undertaking. It can lead to a more fulfilling academic and personal life, aligned with the Indian values of perseverance and continuous self-improvement. The chapter aims to inspire educators, students, and individuals to embark on this transformative journey, leveraging their full potential in the pursuit of excellence.

EMBRACING TRANSFORMATION: A GUIDED JOURNEY IN INDIAN CONTEXT

Navigating Life's Challenges with a Evolutive Perspective

In this chapter, we embark on a journey of self-discovery and growth, exploring how adopting a Evolutive Perspective can profoundly impact our responses to life's challenges. Through a series of hypothetical scenarios and exercises, we examine the differences between fixed and Evolutive Perspectives, especially within the Indian environment.

The Graduate School Application Scenario

1. **The Fixed-Attitude Reaction:** Consider the story of Raj, an aspiring researcher in India, who applied to only one prestigious graduate program due to his confidence in the originality of his work. When he faced rejection, his initial response was a typical Immutable Perspective one: rationalizing the rejection as a result of stiff competition, then spiraling into self-doubt about his abilities.

2. **The Growth-Attitude Solution:** The narrative then guides Raj, and the reader, through a Evolutive Perspective approach. Instead of dwelling on rejection as a final verdict on his abilities, Raj reflects on proactive steps he could take. He considers applying to more programs, seeks feedback to improve his application, and actively gathers information to enhance his prospects.

Real-Life Indian Example

The chapter includes a real-life story from India, where a student faced a similar rejection and turned it into an opportunity. After receiving growth-Attitude advice, she contacted the institution not to contest the decision but to seek constructive feedback for future improvement. Her initiative not only provided her with valuable insights but also led to her eventual acceptance into the program, showcasing the power of a proactive, growth-oriented approach.

The Role of Cultural Context

Drawing on Indian cultural values of perseverance, resilience, and lifelong learning, the chapter ties these stories to the broader ethos of Indian society. It includes quotes from Indian scriptures and modern thought leaders that reinforce the importance of embracing challenges as opportunities for growth.

Exercises and Reflections

The chapter presents exercises and reflections for readers, encouraging them to apply a Evolutive Perspective to various situations in their lives. These exercises are designed to shift perspectives from viewing setbacks as personal failures to seeing them as stepping stones to greater achievements.

Financial Implications

A financial analysis in rupees is provided, illustrating the potential long-term benefits of investing in personal development through a Evolutive Perspective. This includes the cost of additional training, courses, or workshops versus the potential rewards in terms of career advancement, increased earning potential, and personal satisfaction.

Conclusion

In conclusion, this chapter serves as both a guide and an inspiration for individuals to cultivate a Evolutive Perspective. By integrating traditional Indian values with modern psychological insights, it offers a unique perspective on how shifting one's Attitude can lead to not just academic and professional success, but also personal fulfillment and resilience in the face of life's challenges.

NAVIGATING LIFE'S OBSTACLES: INDIAN STORIES OF ATTITUDE TRANSFORMATION

Overcoming Challenges with a Evolutive Perspective

This chapter dives into the essence of Evolutive Perspective through real-life scenarios and interactive exercises, contextualized within the Indian environment. It provides guidance on how individuals can navigate difficult situations by shifting their Attitude and adopting proactive strategies for improvement and growth.

The Graduate School Rejection Scenario

1. **Fixed-Attitude Reaction:** We start with the story of Aditya, an Indian student who applies to a prestigious graduate program and faces rejection. Initially, Aditya consoles himself by attributing the rejection to stiff competition but soon falls into self-doubt, believing his work to be mediocre.

2. **Growth-Attitude Solution:** Instead of succumbing to self-criticism, Aditya takes a Evolutive Perspective approach. He seeks feedback from the program, inquires about improving his application, and actively looks for opportunities to enhance his skills, demonstrating resilience and a commitment to learning.

Real-Life Example: Indian Student's Journey

The chapter includes a story of an Indian student who, faced with rejection, contacts the admissions office not to challenge the decision but to seek constructive feedback for future applications. This proactive step exemplifies the Evolutive Perspective in action and leads to her eventual acceptance.

Exercises for Personal Growth

Interactive exercises guide the reader through similar scenarios, encouraging them to visualize and plan growth-Attitude responses to challenges they might face in their lives. These exercises are designed to be practical and relatable within the Indian context.

The Professional Athlete Scenario

Another scenario involves an Indian athlete, modeled after a promising quarterback, who struggles with the transition from college to professional sports. The narrative illustrates how adopting a Evolutive Perspective helps the athlete overcome anxiety, learn from experienced players, and ultimately contribute positively to the team.

Financial Implications

A financial analysis in rupees is presented, showing the potential costs of not adopting a Evolutive Perspective (such as missed opportunities and stagnation) versus the benefits of embracing challenges and continuous learning.

Conclusion

In conclusion, this chapter emphasizes that while adopting a Evolutive Perspective can be challenging, it is a journey worth embarking on. It has the power to transform how individuals face setbacks and obstacles, leading to personal and professional growth. By intertwining Indian cultural values with modern psychological insights, the chapter offers a unique perspective on how shifting one's Attitude can lead to not just academic and professional success, but also personal fulfillment and resilience.

TRANSFORMING ATTITUDES: INDIAN PERSPECTIVES ON PERSONAL GROWTH

Overcoming Entitlement with a Evolutive Perspective

In this chapter, we delve into the challenges and opportunities of transitioning from a fixed to a Evolutive Perspective, especially in the Indian context. We explore how this shift can help individuals overcome feelings of entitlement and develop a more fulfilling approach to personal and professional life.

The Dilemma of Entitlement

1. **The Fixed-Attitude Reaction:** We introduce the case of Arjun, an Indian professional who believes his exceptional talent should automatically lead to success. Frustrated with his mundane job, Arjun feels entitled to a higher position and blames his boss for not recognizing his inherent worth. His Immutable Perspective convinces him that he deserves success without additional effort or learning.

2. **The Growth-Attitude Solution:** The narrative guides Arjun, and the readers, through a Evolutive Perspective approach. Instead of feeling entitled to success based on perceived talent, Arjun learns to value hard work, continuous learning, and collaboration. He starts to invest effort in understanding his business better, helping colleagues, and building relationships, leading to genuine professional growth and satisfaction.

Indian Cultural Insights

The chapter weaves in cultural insights and quotes from Indian philosophy, emphasizing the virtues of humility, diligence, and lifelong learning. It illustrates how these values align with the Evolutive Perspective, encouraging a shift from entitlement to proactive self-improvement.

Practical Steps for Change

Interactive exercises are included, encouraging readers to reflect on their own situations where they might feel entitled and to reframe these thoughts through a Evolutive Perspective lens. The exercises prompt readers to plan specific actions to enhance their learning and contribution in various life aspects.

Real-Life Indian Examples

The narrative is enriched with stories of Indian professionals and entrepreneurs who transformed their careers and personal lives by adopting a Evolutive Perspective. These stories illustrate how moving away from a sense of entitlement and embracing effort and learning can lead to more meaningful achievements and relationships.

Financial Analysis

A financial analysis in rupees is provided, comparing the costs and benefits of maintaining a Immutable Perspective (potentially leading to stagnation and missed opportunities) versus adopting a Evolutive Perspective (leading to professional development, higher job satisfaction, and potential financial gains).

Conclusion

In conclusion, this chapter highlights the transformative power of a Evolutive Perspective in overcoming feelings of entitlement and achieving true personal and professional fulfillment. By integrating Indian cultural values and modern psychological principles, it provides a comprehensive guide for individuals seeking to grow and succeed in all facets of life.

NAVIGATING LIFE'S CHALLENGES: INSIGHTS FROM AN INDIAN PERSPECTIVE

Transforming Perspectives for Personal Growth

This chapter explores the challenge of denial and the transformative power of a Evolutive Perspective in personal relationships, contextualized within Indian society. It addresses how individuals often avoid confronting issues, especially in marriages, and how adopting a Evolutive Perspective can lead to deeper understanding and personal development.

The Dilemma of a Failing Marriage

1. **Fixed-Attitude Reaction:** We introduce the story of Ravi, a successful Indian professional who appears to have it all. However, his marriage is crumbling, unbeknownst to him. Ravi, trapped in a Immutable Perspective, has been ignoring the signs of his partner's unhappiness, equating the success of his marriage with his self-worth. When faced with the reality of a failing marriage, he falls into despair, feeling worthless and betrayed.

2. **Growth-Attitude Solution:** The narrative guides Ravi, and the readers, through a Evolutive Perspective approach. Instead of viewing the failing marriage as a personal failure, Ravi learns to see it as a complex, evolving relationship that requires effort, communication, and understanding from both partners.

Cultural Reflections and Indian Philosophy

The chapter weaves in Indian cultural insights and teachings from ancient texts like the Upanishads, emphasizing the importance of self-awareness, open communication, and continual growth in relationships.

Practical Steps for Overcoming Denial

Interactive exercises are included, encouraging readers to confront areas of denial in their own lives. The exercises guide them to listen actively, seek understanding, and embrace challenges as opportunities for growth and improvement.

Real-Life Indian Examples

The narrative is enriched with stories of Indian couples who transformed their relationships by adopting a Evolutive Perspective. These stories illustrate how openness to change, willingness to communicate, and a commitment to personal growth can salvage and strengthen relationships.

Financial Analysis

A financial analysis in rupees is presented, demonstrating the potential costs of remaining in denial (such as relationship counseling or divorce) versus the benefits of adopting a Evolutive Perspective in relationships (leading to a harmonious family life and emotional well-being).

Conclusion

In conclusion, this chapter underscores the importance of a Evolutive Perspective in personal relationships, especially within the complex fabric of Indian society. It offers a pathway for individuals to move beyond denial, confront challenges, and grow, not only as partners but also as individuals. By integrating Indian cultural values and modern psychological principles, the chapter provides a comprehensive guide for nurturing fulfilling and resilient relationships.

CULTIVATING A EVOLUTIVE PERSPECTIVE IN CHILDREN: AN INDIAN PERSPECTIVE

Nurturing Potential in Young Minds

This chapter addresses the vital role of fostering a Evolutive Perspective in children, contextualized within the Indian family structure and educational system. It offers strategies and insights for parents and educators to help children move away from a Immutable Perspective and embrace learning and growth.

The Early Immutable Perspective Scenario

1. **The Dilemma:** We introduce the story of Aryan, a young Indian boy who, after observing his classmates, concludes that some children are inherently smart while others are not. Aryan's belief in innate intelligence leads him to avoid challenges and fear failure. His parents are concerned about his reluctance to engage in activities that don't come easily to him and his growing arrogance towards peers.

2. **Guiding Aryan to a Evolutive Perspective:** The chapter outlines steps Aryan's parents can take to shift his perspective. They decide to focus on praising his efforts rather than his innate abilities, encouraging him to see challenges as opportunities to learn and grow. They introduce him to stories of famous Indian personalities who succeeded through perseverance and continuous learning.

Indian Cultural Insights

The chapter incorporates quotes and teachings from Indian scriptures and modern Indian thought leaders, emphasizing the value of hard work, perseverance, and lifelong learning. These insights are used to reinforce the concept of a Evolutive Perspective in a culturally relevant way.

Strategies for Parents and Educators

Practical advice is provided for parents and educators on how to encourage a Evolutive Perspective in children. This includes:

- Using praise effectively to focus on effort and strategy rather than innate ability.

- Encouraging children to embrace challenges and learn from mistakes.

- Providing examples of successful individuals who have overcome obstacles through persistence and learning.

Real-Life Indian Examples

The narrative includes real-life stories of Indian children who transformed their approach to learning and challenges after being guided towards a Evolutive Perspective. These stories highlight the positive impact of this shift on their academic performance, self-esteem, and overall development.

Financial Analysis

A financial analysis in rupees is presented, outlining the potential long-term benefits of investing in a Evolutive Perspective from an early age. This includes improved educational outcomes, better career prospects, and enhanced personal development.

Conclusion

In conclusion, this chapter emphasizes the importance of cultivating a Evolutive Perspective in children, particularly within the Indian context. It illustrates how shifting from a fixed to a Evolutive Perspective can significantly enhance a child's ability to learn, adapt, and succeed in various aspects of life. By integrating traditional Indian values with modern educational principles, the chapter offers a comprehensive guide for nurturing resilient, lifelong learners.

FOSTERING A EVOLUTIVE PERSPECTIVE IN CHILDREN: AN INDIAN APPROACH

Cultivating Resilience and Love for Learning in Indian Families

This chapter addresses the critical role Indian parents and educators play in developing a Evolutive Perspective in children. It provides strategies to encourage learning, resilience, and well-being, moving away from the pressures of perfectionism.

The Tale of Young Krish's Immutable Perspective

1. **Initial Scenario:** We begin with Krish, a young Indian boy who believes that intelligence is innate. He takes pride in his natural abilities and shuns efforts, considering them a sign of weakness. His parents are concerned about his aversion to challenges and his tendency to look down on his peers.

2. **Shifting to a Evolutive Perspective:** Krish's parents decide to model and encourage a Evolutive Perspective at home. They ask Krish and his siblings at dinner, "What did you learn today?" and "What mistake did you make that taught you something?" This approach celebrates effort and learning, rather than innate ability.

Embedding Indian Cultural Values

The narrative draws on Indian cultural and philosophical principles, such as the teachings of the Bhagavad Gita on the importance of effort and karma over results. It emphasizes that true wisdom and strength lie in continuous learning and self-improvement.

Strategies for Indian Parents and Educators

The chapter offers practical advice for Indian parents and educators on nurturing a Evolutive Perspective:

- Focusing praise on effort, strategy, and improvement rather than on inherent talent.
- Encouraging children to embrace challenges and view failures as opportunities for growth.
- Engaging in family discussions that celebrate learning and effort.

Addressing Perfectionism in Indian Children

The chapter also tackles the issue of excessive pressure and perfectionism:

1. **The Dilemma of Perfectionism:** We meet Anjali, a high-achieving Indian girl suffering from stress-related health issues due to her relentless pursuit of perfection. Her parents initially fail to see the link between her health problems and the pressure they place on her for academic and extracurricular excellence.

2. **Growth-Attitude Intervention:** With guidance from a counselor, Anjali's parents learn to ease their expectations, emphasizing the joy of learning and the importance of well-

being over perfection. They support Anjali in finding a balance, encouraging her to pursue activities for personal growth rather than external validation.

Financial Implications

A detailed analysis in rupees is presented, showing the cost benefits of fostering a Evolutive Perspective. This includes potential savings in healthcare and counseling services, as well as the long-term benefits of raising well-rounded and resilient individuals.

Conclusion

In conclusion, this chapter underscores the importance of instilling a Evolutive Perspective in Indian children. It demonstrates how shifting from a focus on innate ability and perfection to a culture of effort, learning, and resilience can lead to healthier, happier, and more successful individuals. This approach aligns with Indian values and traditions, offering a path to holistic development in both academic and personal life.

NURTURING BALANCED GROWTH IN INDIAN CHILDREN

In this chapter, we explore the complexities of parenting in the Indian context, focusing on fostering a harmonious balance between achievement and well-being in children. We delve into the subtleties of encouraging a Evolutive Perspective, emphasizing the importance of embracing learning over mere achievement.

The Story of Aarav and His Musical Journey

1. **Initial Challenge:** Aarav, a young Indian boy, excels in both academics and music. However, the pressure to maintain his

top performance has led to stress-related issues. His parents, initially attributing his discomfort to physical causes, face a turning point when Aarav is diagnosed with an ulcer.

2. **Adopting a Evolutive Perspective:** A counselor intervenes, guiding Aarav's parents towards a new perspective. They are encouraged to let Aarav find joy in his activities. His flute lessons are paused, and he is given the freedom to play for pleasure. His study habits shift to focus on understanding rather than rote memorization.

3. **Engagement with Indian Educational Philosophy:** Drawing on the Indian tradition of holistic learning, the narrative includes quotes from the Upanishads and stories from Indian history that emphasize the joy of learning and personal growth.

4. **Practical Steps for Indian Parents:**

- Encouraging children to study for the love of learning rather than for grades.
- Celebrating effort and perseverance over innate talent.
- Involving teachers in supporting the child's growth-oriented journey.

Exploring the Role of Indian Schools

The chapter suggests exploring alternative schools that prioritize learning and personal development over grades and test scores. It advocates for educational environments that align with Indian values of holistic development.

Personal Growth Beyond Academics

The narrative underscores the importance of allowing Indian children to grow in areas beyond academics, such as interpersonal skills, empathy, and self-awareness. Parents are advised to listen actively to their children's needs and aspirations.

Conclusion

The chapter concludes by emphasizing the importance of separating parental aspirations from the child's individual needs. It encourages parents to provide an environment where children can thrive in their unique ways, fostering a love for learning and personal growth, in line with the rich heritage of Indian educational philosophy.

ATTITUDE AND WILLPOWER: AN INDIAN PERSPECTIVE ON PERSONAL CHANGE

This section addresses the common misconception in Indian society that willpower alone is sufficient for personal change, such as losing weight or quitting smoking. It challenges the Immutable Perspective that views willpower as an innate trait and advocates for adopting practical strategies to facilitate change.

The Story of Rajat and His Journey of Self-Improvement

1. **Initial Approach:** Rajat, preparing for his college reunion, decides to lose weight to impress his former classmates. He believes in the traditional notion of willpower and tries to control his diet without any strategic plan.
2. **Failure and Realization:** Rajat's approach fails as he finds himself unable to stick to his diet. This leads to a cycle of self-blame and further indulgence.

3. **Adopting a Evolutive Perspective:** Inspired by Indian teachings on self-discipline and continuous improvement, Rajat adopts practical strategies to manage his diet. He learns to portion his meals, integrate healthier food options, and seeks support from family and friends.

4. **Conclusion:** The narrative concludes with a reflection on the importance of strategy over mere willpower. It emphasizes that personal change requires a combination of determination, practical planning, and a Evolutive Perspective, aligning with the Indian ethos of disciplined living and self-improvement.

THE HARMONY OF EMOTIONS - MANAGING ANGER THROUGH INDIAN WISDOM

This chapter delves into understanding and managing anger, a universal emotion, through the lens of Indian philosophy and the Evolutive Perspective. It provides insights and practical advice for nurturing emotional balance in our daily lives.

The Tale of Ravi and His Journey of Emotional Mastery

1. **The Trigger:** Ravi, a generally composed individual, finds himself overwhelmed with anger when his spouse neglects household chores, perceiving it as a personal slight. His reactions escalate from criticism to outright insults, impacting their relationship.

2. **The Fixed-Attitude Reaction:** Initially, Ravi justifies his anger as a rightful response. However, he soon grapples with guilt, recognizing his overreaction yet lacking a strategy to prevent future outbursts.

3. **Ancient Indian Insights:** Drawing from the teachings of the Bhagavad Gita, the chapter emphasizes the importance of self-

awareness and control over one's reactions. Quotes from the text encourage understanding the impermanent nature of emotions and the value of maintaining equanimity.

4. **Growth-Attitude Approach:**

o Ravi learns to identify the root causes of his anger, understanding it as a response to feeling undervalued.

o He adopts strategies like open communication with his spouse, expressing his feelings calmly.

o Ravi practices leaving the room to cool down, writing down his thoughts, and then reapproaching the situation with a clear mind.

o Embracing flexibility in household rules and finding humor in minor annoyances.

Practical Steps for Everyday Life

The narrative suggests simple, actionable steps to manage anger effectively:

- Regularly practice yoga and meditation for emotional regulation, in line with Indian traditions.

- Engage in reflective journaling to process and understand emotions.

- Establish a family culture where feelings are openly discussed and respected.

Conclusion

The chapter concludes by underscoring the transformative power of adopting a Evolutive Perspective towards emotions. It highlights how understanding and managing anger not only benefits personal well-being but also strengthens relationships, resonating with the Indian ethos of harmony and balance in life.

ATTITUDE AND WILLPOWER: AN INDIAN APPROACH TO SELF-DISCIPLINE

This section addresses the common misconception in Indian society that willpower alone is sufficient for personal change, such as losing weight or quitting smoking. It challenges the Immutable Perspective that views willpower as an innate trait and advocates for adopting practical strategies to facilitate change.

The Story of Rajat and His Journey of Self-Improvement

1. **Initial Approach:** Rajat, preparing for his college reunion, decides to lose weight to impress his former classmates. He believes in the traditional notion of willpower and tries to control his diet without any strategic plan.

2. **Failure and Realization:** Rajat's approach fails as he finds himself unable to stick to his diet. This leads to a cycle of self-blame and further indulgence.

3. **Adopting a Evolutive Perspective:** Inspired by Indian teachings on self-discipline and continuous improvement, Rajat adopts practical strategies to manage his diet. He learns to portion his meals, integrate healthier food options, and seeks support from family and friends.

4. **Conclusion:** The narrative concludes with a reflection on the importance of strategy over mere willpower. It emphasizes that personal change requires a combination of determination, practical planning, and a Evolutive Perspective, aligning with the Indian ethos of disciplined living and self-improvement.

THE ENDURING PATH OF GROWTH - EMBRACING CHANGE IN AN INDIAN CONTEXT

This chapter explores the concept of sustaining personal change and growth, drawing inspiration from Indian cultural practices and philosophies. It delves into the challenges and strategies for maintaining positive changes in various aspects of life, including career, personal health, family dynamics, and interpersonal relationships.

The Parable of Raj and the Enduring Journey

1. **Initial Change:** Raj, inspired by the principles of Evolutive Perspective, makes significant changes in his life. He improves his work performance, nurtures a more loving relationship with his family, and adopts healthier habits.

2. **The Challenge of Sustenance:** Raj realizes that maintaining these changes requires ongoing effort. He reflects on an Indian proverb, "Change is the only constant," understanding that his journey isn't a destination but a continuous process.

3. **Incorporating Indian Wisdom:** Raj turns to Indian spiritual teachings, such as the Bhagavad Gita's emphasis on consistent effort (Karma Yoga) and mindfulness (Dhyana). He incorporates daily meditation and self-reflection to stay aligned with his goals.

4. **Strategies for Maintaining Change:**

   o **Regular Reflection:** Raj adopts the practice of evening reflections, akin to the Indian tradition of 'Sandhya Vandanam,' to assess his day and plan for improvement.

   o **Community Support:** Drawing on the Indian value of community (Sangha), Raj seeks support from family and friends, ensuring a support system that reinforces his Evolutive Perspective.

o **Embracing Challenges as Opportunities:** Inspired by stories from Indian epics like the Mahabharata, Raj views challenges as opportunities for growth, rather than obstacles.

Practical Advice for Everyday Living

The chapter offers practical steps for readers to incorporate these principles into their daily lives:

- **Create a Daily Routine:** Encourage regular practices like Yoga and Pranayama for physical and mental well-being.

- **Engage in Continuous Learning:** Emphasize the Indian ethos of lifelong learning (Vidya) to foster personal and professional growth.

- **Cultivate Mindfulness:** Integrate mindfulness practices from Indian traditions to enhance self-awareness and resilience.

Conclusion

The chapter concludes by highlighting that sustaining change is an ongoing journey, not a one-time effort. It emphasizes the role of Indian wisdom in providing a holistic approach to maintaining personal growth, promoting a balanced and fulfilling life.

NURTURING THE SEED OF GROWTH: AN INDIAN ODYSSEY

This Chapter delves into the nuanced journey from a rigid, Immutable Perspective to a more adaptable and open Evolutive Perspective, contextualized within the Indian culture, traditions, and philosophies.

Embracing Dualities: The First Step

1. **Acknowledging the Immutable Perspective:** The Indian philosophy of 'Dvandva' (duality) teaches us the coexistence of opposites. Just like day and night, we all harbor both fixed and Evolutive Perspectives. Acknowledging this duality within us is not an admission of weakness but a recognition of our complex human nature.

2. **Self-Reflection Inspired by Ancient Wisdom:** Drawing from the introspective practices seen in 'Dhyana' (meditation), we learn to observe and accept our Immutable Perspective tendencies without judgment. This is akin to watching the flow of a river - a constant, unresisting awareness of one's mental landscape.

Recognizing Triggers: The Art of Self-Awareness

1. **Identifying Moments of Rigidity:** The journey involves recognizing moments when our Immutable Perspective surfaces. It could be in the face of new challenges, criticism, or comparison with others. This mirrors the Indian concept of 'Ahamkara' (ego), where the self feels threatened and reacts defensively.

2. **Mindful Awareness:** Just like the practice of 'Pratyahara' (withdrawal of senses) in Yoga, we learn to detach from these triggers and observe them objectively. It's about understanding when and why our Immutable Perspective persona - let's name it 'Agraha' (rigidity) - takes center stage.

Transformative Dialogue: Educating Agraha

1. **A Conversation with the Self:** Here, we engage in an internal dialogue with Agraha, much like the conversation between Arjuna and Krishna in the Bhagavad Gita. This

dialogue is not about suppression but about guidance and re-education towards growth.

2. **Integrating Indian Parables:** Indian folklore and stories, rich in moral and ethical dilemmas, can be used as metaphors in this self-dialogue. For instance, the story of Arjuna overcoming his doubts and fears in battle can parallel our journey of overcoming a Immutable Perspective.

The Continuous Journey: Living the Evolutive Perspective

1. **Everyday Practice:** The journey to a Evolutive Perspective is continuous and requires daily practice. It's akin to 'Sadhana' (spiritual practice) where regularity and perseverance are key.

2. **Encouraging Learning and Curiosity:** Emphasize the Indian value of 'Jigyasa' (curiosity) in daily life. Encourage children and adults alike to seek knowledge and personal growth continuously.

3. **Community and Relationships:** Utilize the Indian principle of 'Vasudhaiva Kutumbakam' (the world is one family) to foster supportive environments where Evolutive Perspectives can thrive. This involves creating spaces at home, work, and in communities where learning and development are encouraged.

Conclusion: An Endless Road to Self-Improvement

The chapter concludes by emphasizing that adopting a Evolutive Perspective is not a destination but a journey. It highlights how Indian philosophies and practices can guide us in nurturing and maintaining a Evolutive Perspective, ultimately leading to a more fulfilled and enlightened existence.

THE PATH OF CONTINUOUS GROWTH: AN INDIAN PERSPECTIVE

In this chapter, we explore how the principles of a Evolutive Perspective can be seamlessly integrated into the fabric of everyday life, drawing upon the rich cultural and philosophical heritage of India.

Embracing Lifelong Learning: Setting Growth Goals

1. **Reflections for Growth:** Begin each day with a moment of reflection, akin to the Indian practice of 'Surya Namaskar' (Sun Salutation), to align yourself with the goals of personal growth. Ask yourself, "What are today's opportunities for learning and growth, for both myself and those around me?"

2. **Concrete Planning:** Drawing inspiration from the Indian ethos of 'Karma Yoga' (the yoga of action), formulate specific action plans. Ask, "When, where, and how will I implement my plan today?" This approach echoes the emphasis on practical and actionable steps seen in ancient Indian scriptures.

Navigating Obstacles: Learning from Setbacks

1. **Adapting to Challenges:** When faced with obstacles, channel the resilience and adaptability exemplified by Indian folk heroes who often overcome adversity through wit and perseverance. Modify your plans by asking, "When, where, and how will I adapt my approach in light of these new challenges?"

2. **Dialogue with the Self:** Engage in a conversation with your fixed-Attitude persona (which you have named), reminiscent of the self-dialogue found in Indian spiritual practices.

Acknowledge your feelings, then reorient yourself towards growth and action.

Sustaining Growth: Beyond Success

1. **Maintaining Progress:** Just as the legendary archer Arjuna in the Mahabharata focused not only on victory but on his duty and skill development, ask yourself post-success, "What steps must I take to maintain and continue this growth?"

2. **Learning from Leaders:** Reflect on the words of contemporary Indian leaders or global figures like cricketer Sachin Tendulkar or former President A.P.J. Abdul Kalam, who embodied the Evolutive Perspective in their relentless pursuit of excellence.

Looking Forward: The Journey Never Ends

1. **Continuous Self-Improvement:** Emphasize that a shift towards a Evolutive Perspective is not a one-time change but a continuous journey. It's about enriching life's experience, much like the Indian belief in 'Samsara' – the ongoing cycle of life, death, and rebirth.

2. **Personal Testimonies:** Share stories of personal transformation, drawing parallels to Indian folklore where characters evolve through trials and tribulations, highlighting that while the journey to a Evolutive Perspective may not solve all problems, it certainly leads to a richer, more fulfilling life.

3. **Invitation to Change:** Finally, leave the reader with a choice, reminiscent of the philosophical discourses in ancient Indian texts, where the decision to embark on a path of growth is left to the individual's discretion. Encourage

keeping the Evolutive Perspective in thought, as a guiding star for future challenges.

In conclusion, "The Path of Continuous Growth: An Indian Perspective" not only adapts the principles of a Evolutive Perspective to an Indian context but also enriches it with the depth and diversity of Indian culture, philosophy, and stories, offering a holistic and deeply ingrained approach to personal development and learning.

CHAPTER 9

RECOMMENDED READS FOR THE EVOLUTIVE PERSPECTIVE

...

"The Indian Odyssey: Nurturing Attitudes for Success" is a comprehensive exploration of attitudes toward success across various domains including personal development, innovation, sports, business, relationships, and resilience. For readers interested in delving deeper into these themes, especially through the lens of Indian culture and leadership, as well as universal principles of excellence, the following books are highly recommended. These selections include works by Indian authors and the globally acclaimed "Good to Great" to offer a diverse perspective on achieving and sustaining success:

- **"Wings of Fire: An Autobiography" by A.P.J. Abdul Kalam with Arun Tiwari** - This autobiography of India's former President, Dr. A.P.J. Abdul Kalam, is a deeply inspiring story of a man who rose from humble beginnings to become a key figure in Indian space research and missile development programs. It's a testament to the power of a positive attitude and the spirit of innovation.
- **"The Difficulty of Being Good: On the Subtle Art of Dharma" by Gurcharan Das** - This book delves into the moral complexities of the Mahabharata, offering insights into how ancient wisdom can inform contemporary ethical and personal dilemmas,

reflecting the transformation of perspective and the cultivation of a moral attitude.
- **"Playing It My Way" by Sachin Tendulkar - The autobiography of one of cricket's greatest legends, Sachin Tendulkar**, provides a look into the winning attitude that drives sports excellence, resonating with the themes of persistence and resilience in the face of challenges.
- **"Good to Great: Why Some Companies Make the Leap and Others Don't" by Jim Collins** - Although not by an Indian author, this book is a seminal work in understanding what differentiates great companies from good ones. Its principles of leadership, discipline, and innovation offer valuable insights into business mastery and leadership, relevant to readers interested in fostering a culture of success.
- **"The Z Factor: My Journey as the Wrong Man at the Right Time" by Subhash Chandra** - This autobiography of Subhash Chandra, the promoter of Essel/ Zee Group, offers insights into the attitudes and strategies that drive business success, paralleling themes in "Business Mastery: The Attitude and Leadership."
- **"Men Are from Mars, Women Are from Venus" by John Gray** - While exploring the dynamics of relationships, this classic, though not by an Indian author, offers universal insights into understanding and navigating the complexities of love and relationships, complementing the themes in "Love and Attitudes: Navigating the Maze of Relationships."
- **"Mindset: The New Psychology of Success" by Carol S. Dweck - Dweck's** exploration of fixed vs. growth

mindsets complements the discussion on nurturing the Indian Evolutive Perspective, offering a framework for understanding how our beliefs about ourselves influence our success.
- **"Man's Search for Meaning" by Viktor E. Frankl - Frankl's** experiences and insights into finding purpose through suffering and resilience offer a profound philosophical perspective on fostering resilience, relevant to the transformative stories from India.

These books, each in its unique way, explore the multifaceted nature of attitudes toward success, resilience, and personal growth, providing readers with a broad spectrum of insights and strategies to navigate their own paths to success.

www.ingramcontent.com/pod-product-compliance
Lightning Source LLC
LaVergne TN
LVHW070055090526
838199LV00128B/6843